W9-BXT-272

MARK TWAIN

GOD'S FOOL

MARK TWAIN

GOD'S FOOL

By HAMLIN HILL

HARPER & ROW, PUBLISHERS

New York, Evanston, San Francisco, London

MARK TWAIN: GOD'S FOOL. Copyright © 1973 by Hamlin Hill. Previously unpublished material controlled by The Mark Twain Company: Copyright © 1973 by The Mark Twain Company. All rights reserved. Printed in the United States of America. No part of this book may be used or reproduced in any manner whatsoever without written permission except in the case of brief quotations embodied in critical articles and reviews. For information address Harper & Row, Publishers, Inc., 10 East 53rd Street, New York, N.Y. 10022. Published simultaneously in Canada by Fitzhenry & Whiteside Limited, Toronto.

FIRST EDITION

Designed by Dorothy Schmiderer

Library of Congress Cataloging in Publication Data

Hill, Hamlin Lewis, 1931–
 Mark Twain: God's fool.
 Source notes: p. 275
 1. Clemens, Samuel Langhorne, 1835–1910.
I. Title.
PS1332.H5 818′.4′09 [B] 72-9754
ISBN 0-06-011893-8

CONTENTS

ILLUSTRATIONS

Illustrations follow page 100.

ACKNOWLEDGMENTS

Comedians, in whatever media they work, are supposed to be essentially tragic figures who sublimate their grief in laughter. While Mark Twain fits the stereotype, in writing this volume I have been constantly aware of a sort of biographical invasion of privacy entailed in bringing personal tragedy and frustration to public scrutiny. The intimate life of an aging author, whose rages, tantrums, and sorrows in his last decade were at the very least unpleasant, might seem to deserve a respectful silence. But precisely because the writer was Mark Twain, whose life and literature were remarkably intertwined, the true facts of his final ten years seem all the more to deserve public discussion, especially so because of the wealth of material that has become accessible to scholarly research in the past several years.

A solution to the dilemma has seemed to me to present as much of the detail and evidence as possible in the language and writings of the principals in the biography. "Dramatize, dramatize," Henry James told himself; and I have tried to follow his suggestion by including here, wherever I could, the comments of Samuel Clemens, his wife, Olivia, his daughters, Jean and Clara, and his secretary, Isabel Lyon. Most of them wrote voluminously, and it has seemed judicious—especially because of the mystique which

surrounds Mark Twain—to allow each of them to speak for himself.

Readers may question the propriety of revealing these facts; they may be repelled by the behavior of some of the actors in the tragedy. But if I have succeeded in presenting the evidence predominantly in the voices of the participants, readers will at least not question the truth of the discomforting facts in this book and, hopefully, will admire even more Mark Twain's attempts at humorous literature in the midst of such a ceaselessly unhumorous existence.

Research for this book has been carried out almost exclusively at the Mark Twain Papers, Bancroft Library, the University of California at Berkeley, on a John Simon Guggenheim Fellowship generously supplemented by a research leave from the University of Chicago. To the Estate of Samuel L. Clemens I am obviously grateful for permission to quote liberally from the unpublished writings of the Clemens family. The original documents cited and quoted here are located in the Mark Twain Papers and in the following collections as specifically acknowledged in the source notes: Professor Bigelow P. Cushman, Newtown, Connecticut; Mrs. Olivia Lada-Mocarski, Murray Hill, New Jersey; the Henry W. and Albert A. Berg Collection of the New York Public Library (Astor, Lenox, and Tilden Foundations); the American Literature Collections, Yale University Library; the Clifton Waller Barrett Collection, Alderman Library, the University of Virginia; the Mark Twain Memorial, Hartford, Connecticut; Harvard University Library; Princeton University Library; Columbia University Library; the University of Texas Library; the Louisiana State University Library; the library of the University of California at Los Angeles; the Henry E. Huntington Library, San Marino, California; Washington University Library; Brown University Library; the Lilly Collection of the Indiana University Library; the DeVoto Papers at Stanford University Library; the University of Wisconsin Library; and the Folger Shakespeare Library. Mr. Robert Rosenthal, curator of Special Collections at the Regenstein Library, the University of Chicago, and Mrs. Sylvia Mechanic of

the Brooklyn Business Library answered my questions patiently; and Mr. John Kohn of the Seven Gables Bookstore, New York, provided translations of Jean Clemens' letters to Marguerite Schmidt quoted herein. In Florence, my work was helped immeasurably by Clara Louise Dentler, Mary Forman of the British Consulate, former U.S. consul Willard Cootes, and Mr. Sergio Era of the American Cultural Center. Carolyn Keene performed the same services in Rome, checking the unpublished autobiography of her father, Francis Keene (U.S. consul in Florence during the Clemenses' residence there), for references to Mark Twain.

In the Mark Twain Papers, Michael Frank, Al Gribben, Bruce Hamilton, and Robert Hirst helped with their knowledge of important material which might otherwise have escaped my attention. Frederick Anderson, editor of the Mark Twain Papers, read through the entire manuscript, making valuable suggestions and corrections at every stage of the composition of the book. Walter Blair, of the University of Chicago, also read the manuscript and provided me with the benefit of his lifelong study of Mark Twain and with his insights about the appropriate methods for handling the material. I hope the final product shows how indebted I have been to their comments and concerns.

Every man ought to be as fortunate as I am in having a family whose willingness to indulge him exceeds all the limits of good sense. My wife, Arlette, and my daughter Cynthia read this book in manuscript, giving me the benefit of their responses and persuading me to alter its form. My other children, Scott, Sondra, and Bill, while they did not participate in the long process of writing, revising, and proofreading, allowed themselves to be uprooted and moved across the country against their own wishes with a good cheer that their father will always remember and cherish.

H. H.

"Ah, well, I am a great & sublime fool. But then I am God's fool, & all His works must be contemplated with respect."
 —Mark Twain to William Dean Howells, *Mark Twain–Howells Letters,* p. 215.

"I have reached the positive conviction that one should not withhold information about the great ones—artists, authors, explorers and statesmen. . . . their habits and lives can bring help and inspiration, if one does not overdo the idea of sacred secrecy."
 —Clara Clemens Samossoud to Hattie Whitmore Enders, March 3, 1948 (MTM).

INTRODUCTION

In 1912, two years after Samuel Clemens' death, Albert Bigelow Paine published his massive, multivolume, official biography, *Mark Twain: A Biography,* a life story that Paine had worked on, as a visitor and finally as a member of the Clemens household, for a half dozen years prior to its publication. The work was encyclopedic in its scope, especially for the years after 1906 when Paine was in almost daily contact with his subject; and although in the succeeding sixty years scholars and biographers have corrected, reevaluated, and contradicted many of Paine's conclusions about the life and works of Mark Twain, that last decade of his life has remained substantially unexamined largely because one-third of Paine's biography presented his firsthand account of the years 1900 to 1910.

Paine was the victim of a fastidious Victorian sense of propriety, and much of his editing of the writings of Mark Twain consisted of removing from the unpublished material what he considered to be blasphemies and vindictiveness. He was also the officially chosen guardian of an image which Clara Clemens, her father's only surviving daughter, believed the public expected of Mark Twain. Exactly the extent to which Clara, and Paine, nourished that image for material advantage, or the extent to which they both believed in it, is irrelevant here. Whatever their reasons, they

managed to impart a representation of Mark Twain, "the Belle of
New York," the beautiful aging spokesman for the oppressed, the
"King" of a devoted family and world, the playlike cynic whose
twinkling eye betrayed his warm underlying sympathy and essen-
tial humanity.

More effusively than anyone else, Mary Lawton, an actress and
close friend of Clara's, gave expression to this sentimental and
sycophantic version of the aura of Mark Twain's last decade:

> From the very beginning of my intimacy in the
> Clemens household, the doings of that delightful
> family were an everlasting joy to me. . . .
> What a romance it was! How unlike anything
> else! One glimpsed another world—one breathed
> a better air. It was something too precious to be
> lost.

Similar, if less gushy, statements about the Clemens family life
could be culled from Paine, Clara's *My Father, Mark Twain,* and
Caroline Harnsberger's *Mark Twain, Family Man.*

Now that none of the family is alive, it is possible to re-examine
the last ten years of Samuel Clemens' life, to remedy some of the
deliberate omissions from his official biography, and to publish
biographical information that was essentially unavailable before.
If, as one example, a reader looks in the index to *Mark Twain: A
Biography,* he will find one—only one—reference to Isabel Lyon,
Mark Twain's secretary, who was a member of the Clemens house-
hold from November 1902 until March 1909. She wrote Clemens'
letters, managed his house, kept his books, took his dictation, and
was, as Clemens himself said, the person, with the exception of his
wife, Olivia, he knew most intimately in all the world. The
reasons for Miss Lyon's expurgation from the official biography
will appear later in this volume. And these reasons are a part of
Clemens' life which until now has never been thoroughly ex-
plored. Other unexplored areas abound. Some are unflattering to
Clara and Jean; some question the stability of the Clemens family;
and several show Clemens in vindictive and occasionally alcoholic
rages, explicable only as indications of increasing infirmity.

Mark Twain was immensely interested in his destination after death. The truth is inescapable that, wherever he went after he died, much of the last decade of his life he lived in hell.

The raw materials for a biography of this period present substantial difficulties. Every scrap of paper was apparently scrupulously saved. For these years alone there are, in the Mark Twain Papers at Berkeley, half a dozen notebooks, three file-cabinet drawers of Clemens' letters, five file-cabinet drawers of correspondence to Clemens and his family, a drawer of clippings and documents and two of autobiographical dictations, the unpublished manuscripts, two sets of notebooks which Isabel Lyon kept (one, called Diaries here, are personal, effusive, intimate; the other, containing dictations, letters, reminders of appointments Clemens had, are formal and businesslike—Daybooks), and the legal and business papers. Literary materials for the decade—including the recently published *Mysterious Stranger Manuscripts, Mark Twain's Which Was the Dream?,* and *Mark Twain's Fables of Man* as well as *The Man That Corrupted Hadleyburg, Christian Science, The $30,000 Bequest, What Is Man?,* the *Autobiography,* and an enormous number of shorter works—are a shelf in themselves.

To reduce these materials to workable and coherent dimensions it has been necessary to divide this biography into three felicitous chronological periods—"Indian Summer," "Götterdämmerung," and "The Derelict."

During "Indian Summer (1900 to Summer 1904)" Samuel Clemens and his family confronted the twentieth century, trying to maintain the equilibrium they had developed until the last decade of the nineteenth. The Clemenses' eldest daughter, Susy, had died, Clemens had gone into bankruptcy with the failure of his publishing company, and had lectured and written his way out of his debts. Jean, the youngest daughter, had become afflicted with persistent attacks of epilepsy. Olivia's health was unstable. But the family, residing in London as 1900 arrived, managed to preserve the appearance of stability until Olivia died in Florence in June 1904. The family was homeless—even without a country—

as it floated from London to New York City to Lake Saranac to
Riverdale-on-the-Hudson and finally to Florence, and it was dis-
integrating as steadily as an iceberg in the Gulf Stream.

After Olivia's death—in "Götterdämmerung (Summer 1904 to
Summer 1907)"—there really was no Clemens family any longer.
Clara and Jean both developed symptoms to fascinate a clinical
psychiatrist, of which their estrangement from their father was
only the most obvious and most enduring manifestation. Mark
Twain, the comic voice of Samuel Clemens, found what was
perhaps its most significant expression in a frenzy of autobio-
graphical dictations and unfinished fantasies which attempted to
work out and explain, for his own rather than an audience's
benefit, the destruction of his world. He had said in the 1880s that
everything he touched turned to gold; in the first decade of the
twentieth century everything turned to ashes—his business invest-
ments, his literary endeavors, and his volatile and unpredictable
relations with his family and his oldest friends. His temper flared
often, unpredictably and uncontrollably, but in a final and phos-
phorescent burst of energy Mark Twain was able to direct his
energies for one last time toward literary impulses and into cre-
ative channels.

Finally, "The Derelict (Summer 1907 to 1910)" charts the last
stage in Samuel Clemens' life. His literary career was ended except
for an occasional and completely unsustainable flash here and
there—as in the poignant "Death of Jean" or his testament of icy
resignation, "The Turning Point of My Life." His daughter
Clara, Isabel Lyon, Ralph W. Ashcroft—his business adviser—and
Paine all sought to establish pre-eminence in his affections and in
his estate. His memory faltered so much that he was unable on
many occasions to keep track of the time or his public façade; the
comic mask of Mark Twain dropped almost completely. And in
rural Connecticut, at the home called Stormfield, he led a life
insulated from the outside world by a protective coterie that was
more protective of its own interests than of Samuel Clemens'
welfare and fought a vicious internecine war to gain his favor.
Jean, the daughter whose personality was most sympathetic to that

of Clemens', was shuttled to asylums and rest homes and was allowed to live with her father at Stormfield for only the last few months of her life. When Jean died, Clemens had literally nothing left. He had banished Miss Lyon—the only person who had shown any unselfish concern for him—and Clara had married and left his house. Death would be exactly the blessing he had proclaimed it to be for years.

In treating each of these three segments of Samuel Clemens' last decade I have combined what seem to be the three dominant facets of his personality—his financial and business career, his literary activities and endeavors, and his domestic life—in order to suggest their inseparable relationships. In his own mind his business investments and his literary productions were equal. He looked on his manuscripts as many of us would on a portfolio of blue-chip stocks or well-located real estate. His concern for copyright was, as he repeated over and over, a concern for the welfare of his family after he was dead. Thus each strand of the tripartite division is inextricable from the other two. Nevertheless, clarity may best be served by a brief discussion here of the business, literary, and family entanglements as distinct parts of his life.

Clemens had been, in his own mind, a businessman his whole life. It apparently never mattered that most of the investments he poured his money into were visionary and ultimately worthless. His career was checkered with payments to Kaolatype (a chalk engraving process), the Paige typesetter, Plasmon (a food supplement), self-adjusting suspenders, self-pasting scrapbooks, and a history game, to name only a few of the projects. Get-rich schemes were never far from the forefront of his mind, and he was willing to drop all literary endeavors to scheme and plot an overnight fortune by speculation.

Clemens was ambivalent about the participants in his wildcat schemes—James W. Paige, Charles L. Webster—and most co-investors were ultimately to be suspected and accused of various felonious intentions on the Clemens pocketbook. Andrew Carnegie and John D. Rockefeller (outstandingly different from Samuel Clemens in the success of their enterprises) were targets of

his scorn. In the twentieth century Clemens would still find stock waterers, duplicitous bookkeepers, and confidence men behind almost every business enterprise he engaged in. But if he continued to suspect his associates, he never questioned the motivations or the morality which underlay their search for instant wealth.

And he found among his business associates two or three whom he could admire and emulate without risking his friendship by recriminations and threats. Henry H. Rogers, J. Y. W. MacAlister, even Katharine Harrison were important figures in Clemens' last decade because they were above suspicion. Rogers, whom Clemens was almost always to address as "Mr. Rogers" in the hundreds of letters he wrote, was the formidable vice-president of Standard Oil and, according to the popular and muckraking press, a robber baron of Wall Street. Clemens had no difficulty overlooking the possible moral ambiguities involved in his friendship with Rogers; indeed, he refused to contemplate the publication of an exposé of Standard Oil and Rogers. However strong his Presbyterian conscience, Clemens was a moral relativist when it came to friends who could be of financial assistance to him. The most puzzling aspect of his relationship with Rogers was Clemens' apparently total insensitivity about his demands on the oil magnate's time and energies. Almost as if Rogers and his executive secretary, Miss Harrison, were office boys, Clemens requested them to make stock purchases and sales, dividend collections, and engage in complicated business manipulations for him. Miss Harrison was an agent who had access to the Clemens safety-deposit box; Rogers and she both had powers of attorney and negotiated literary contracts as well as purely financial investments. It is not true that Clemens deliberately exploited their friendship for his own material gain. But he did manage to "use" Rogers, in the most pejorative sense of that word, to his own advantage, contributing his friendship and his performance as the court jester for a group of millionaires as his share of the relationship.

Miss Harrison puzzled him. She was a woman of a kind who brought his simplistic and Victorian notions of womanhood into

question. A severely masculine, almost robotlike efficiency expert, Miss Harrison terrified and fascinated many people. She actually ran Rogers' day-to-day business (including the "S. L. Clemens Account"), which occasionally involved business deals of millions of dollars. She worked with the calm and stern precision of a machine, juggling figures and details that would have produced a month of migraine headaches in the Clemens women. Miss Harrison is a minor character in the Clemens biography, but her shadow, the masculine, self-sufficient, aggressive female, would appear in the writings of Mark Twain in *The $30,000 Bequest*, "Hellfire Hotchkiss," "Wapping Alice," and other works as a puzzling and intriguing counterpoint to those fictional versions of the Clemens women, Joan of Arc, the little heroine of *A Horse's Tale*, and the Eve of *Eve's Diary*.

MacAlister had become a close friend during the London stay that opened the last decade of the writer's life. Secretary of the Royal Medical Society, MacAlister was responsible for attracting Clemens' eye to the speculative possibilities of Plasmon, a skim-milk derivative that was to be his major financial investment of the twentieth century. Clemens invested in both the British and American corporations founded to promote the health food, became involved in extensive litigation over the control of the American branch, and found Ralph W. Ashcroft, a young Liverpudlian whose photographs bear an uncanny resemblance to George Washington Cable, among the company's officers, taking him as his own representative and making him one of the original directors of the Mark Twain Company—an organization Ashcroft himself conceived. There would be reason, in the last year of his life, for Clemens to regret his appointment of Ashcroft as his business manager, but MacAlister was not to blame for that possibly misdirected confidence. MacAlister received some of the most intimate and most humorous of the letters that Clemens wrote in the last years of his life. And he became increasingly important to Clemens. He suggested an investment in Lysoform, an antiseptic soap, which Clemens adopted, and he sent his brother, a physician, to examine Olivia in her last illness in Florence. On occasion he

became Clemens' agent with Chatto & Windus, the humorist's English publishers.

It was not his friends and allies who kept Clemens' zestful mania for speculation alive in the twentieth century, however. Most often Rogers, MacAlister, and Miss Harrison were conservative and served as restraining influences on his excesses. It was his "enemies" who provided the spice.

Clemens' suspicions and disputes with business associates extended to his publishers. As he moved to the final contracts with Harper & Brothers which exchanged a guaranteed annual income for a virtual monopoly on his writings, Clemens used Rogers as his negotiator with Colonel George Harvey and Frederick Duneka of that publishing house, with Francis E. Bliss of the American Publishing Company, and with Robert Collier of Collier's. His own interests seemed almost monomaniacally centered on the monetary aspects of his writing: the price per word for his occasional writings, the return on complete sets—retail and subscription—of his works, the retention of copyright in his own name, and the right to reconsider all agreements every five years. In spite of Rogers' watchful eye, Clemens was to accuse all his publishers of dishonesty and corruption.

His literary instincts, aside from the commercial value of the results, atrophied during his last decade. Always uncertain and uncomfortable with fiction, Clemens more and more emphasized the autobiographical voice during his last years. His autobiographical dictations were the most obvious example, but his letters, diaries, essays, and literary polemics were only slightly disguised versions of that same voice. The "fiction" of the decade was almost obsessively fantastic projections of himself and his family and was almost always abortive and unfinished. Realistic fiction, Hannibal and the Mississippi River, were lost to him as resources for writing; instead, anti-imperialism, anti-vivisection, vituperation against Mary Baker Eddy, and similar outbursts, largely lacking the humor characteristic of Mark Twain to provide distance and equanimity, were the major products. And the autobiography itself was the purest form of this confessional mode. It

was Samuel Clemens with relatively few of the usual modifications
which the comic mask of Mark Twain allowed. In its associational
pattern it resembled psychoanalytic therapy as much as anything
else. The picture which accompanies its creation, the "King" (as
he was called by his court) propped up in bed dictating to a
shocked stenographer, Miss Josephine Hobby, and attended by
Paine and Miss Lyon, would be ludicrous except for Clemens'
attempts at complete honesty and truth and the artistry that
shaped many passages. Almost as if to reinforce the deathbed
image of the dictations, the recumbent speaker convinced himself
that he was talking "as from the grave" with complete candor and
unrestraint.

Whatever the posture of the author, the autobiographical writ-
ings of these years are an amazing achievement. They required,
first of all, an immense ego—the self-assurance that generations yet
unborn would be interested in the rambling reminiscences of a
septuagenarian, even if he was America's greatest humorist. Per-
haps vanity is a better word than self-assurance; Mark Twain had
an abundance of both. In addition, the autobiography required
narrative skill to blend the oral, associational manner of Huck
Finn floating down the Mississippi on a raft with the sarcasm, the
critical perspective, the pessimism of a man in his seventies. Once
he found the proper method, he wandered along constructing a
testament that runs to hundreds and hundreds of pages and repre-
sents a remarkable, and perhaps unique, combination of the oral
method with the perspective and the material of the astute and
complex cynic. Finally, for Mark Twain at any rate, the attempt at
complete honesty was new and unusual. In the nineteenth century
no American writer demeaned himself more to his various audi-
ences—or calculated his audiences' tastes so accurately. It required
a maturity which his readers had rarely seen for him to speak as
Samuel Clemens rather than as Mark Twain; and during this final
ten years of his life he attempted more and more often to strike
through the mask.

The impulse to be humorous choked a man whose sense of rage
at the world in which he lived grew and grew to mammoth pro-

portions and whose methods for dealing with that world were more often sarcastic and indignant rather than ironic or satiric. The very fact that so many of his fantasies were unfinished, even though Clemens worked on them compulsively and repeatedly, is testimony to the failure of his comic pose. What the literature of the final decade tells about his personality more strikingly than anything else is that he was struggling desperately to cast off the public image of himself which he had spent almost forty years perfecting.

And although it was extremely difficult for him to separate his public and his private manner, it was impossible for him to relinquish the public image he had developed for his family. The Clemens family was blessed, according to Clemens' and most of their associates' accounts, with utter harmony, complete understanding, and idyllic relationships. His wife, Olivia, was, to his mind, a delicate figurine, the Victorian ideal of a "lady." As he told T. R. Lounsbury in the month after her death, his "reverent & quite conscious worship" of Olivia was heightened by "the frailty of her body, which made us nurse her, & tend her, & watch over her & hover about her."

The truth is that Olivia's body was less frail than her mind; most of her lifelong illnesses originated from "emotional" rather than organic sources. When she was seventeen she was cured of "paralysis" by a faith healer. In her final illness Clemens himself finally admitted that she suffered from "nervous prostration"—the Victorian euphemism for a nervous breakdown or neurasthenia.

But in spite of her supposed frailty, Olivia was a strong-willed, passionate, even sensual woman. Her letter to her husband about the young writer Marie van Vorst (printed on p. 41) is neither docile nor ameliorative. The evidence of Letter VIII of "Letters from the Earth"—regarding masculine and feminine sexual capacities—must have some autobiographical basis:

> From the time a woman is seven years old till she dies of old age, she is ready for action, and *competent*. As competent as the candlestick to receive the candle. . . .

> But man is only briefly competent; . . . After
> fifty his performance is of poor quality, the in-
> tervals between are wide, and its satisfactions of
> no great quality to either party; whereas his
> great-grandmother is as good as new.

Olivia was indisputably a warm, independent, and occasionally antagonistic wife, whom Clemens forced into the Victorian mold of idolized invalid.

Her letters to the Southern novelist Grace King and to Mrs. Franklin Whitmore (the wife of Clemens' business agent in Hartford) are plaintive in their desire for a visit, for a friend whom Olivia could talk to or confide in. The urge for companionship evidently unavailable within her family was compounded by Clemens' unwillingness to introduce her into the worlds of his business or literary associates. Olivia and Mrs. Howells were not close friends, nor were she and her daughters more than casual acquaintances of Mrs. Henry Rogers and the Rogers girls. Clemens seems to have concluded that both his business and his literary relationships were not on a plane suited to his family; and although Olivia was not chained to her psychological sickbed, she was no doubt with her own contrivance locked in a marriage which near the end of her life was lonely and which focused all her attentions and energies on her husband.

Susy, the oldest daughter, who had died of meningitis in 1896, was by Clemens' own account a precocious and doting child; but we know that in her adult years she would listen in her bedroom until her father had left the breakfast table before she would come downstairs in the morning and that she fled from one of his lectures at Bryn Mawr, mortified by his performance.

Clara, the second daughter, was Clemens' Gentle Ben, the daughter who took her mother's place after Olivia's death. But Clara was discouraged by her father from pursuing the musical career she wanted and from contemplating marriage. Hypochondriacal and emotionally unpredictable, Clara was in and out of sanitariums during the last six years of her father's life, suffering from the symptoms of "nervous prostration" disturbingly similar

to her mother's, and, like her mother, able to see almost any visitor except Clemens. When out of the sanitarium, she pursued an expensive singing career, paid for (to the total of approximately $15,000 in the two-year span from early 1907 to early 1909) from the pockets of the father whose presence she could not tolerate. When she was at home with her father she was the domineering "commander-in-chief."

Clara had always been the daughter who dared confront and defy her father most openly. When she had attended a military ball in Berlin in 1893, Clara found herself alone in a side room with forty young German officers. Clemens became forty times more furious than he would have been if she had been in the room with only one. And the hysteria and intemperance of his chiding and lecturing of his daughter—she was Mark Twain's daughter and must be above suspicion—seems excessive and vain to the contemporary reader.

Later in her life, when the family was living in Florence in late 1903 and early 1904, Clemens and Clara stopped at a sidewalk restaurant. Clemens noticed that several young men were paying marked attention to Clara, looking at her with what he considered undue interest. Persuaded that the ornamental decorations on Clara's hat were the source of the attraction, he "became so enraged that, when they returned to the villa, he found a pair of scissors and sheared off every piece of fruit from her hat." Such behavior cannot help but suggest that Clemens was unprepared for his daughter to grow up and establish a life for herself. He would require that, even when she was approaching the age of thirty, she have chaperones meet her at trains, escorts supervise her abortive early concert tours—to be under almost constant surveillance. He may have felt that her behavior justified this scrutiny, but it seems just as likely that he resented and tried to stifle any acts of independence or maturity. Clara's long interview with a London newspaper during a concert tour—headlined "Penalties of a Father's Fame"—described in terms not altogether comic the unpleasantness of being Mark Twain's daughter and proved that she was unhappy with the restraints and restrictions he had im-

posed on her as a result of his urgent need to keep Clara depen-
dent on him.

Jean, the youngest daughter, was an epileptic who might almost
be labeled the daughter Mark Twain wanted to forget. Like him,
she was endowed with a native wit, a vigorous and energetic
personality, and a charm that manages to shine through the scanty
record of her life. But her epileptic attacks became more and more
violent and finally homicidal, resulting in attempts to kill sixty-
year-old Katy Leary, the Clemenses' housekeeper since 1880. Her
father banished her from his household—first to a two-year exile in
a "home" in Katonah, New York, then to Gloucester, Massachu-
setts; Greenwich, Connecticut; Berlin, Germany; Babylon, New
York, and Montclair, New Jersey—in spite of her pathetic requests
to be allowed to return to live with him at Redding, Connecticut.

Jean's epilepsy and the neurasthenic illnesses of Olivia and Clara
must suggest that in being forced to appear as models of propriety,
to assume the roles of Mark Twain's Family, to be subjected to but
not share the author's prominence, they became twisted people.

As his own family relationships disintegrated in the last few
years of his life, Samuel Clemens cultivated the friendships of
barely adolescent girls called "Angel Fish" separately and "The
Aquarium" in the mass. Although Clemens had said as early as
1866, "Young girls innocent & natural—_I_ love 'em same as others
love infants," his interest in the Angel Fish was more than avuncu-
lar, was even—in those final months when his mind tended to
wander, his memory lapsed, and symptoms of senility became
obvious—latently sexual. But in addition there must have been on
his part some sense of recapturing in those young girls the child-
hood of his own daughters which was lost, a period when he was
still an object of adoration and obedience. Lear-like, he had laid
waste to his kingdom, alienated his most loyal subjects, replacing
them with people who were more interested in their own future
share of his estate than in his well-being. The "King" was left in
the enormous empty mansion he had built in Redding, more
alone than he had ever been before.

As the body of Jean was carried for burial from Stormfield to

Elmira, New York, Clemens, too sick and infirm to accompany her, wrote one of his final essays:

> The snow continued to fall. At six o'clock the hearse drew up to the door to bear away its pathetic burden. Payne playing Schubert's "Impromptu," which was Jean's favorite. Then he played the Intermezzo; that was for Susy; then he played the Largo: that was for their mother. . . .
>
> From my windows I saw the hearse and the carriages wind along the road and gradually grow vague and spectral in the falling snow, and presently disappear.

In the circumstances, his ability to retain even a spark of humor and to write even unfinished fantasies was remarkable. God's fool, like Jay Gatsby, managed to come out all right in the end, which was his triumph; but he sustained himself by a microscopic margin in the last ten years of his life.

I. INDIAN SUMMER

(1900 to Summer 1904)

The 20th Century is a stranger to me—I wish
it well but my heart is all for my own century.
I took 65 years of it, just on a risk, but if I
had known as much about it as I know now
I would have taken the whole of it.
 —*Mark Twain's Notebook,* p. 372.

i

On January 1, 1900, fourteen correspondents to the London
Times wrote letters debating whether a new century had begun
that morning. Samuel L. Clemens (who, incidentally, sided with
the group that believed the twentieth century would not com-
mence until New Year's Day, 1901) was living in an apartment at
30 Wellington Court, taking personal stock of himself, his ailing
family, and his own homesickness. To his old friend Princeton
professor Laurence Hutton he complained on New Year's Day of
1900:

> I am getting heart-breakingly anxious to get
> home—to get home and never budge again. I am
> due to die this year, according to a trustworthy
> prophecy of thirty-five years' standing, and I
> must not get caught out, on the wrong side of
> the water.

And even if it was not a new century, it was a sensible year for
Clemens to be taking stock.

He had been born in Florida, Missouri, in 1835 but had spent
his childhood in Hannibal, on the Mississippi, storing up the

memories which would serve him as the reservoir for his most important writings. His formal education ended early—at the death of his father—and he became an apprentice newspaperman in Hannibal and in Keokuk and Muscatine as his older brother, Orion, struggled hopelessly to make a success of editing papers in those towns. Giving up journalism for the more lucrative profession of piloting, Clemens worked the St. Louis-to-New Orleans route along the Mississippi until the Civil War closed the river. In 1861 he traveled with Orion (paying both fares) along the Overland stage route to Nevada, where the older brother became secretary to the governor of the territory and the younger one pursued evanescent fortunes in silver. In 1863 Sam Clemens became a reporter for the lively Virginia City *Territorial Enterprise* and first used the pseudonym "Mark Twain," which would become both his gold mine and his albatross in later years. Moving to San Francisco, he wrote comic articles for a number of California papers and journals—the *Golden Era,* the *Californian,* the *Alta California,* and the *Call* among them—until, in 1867, he boarded the *Quaker City* to report for his Western audience the "pleasure" trip to the Holy Land of his Eastern fellow travelers.

But in the contest between the brash, self-confident Western journalist and the Eastern seaboard, it was Mark Twain who ultimately lost. A Hartford, Connecticut, subscription publishing house, the American Publishing Company, asked him to make a book of the travel letters he had written. A surrogate "mother," Mary Mason Fairbanks, undertook the impressive task of "refining" both Clemens and his prose. Smitten with a portrait of Olivia Langdon that her brother carried on the *Quaker City,* Sam Clemens wooed and won the Elmira, New York, girl over the objections of her family; and after a brief residence in Buffalo, New York, the couple settled in Hartford.

Success and fame came in a torrent. *The Innocents Abroad* (1869) was a best seller, as was its successor, *Roughing It* (1872). *The Adventures of Tom Sawyer* (1876), *Life on the Mississippi* (1883), *Adventures of Huckleberry Finn* (1885), and *The Trag-*

edy of Pudd'nhead Wilson (1894) all exploited the memories and the earlier career of Mark Twain for fictional and travel-narrative purposes. But other modes of writing interested him, too. Romances such as *The Prince and the Pauper* (1881) appealed to his genteel audience and his family, if not to the usual reader of his writings. And the fantasy called *A Connecticut Yankee in King Arthur's Court* (1889) also included moral and sociological preachments which suggested Clemens' increasing concern for political and economic issues.

After the death of their infant son, Langdon, in 1872, Clemens and Olivia had three daughters—Susy, Clara, and Jean—and lived in their Hartford house in a style that seemed almost a deliberate revenge for the poverty of his own childhood. And in spite of his literary successes, schemes for speculation became as habitual to Samuel Clemens as was the corollary loss of the money he invested. Apparently nothing in the way of poor investments, misplaced trusts, and absurd inventions could cool the fever that burned in him for immense wealth.

The world applauded in 1885 as Clemens' publishing company removed the shadow of bankruptcy from the family of dying Ulysses Grant by publishing his *Memoirs* at a spectacular profit. But the sales machinery developed to market Grant's two-volume account of his role in the Civil War was so elaborate and extensive that Clemens merely transferred the specter of insolvency to his own family when later books failed to sustain the company's early success. And when his publishing house failed during the Panic of 1893, the world applauded again as the sixty-year-old author vowed to pay back all his debts in full. By a strenuous round-the-world lecture tour and through the vigorous and conservative business management of Henry Huttleston Rogers, Clemens had managed to recover from his bankruptcy, with all creditors paid in full, shortly before the end of the nineteenth century.

But the cost had been immense, especially to the conscience of the writer. While he was in London at the end of the lecture tour that paid off his debts, word came that Susy, the eldest daughter,

had died of spinal meningitis in Hartford. Clemens blamed himself for her death, and neither he nor Olivia could contemplate moving back into the house in Hartford in which she had died.

So since the mid-1890s he and his family had lived in Europe—in London and Vienna and Florence and Sanna, Sweden. His wife and the two surviving daughters had not been in the United States since Susy's funeral. And except for the travel volume which came from the round-the-world trip, *Following the Equator,* Mark Twain had produced no major literature since 1894.

But 1900 was to be a watershed year for the man who sat at his desk on New Year's Day writing old friends. He was to celebrate his sixty-fifth birthday that November; he was to take his family "home"—or at least to return them to the United States—in October; he was finally debt-free. And he was on the brink of a "new" career as the social conscience and the political gadfly of the United States. Nevertheless, the paradoxes and inconsistencies in the character of the nineteenth-century humorist were not reconciled. His energy and his ego both were still boundless, and he had learned no permanent lessons from the wildcat speculations which had bankrupted him in 1894. His schemes, literary and non-literary, bubbled forth in random and contradictory confusion.

ii

In spite of his boundless energy, Clemens was beginning to feel old. One of the aphorisms he struggled over in 1900 went, "The age at which we notice, with a sigh, that we are beginning to say, 'it's not worth while, now'—60." Throughout the year, he was to be plagued by gout, toothache, and a persistent bronchial cough, which did nothing to improve his disposition. As 1900 began, Olivia had been bedridden for two weeks with influenza and bronchitis until mid-January. As Clemens told Henry Rogers, ordinary doctors would have bungled her treatment and had her "booked for the season or the grave," just as he claimed that they had assassinated his daughter Susy in 1896. It was no comfort that

Joe Twichell, the Hartford minister who was one of the Clemenses' closest friends, sent gossipy funereal letters cataloguing the deaths and lingering illnesses in Hartford among neighbors and acquaintances: Ward Cheney, Henry Robinson, Lizzie Robinson, Charles Smith, a neighbor named Fellows, Thomas Beecher, Charles Dudley Warner, General Franklin. As Twichell put it, in a phrase echoing unconsciously Mark Twain's own fascination with solipsism, "So the world melts away around us." Finally, inside the front cover of Notebook 34 for 1901—Clemens listed an imposing array of illnesses, some facetious and exaggerated but some recent and actual, with which he had been afflicted.

Mortality might have intruded itself on Clemens' thoughts less harshly had it limited itself to him and his contemporaries; but the health of his daughters diminished whatever reconciliation he might have developed about his own hacking coughs and swollen feet. Jean, the younger daughter, was in precarious health. Although Clemens told Hutton in his January 1 letter, "Clara is pretty fairly well; Jean is improving satisfactorily: both danced till 1 o'clock this morning, seeing the Old Year out and the New one in," the report was a cheerful bluff. Jean, whose epilepsy resulted in seizures as often as twice a day in 1899 and never farther apart than six weeks from mid-1899 to mid-1902, was under the almost daily care of Jonas Henrik Kellgren, at the Swedish Institution, 49 Eaton Square. Extant bills from Kellgren occasionally mention "Mrs. Clemens" as a patient, but the vast bulk of the $900 charges was for tri-weekly osteopathic treatments for Jean.

Although the epilepsy was a closely guarded family secret, it literally controlled the plans of the Clemenses for 1900. Desperately homesick though they were, they remained abroad because the Kellgren treatment was the only one that seemed to work for Jean. Clemens explained to Rogers:

> Jean's head got a bad knock when she [was] 8 or 9, by a fall. Seven years ago she showed capricious changes of disposition which we could not account for; and four years ago the New York experts pronounced her case *epilepsy*. . . .

> And so, this is the situation. We are obliged to
> believe that in time (indefinite) Kellgren can
> accomplish the cure. Nobody else can do it, ex-
> cept, possibly, an osteopathist. If the osteopath-
> ist can do it, we can go home; otherwise we
> must stay here, and stick it out.

The attempt to find an American osteopath began with well-
meaning but bumbling Joe Twichell, who, instead of getting
detailed descriptions of osteopathic treatments, sent "a copy of a
medical journal containing matter of interest (disagreeable inter-
est) to osteopathists." Clemens even contemplated the possibility
of training an osteopath who would join the entourage as family
physician: "the young man is a Swede . . . has studied and
worked four years with Kellgren, and is now head of the establish-
ment (under Kellgren) This gentleman wishes to take your
course and acquire your diploma as his purpose is to practice in
America."

That scheme did not work out either; and on April 23 Clemens
commissioned his nephew, Samuel E. Moffett, to make inquiries
about the ability of American osteopaths to treat "the worst form
of the non-hereditary" epilepsy. While awaiting Moffett's reply,
the family presumed that it was compelled to follow Kellgren to
his summer institute in Sanna, Sweden (where Jean had under-
gone treatment during the summer of 1899 while the rest of the
family swatted flies most of the day). Mrs. Clemens was "strongly
inclined to put in a good deal of time gadding around over
Sweden & Norway." The lightheartedness and the incongruous
idea of Mrs. Clemens "gadding about" were undoubtedly the re-
sult of two encouraging developments: Kellgren concluded in
early May that "Jean passed the main crisis and turned a corner—
an event which we have been anxiously watching for for 6 or 7
months." In addition, on May 17, Clemens decided that Dr.
George N. Helmer, a New York osteopath, would be a satisfactory
substitute for Kellgren. As he told Moffett on that day, "Your pre-
liminary letter and a letter from Helmer have given us great

satisfaction. When we elect to go home, now, we can go with confidence."

Adding to the mood of cheerfulness, on June 7 the family "decided to remain in England instead of going to Sweden; in London, almost . . . so that my daughter may come to the doctor three times a week." The family settled into Dollis Hill House, at the edge of London, with a large park surrounding the residence, in early July. Jean continued to have seizures, however, and the bursts of high spirits alternated with spells of deep gloom and depression. Clemens had told his sister Pamela on April 25, "I cannot think why God, in a moment of idle and unintelligent fooling, invented this bastard human race; and why, after inventing it, he chose to make each individual of it a nest of disgusting and unnecessary diseases, a tub of rotten offal." And in early June, to the widow of his childhood friend Will Bowen, Clemens wrote, "I should like to call back Will Bowen & John Garth & the others, & live the life, & be as we were, & make holiday until 15, then all drown together."

iii

It is significant as a corollary to his rapacious business instincts that Samuel Clemens almost never consulted his wife or family about investments which directly affected their security, future, and well-being. The family might participate in his literary projects as audience, advisers, and "purifiers" of texts, but Clemens chose to exclude them from his non-literary plans almost as if he was aware that his business partners would have to endure the worst attacks of his suspicions and wrath. He was willing to invest substantial sums on high-risk projects, but he was never able to accept responsibility for the loss of any money that such risks involved. It is fortunate that he kept his family out of these affairs and found instead "outsiders" like Charles L. Webster and James W. Paige on whom to exhaust his vituperation.

Still, by the beginning of 1900, in spite of all the calamitous reverses, he could not control any more than he could in the 1880s those impulses that led him to financial speculation and vengeful litigation. If anything, the amount of time and energy he spent on such affairs increased in the period from 1900 to 1906 as his creative output dwindled and in spite of all the common sense and the sage counsel his friends could give him.

His financial savior, Henry Rogers, and Rogers' son-in-law, William E. Benjamin, interceded for Clemens, handled his accounts, sold his real estate, and finally managed to put a solid foundation under his feet just before the beginning of the twentieth century. It is no less than ludicrous that Clemens' first speculative enterprise after Rogers had "saved" him was a plot to gain control of Plasmon, a health food that would instantaneously relieve a famine in India, according to Clemens, and sweep the world to its promoters' vast profit as surely as Beriah Sellers' eye-water was expected to do in Mark Twain's 1873 novel, *The Gilded Age*.

Clemens' interest in Plasmon was a coincidental product of Olivia Clemens' illness in the first months of 1900. He first encountered, consumed, and attempted to buy stock in this skim-milk derivative in 1898 in Vienna. In 1900 he wrote his distant cousin, Dr. James Ross Clemens, that Olivia was out of bed and recovering from her respiratory ailments: "I think she only needs that Vienna albumen, now. Where does one get it?" Although he did not know the brand name, he made up for his ignorance with enthusiasm. He put his entire family on Plasmon—a "pound of powder contains the nutriment of 16 pounds of the best beef"— bought £5,000 of stock in the British branch of the Berlin-based company, and accepted membership on its board of directors. On March 10 he told his close friend and co-investor in the company, J. Y. W. MacAlister, that they should "deliver in Calcutta or Bombay, carriage free, 2,500,000 pounds of Plasmon per month" to end a famine in India and, coincidentally, receive worldwide free advertising for the product. Two days earlier he had proposed

to MacAlister a convoluted mathematical formula for the found-
ing and funding of the American branch of the company. Andrew
Carnegie, Sir Thomas Lipton, and possibly even the Archbishop
of Canterbury would all be asked to subscribe for stock. William
James would get both barrels—a recommendation to go to Sanna
for Kellgren's osteopathic treatment and, while there, a diet of
Plasmon, vegetables, and fruit. And in his enthusiasm Clemens
calculated the possibilities of mixing Plasmon with Bovril, a
health food extracted at that time from horse meat, down to the
precise "average cost" of each Bovril horse.

Such ebullient scheming was integral to Clemens' personality,
balancing the moods of black despair. His stubborn inability to
have learned any lesson from the Paige typesetter or any of his
other doomed and bizarre schemes which resulted in bankruptcy
was completely typical. By cautious and careful management
Rogers had built up an account in Mrs. Clemens' name of $57,151
by June 30, 1900; the audacity required to remove promptly
almost a fourth of this capital for investment in an untried enter-
prise—one which Rogers greeted with stony silence, at that—was
monumental.

Sounder heads than Clemens', it must be admitted, were in on
the British Plasmon syndicate. And if the famine in India was not
dramatically relieved, the British branch of the company was set in
motion in a conservative and orderly fashion. Samuel Bergheim,
the London director, secured an underwriting of £240,000 from
the Exploration Company, an investment corporation and holding
company. When the guarantee was withdrawn and shares offered
to the public, Clemens regretted his inability to keep the organiza-
tion private with its investment divided up among a few di-
rectors so that Plasmon might model itself on "the history of
Vasilene, which pays a monster income, and has not been greatly
advertised." Clemens must have admired one design of Mac-
Alister's which could almost match his own plot to deluge India:
Plasmon secured the endorsement of Sandow the Strong Man,
who would recommend "a special Plasmon-Sandow breakfast

food" to the world. And in fact, the world's strongest man, as Sandow was billed in his popular exhibitions, did endorse a special brand of Plasmon in England.

<center>iv</center>

The nineteenth-century humorist, Mark Twain, lay fallow in the early months of 1900. The illnesses of his family and the speculative fever of Plasmon were enough to occupy his entire time (though there is an interesting correlation between his most frantic periods of composition and the worst of his vicissitudes). His literary interests were stirred, however, by an attractive proposal to edit a magazine. Samuel McClure, of the vast McClure syndicate, attempted to interest him in assuming a titular editorship of *The Universal Magazine,* tantalizing the potential editor with promises of a guaranteed annual salary of $5,000 plus $150 a thousand words for his original contributions; then he offered an option of 20 percent of the new magazine's stock. On the envelope of the letter, Clemens wrote a list of questions and possible objections:

> . . . I could not take a Dept., for the pub. would expect it to be "comic" (my Galaxy experience) and humor should be used sparingly for best effect—as a Roman punch to sauce the meal, not as the meal itself. If I edit the whole magazine (with grave help) no one will expect it to be comic.
>
> ———————
>
> Other Ed to do all correspondence;
> ask for articles;
> arrange terms;
> make up each number and submit it
> to me for approval or disap[1]. . . .

Since Clemens was bothered about the demand on his time, McClure reassured him that in a month "you might have as much

reading as would make an ordinary book—that is to say a day's
reading—at the outside two days' reading." A few days later, how-
ever, the mercurial McClure suddenly decided that Clemens'
duties would include the choice of illustrations, paper, the compo-
sition, and the layout of the magazine; in short, McClure said,
"there is practically no instance where the editors-in-chief of a
magazine are out of practically physical contact with their busi-
ness." This was enough to douse the interest Clemens originally
felt for the project; and the most fascinating vestige of the scheme
is the "manifesto" he wrote for the journal, underscoring the
necessity for humor to be mixed sparingly with "grave company;
its cheerful dress gets heightened color from the proximity of sober
hues."

But McClure was also interested in securing the exclusive right
to publish Mark Twain's future books, and to this part of the plan
the humorist registered no objections—nor apparently did Henry
Rogers—until the *Universal Magazine* part of the enterprise col-
lapsed. This was surprising, because Rogers had been working
diligently on a series of contracts which would untangle Clemens'
copyrights and place all publishing rights, ultimately, with Harper
& Brothers.

Undoubtedly the complex and confusing arrangements between
Harper's, the American Publishing Company, and the Clemenses
which Rogers worked out after the bankruptcy proceedings in the
late 1890s were becoming awkward and cumbersome. Harper's
was in the process of publishing *The Man That Corrupted
Hadleyburg and Other Stories* (as was Chatto & Windus in En-
gland), but the American Publishing Company was gathering
material to include in Volume XXII of its collected subscription
editions—*How to Tell a Story and Other Essays,* which was not
identical to the Harper 1897 *How to Tell a Story.* Clemens' letters
to Francis E. Bliss of the American Publishing Company, to
MacAlister, who was apparently assisting the author with the
English edition, and to Colonel George Harvey, editor of *Harper's
Weekly* and head of Harper & Brothers, suggest that copyright
problems, confusing provenances, and conflicts of interest lurked

not far beneath the surface. A half dozen stories and essays are duplicated in the two volumes, with varying and contradictory copyrights. The problem of conflicts between his publishers would not be solved for several years (and then only to Clemens' temporary satisfaction), but the various McClure schemes and proposals seem to have impelled the author's thinking toward a single and solidified publishing contract as early as 1900.

v

A former residence of Gladstone's, Dollis Hill, thirty minutes from central London, was surrounded by huge trees and vast expanses of lawn. The family loved its charm, and Olivia wrote that

> Jean has a hammock swung between two such
> great trees, & on the other side of a little pond,
> which is *full* of white & yellow pond-lilies, there
> is tall grass & trees & Clara & Jean go there in
> the afternoons, spread down a rug on the grass
> in the shade & read & sleep.

Clemens told Twichell, "I am the only person who is ever in the house in the daytime," and later during the summer he decided that the substantial, solidly built brick house "comes nearer to being a paradise than any other home I ever occupied." Even though it sounded arcadian in its repose and splendor, Dollis Hill had some minor vexations—no telephone, erratic mail deliveries, confusing street names in the vicinity.

But Mark Twain was able to turn the annoyances to literary use. In the unpublished fragment "Travel Scraps" he explained the dilemma of having to order groceries and supplies by mail from the great Whiteley's:

> He will send you anything you want: a bishop,
> a cook, a cow, a kangaroo; set of furniture; beef,
> ham, butter, ice, any brand of eatable or drink-
> able the globe affords; an orchestra, a nigger

show, a banquet, with table-ware, flowers, wait-
ers, after-dinner speakers; a bride, a groom,
bridesmaids, groomsmen, wedding-clothes, bridal
presents; cradle, cat, dog, doctor, rat-poison, rats,
whetstone, grindstone, tombstone, hearse, corpse
—anything you want; but you must order to him
a day and a half in advance, to make sure.

These were minor, and comic, harassments, though, compared to
the world situation, which was beginning to attract his attention
and to arouse his anger.

The Boer War, the Boxer Rebellion, and the Philippine strug-
gle for independence had all brought forth Mark Twain's private
comment in letters to Howells, Twichell, and Rogers. Twichell
confirmed his own mood of despair: "Mark, *what* a world tumult
is on hand just now! And what a black appalling cloud Pekin lies
under! Nothing like it since the Indian Mutiny. I dread the tale
of shuddering horrors presently to unfold." And Twichell even
praised his friend for "the way you throw your rotten eggs at the
human race. . . . For enthusiasm of misanthropy you beat us out
of sight." But what Twichell approved, as became obvious in early
1901, was private rather than public criticism of the aggression of
the United States and England. And the evidence suggests that in
early 1900 Mark Twain agreed.

For, some time that summer, he composed "The Missionary in
World-Politics," a bitter rehearsal of "To the Person Sitting in
Darkness" and "To My Missionary Critics." Twain attacked the
Christian missionaries in China more astringently than he ever
had before, even in *Following the Equator,* and concluded with
the prophecy, "The future is blacker than has been any future
which any person now living has tried to peer into." He did not
offer the letter for publication, however, though a letter to
C. Moberly Bell, editor of the London *Times,* accompanied the
manuscript. As interesting as the decision not to publish at all was
the injunction to Bell for total anonymity: "Don't give me away,
whether you print it or not."

If anonymity or self-censorship in print were necessary, Mark

Twain still needed a literary outlet for his indignation. He took up his manuscript of "Chronicle of Young Satan," one of the *Mysterious Stranger* fragments, which he had begun in Vienna in 1897, and wrote six and a half chapters that summer of 1900. Whether because he could never satisfactorily complete any of the fragments or from fear of identifying himself with unpopular views, he would never submit any of *The Mysterious Stranger* for publication. In the 1900 segment Philip Traum, the young angel who appears in the Austrian village to comment upon human behavior, notes with scorn the missionaries' exploitation of the Chinese and the indefensible English position in the Boer War. The paragraph on the missionaries in China was pungent:

> The Christian missionary will exasperate the Chinese; they will kill him in a riot. They will have to pay for him, in territory, cash, and churches, sixty-two million times his value. This will exasperate the Chinese still more, and they will injudiciously rise in revolt against the insults and oppressions of the intruder. This will be Europe's chance to interfere and swallow China, and her band of royal Christian pirates will not waste it.

This prophecy was delivered by a fantastic stranger in a romance which, since Mark Twain may in 1900 still have intended to publish it, insulated its author from direct criticism. Probably the most important single fact in Mark Twain's life in 1900 was his tentative, exploratory removal of his fictional disguise, which he was unable to make in this case.

Of course it is true that Mark Twain had always been a moralist; as countless earlier statements had, his prospectus for the abortive *Universal Magazine* made that fact clear in 1900:

> I think I have seldom deliberately set out to be humorous, but have nearly always allowed the humor to drop in or stay out, according to its fancy. Although I have many times been asked

> to write something humorous for an editor or
> a publisher I have had wisdom enough to de-
> cline. . . . I have never tried to write a humor-
> ous lecture; I have only tried to write serious
> ones.

"I have," he said in 1900, "been forced by fate to adopt fiction as a medium of truth." It was vital to the rest of his literary career that the fictional mode and voice be discarded at least part of the time, that he break through the largely self-imposed comic public image, that he gain confidence in his own personal voice—the autobiographical mode—as a means of expressing unpleasant truths. Very shortly he would have the opportunity to test his "real" voice.

Idyllic as Dollis Hill was, in mid-October, after almost a decade of residence outside the United States, the Clemens family returned home. Finally convinced that Jean could receive proper treatment in New York City, they sailed on the *Minnehaha*. Clemens was interviewed, both before his departure and after his arrival, like a victorious hero or a major prophet. Just as he was leaving England, he said in an interview for the New York *World* on October 6, when asked for his views on imperialism, that he was "at the disadvantage of not knowing whether our people are for or against spreading themselves over the face of the globe." But in a dockside interview in New York on October 15, he shrugged off his diffidence and public reservations: "I am an anti-imperialist. I am opposed to having the eagle put its talons on any other land." Not only was the initial interview reprinted widely (Mark Twain subscribed to several clipping services whose documents survive in the Mark Twain Papers) but, more important, his outspoken criticism received editorial approval. One anonymous clipping, "Mark Twain Wavers, Too," expressed admiration at the courage it took to voice his honest anti-imperialism, "even if it costs him the severing of lifelong ties." When he pressed charges against an extortionate hackman, the Springfield (Massachusetts) *Republican* (a newspaper not usually sympathetic to Mark Twain) commented about his "courage in standing up for the

rights of the citizen. . . . But it is to be feared that so few will dare to imitate the example that the public will settle back into its easy-going ways" (December 2, 1900). When he castigated with savage irony the municipal government of New York at a speech at the St. Nicholas Club, another unidentifiable editorial praised his willingness to satirize "New Yorkers to their faces as few after-dinner speakers have the courage to do." Mark Twain was to have ample opportunity to display his courage.

vi

When the *Minnehaha* docked, a reporter for the New York *World* with a keen eye for descriptive detail catalogued Mark Twain's appearance:

> There was the familiar bushy hair, the twinkling, semi-mysterious eyes, the peculiar drawling voice, half Yankee, half Southern, the very low turn-down collar of the West and the immaculate shiny silk hat and long frock coat of the effete East. He looked as young as he did twenty years ago, and younger than he did when he shook American dust off his feet in 1891.

Olivia, nearing her fifty-sixth birthday as the family returned to the United States, had lost the fragile and delicate beauty that had marked her earlier portraits. High collars and severely tailored clothing accented the healthy vigor, even portliness, of her features, as did her upswept hair. Everything about her photographs of the period suggests authoritative well-being. Clara and Jean, who were twenty-seven and twenty-one years old, were pretty. Clara was stately, even patrician, with a fuller face than the other women of the family, which muted the Roman nose and angularity of her mother and sisters. Jean had been photographed with her dog "The Professor" in 1898 and looked like a Gibson girl: mutton-chop sleeves on her lace blouse, her dark hair pulled

back by a single bow and hanging down her back, her eyes demurely downcast, and her features classically beautiful. By 1901, in another photograph, she was wearing her hair up, and her illness was presumably responsible for the increasingly masculine austerity of her features.

Clemens made a triumphal entry into the social life of New York City on his return to the United States. But there were ominous undercurrents, as he recalled in 1906:

> We took No. 14 West 10th Street, just out of Fifth Avenue, for a year, and there the over-taxing of Mrs. Clemens's strength began. The house was large; housekeeping was a heavy labor—as indeed it always is in New York—but she would not have a house-keeper. She had resisted, and successfully resisted, all my persuasions in that direction from the day that we were married. Social life was another heavy tax upon her strength. In the drive and rush and hurly-burly of the mid-winter New York season my correspondence grew beyond my secretary's strength and mine, and I found that Mrs. Clemens was trying to ease our burden for us. One day I wrote thirty-two brief letters with my own hand, and then found, to my dismay, that Mrs. Clemens had written the same number. She had added this heavy labor to her other labors and they were already too heavy for her.

While the house and the epistolary duties may have been a burden to his wife, every indication is that the vast bulk of Clemens' own social activity occurred away from home and apart from his wife.

He wrote, he spoke at political rallies, he dashed off letters to the editors of newspapers with the frenzy of a demented spinster, and he paraded with glee and relish wherever the spotlight of publicity shone. His speechmaking schedule and after-dinner itinerary literally made him ill during the winter of 1900–1901, and it took him away from his family and the sequestered existence they

had enjoyed in London. Clubs honored him with testimonial dinners—the Lotos, the Aldine, the St. Nicholas, and the Press Club. He spoke—and spoke—to the Nineteenth Century Club, to the Berkeley Lyceum, to the City Club, and to a Lincoln's Birthday celebration at Carnegie Hall. For a man entering his sixty-fifth year, his stamina was almost beyond belief. He told MacAlister, "I declined 7 banquets yesterday (which is double the daily average)." The public figure, dormant during his European exile, appeared again with a compulsiveness which suggests that he hoped to compress into a single winter's schedule all the banquets, ceremonies, and public gatherings he had missed in the preceding six years.

The craving for public acclaim may have been reinforced by private distress. Perhaps Jean's condition, which was to become so repellent to him in the coming years, drove him from the house on the pretext of outside engagements. Possibly Clara's singing career, which was budding that winter of 1900–1901, offended him as a sign of her increasing maturity and independence. It is curious that when Clara's debut as a concert singer occurred on January 22, 1901, "ailing" Olivia was able to make the trip—twice, when the first date was canceled—to the Columbia Theater in Washington, D.C.; Samuel Clemens was not. Shortly after, Clara had her second recital, in Hartford, where she received a "wonderful reception" in spite of the bronchitis which, together with sore throats and tonsillitis, would plague her concert appearances and cause the cancellation of most of them. A concert was scheduled for Boston in mid-February but had to be canceled. There is no indication that Clemens attempted to attend any of these several appearances—and, indeed, he would studiously avoid later ones, playing billiards while Clara sang. And even at this fledgling stage of her career, her father preferred the company of Henry Rogers and a gang of cronies on the yacht *Kanawha,* or an assembly of reformers attempting to wrench Tammany Hall loose from the controls of New York City, or a Congressional hearing on a new copyright law to the society of his own family. Indeed, Mrs. Clemens made it clear to Grace King, one of her few confidantes,

that Clara was pursuing her concert career with less than total parental approval; the daughter had decided "to give up her concerts for this Winter. We are very glad. We do not oppose her, for of course that is not best, but we are very sorry indeed that she wants this public life."

Clara's father nevertheless received further impetus to exploit his own public life in the winter of 1900–1901. Critics who reviewed *The Man That Corrupted Hadleyburg*, published in late 1900, noted and generally approved the seriousness of the volume. William Archer, in a review that appeared in both the London *Morning Leader* (on September 22) and in the November issue of *The Critic*, lauded the title story as "a fable designed to drive home an ethical lesson." In *The Academy* (September 29, 1900), the reviewer said that "Mark Twain, censor and critic, is rapidly taking the place of Mark Twain, fun-maker. . . . Mark Twain, now that he has given up purely funny yarns, remains the one man (barring Mr. Dooley) who is encouraged or permitted to say things like this." *Blackwood's* disapproved of the "new" Mark Twain, while recognizing the qualities he espoused: "He is too fond of being didactic, of pointing morals, of drawing lessons." And *The Book Buyer* for September noted, and praised, the "more serious papers that have come from his pen in recent years. . . . Mark Twain's humor has grown more quiet with the passing of the years, but more subtle as well, more philosophical, with a substratum of wisdom that gives a higher value."

The point is not that all these critics were nearsighted; anyone in 1900 could have compiled a substantial anthology of Mark Twain's "serious" or "philosophical" or "moral" writings. Nor is it the essential point that, almost without exception, critics and interviewers and reviewers were emphasizing for the first time these qualities in the humorist's writing and speeches. What is significant is that Mark Twain, an author more sensitive than most of his image in the eyes of his audience, was becoming persuaded that a vocal dissident minority was respectable and even proper. It seems impossible that such a chorus of approval as the one that greeted his social criticism in late 1900 could have escaped his

attention. As the year ended he was to discover that his own public view was the popular one and that what was required of him was not the courage to defend an unpopular cause but the instinct to perceive accurately the true sentiment and tenor of the American public.

vii

On November 27, 1900, in the midst of the speechmaking schedule that left him physically ill, he wrote "A Greeting from the Nineteenth Century to the Twentieth Century," which appeared in the New York *Herald* on December 30 as "taken down in shorthand by Mark Twain":

> I bring you the stately matron named Christendom, returning bedraggled, besmirched and dishonored from pirate-raids in Kiao-Chou, Manchuria, South Africa & the Philippines, with her soul full of meanness, her pocket full of boodle and her mouth full of pious hypocrisies. Give her the soap and a towel, but hide the looking-glass.

Fifty words, reproduced in the *Herald* in Mark Twain's own handwriting, giving them an added stamp of authenticity and honesty. As soon as the Salutation appeared, a correspondent named Abner Goodell wrote Clemens, "In my opinion it is, so far as I know, the best thing you ever did. Indeed, I rank it with Lincoln's immortal speech at Gettysburg." Clemens' reply thanked Goodell for his letter but predicted, "I shan't receive many of its kind." But the day Clemens wrote Goodell, another letter arrived—from Andrew Langdon, Olivia Clemens' uncle. Langdon wrote:

> In all the books you have written, in all the
> speeches you have made, I have never seen
> So much good sense

> So much Christianity
> So much manhood
> So much Godliness—as in the ten lines of your
> Salutation speech to the Twentieth Century.

Perhaps the two accolades combined with the approving comments on his public morality in the newspapers earlier that autumn were sufficient to persuade Clemens to propel himself onward in his new role. Certainly such hearty approval by a Langdon must have been influential. The first exploratory statement and the two letters which closed the year were to be followed almost immediately by a critical test—"To the Person Sitting in Darkness"—a test which Mark Twain was to pass victoriously.

On Christmas Eve, 1900, the writer culled from the New York *Sun* a series of articles and notes which were to preface "To the Person Sitting in Darkness"; and he replied to a lunch invitation from Brander Matthews, professor at Columbia University, sympathetic critic, and close friend:

> I have ended my holiday at last and put on my
> overalls and devoted myself to a long and steady
> siege of work. My work-day stretches from 11:30
> A.M. till 7 P.M., and so my lunching days are over,
> for many months to come.

As he worked, additional praise came from correspondents; and his replies indicated his own sense of newfound mission. To one he announced, "It is my belief that the things which I have been saying tally with the feelings and opinions which reside in the hearts of all the intelligent men in the nation, but I shall not expect many of them to come out and confess it"; to another he expressed thanks for the approval of the "Salutation": "In speaking for the silent men, you do me a helpful office; we can always speak with more courage when we know that we have backers. The silent approval of straight men is a prodigious support; we only need to know that it exists."

He was to know soon enough the support that his attack on Christian missionaries could command, for, when the *North*

American Review appeared in February, he was deluged with letters from all over the United States, from Canada, England, and Australia. As one would suspect, he kept close tally on favorable letters (which he marked with a + or a #) and the negative ones (marked with a cross in a circle or the word "against").

Of the roughly fifty letters that survive, almost all were enthusiastically favorable. Mark Twain was "the voice of the People"; he had spoken "ringing words of truth [which] have caused an awakening that nothing else has been able to do." One of the correspondents, Edmund Norton, wrote:

> I knew you had the *ear* of the *great audience* and if you saw the *things* I did may-be some day you would tell them and they could not help hearing and their conscience would smite them unawares.
>
> After a while the mask dropped; I saw the *man;* I knew he saw the *things* and he *said* so, while I thanked God it was a man. . . .

On the margin opposite this fulsome praise Clemens wrote, "Read it, Livy, and return to me."

Did Mrs. Clemens disapprove the assault on missionaries? A few—a very few—of the correspondents did; but Clemens, like Colonel Sherburn in *Huckleberry Finn,* noted the anonymity of most of his assailants, who signed themselves "A sister," "Students," "Rob Roy," and "Mulberry Sellers." Clemens would have been especially interested in having his wife read the commendations, for one reason because the most important detractor of Clemens' position could almost certainly count on Mrs. Clemens' attention. Joe Twichell was, throughout all of 1901, a constant and unremitting critic. Twichell wrote his first criticism before the end of January, for on the twenty-ninth Clemens rebuffed him: "I'm not expecting anything but kicks for scoffing, and am expecting a diminution of my bread and butter by it, but if Livy will let me I will have my say." Nevertheless, Twichell kept up the needling:

> But the rest of your milk is also pretty sour it seems to me, old fellow. Really you are getting quite orthodox, on the doctrine of Total Human Depravity anyway.

> [An honorary Yale degree] will be in its intention the highest public compliment, and emphatically so in your case, for it will be tendered you by a corporation of gentlemen, the majority of whom do not at all agree with the views on important questions which you have lately promulgated in speech and in writing, and with which you are identified in the public mind.

> [To Mrs. Clemens:] Of course, I didn't believe a word of it [an attack on the human race, probably "The Stupendous Procession"]—any more than he did.

Exasperated by the carping of Twichell, Clemens could not resist pointing out that the complacent clergyman might examine his own responsibilities:

> *I* can't understand it! You are a public guide and teacher, Joe, and are under a heavy responsibility to men, young and old; if you teach your people—as you teach me—to hide their opinions when they believe the flag is being abused and dishonored, lest the utterance do them and a publisher a damage, how do you answer for it to your conscience? You are sorry for me; in the fair way of give and take, I am willing to be a little sorry for you.

The retort, even though it did not silence the friendly antagonist, suggests a growing self-confidence on Mark Twain's part.

And Mrs. Clemens remained loyal to her husband. On February 15, 1901, she wrote Grace King:

> many of our friends do not approve [the stand of her husband], on the other hand very many do.

He receives more letters of approval than of dis-
approval—in fact ten to one I should think.

Twichell could have mustered slightly greater support from the
newspaper and magazine editorials than from Clemens' personal
mail. On February 9, 1901, *Harper's Weekly* allowed John Ken-
drick Bangs to comment on "To the Person Sitting in Darkness";
Bangs mourned his discovery that "the great purveyor of sunshine
to his fellow men [was] joining the ranks of the prophets of evil,
spreading the gospel of discontent, and being governed by his
disgusts rather than by his admirations." The New York *Times*
was opposed to Mark Twain's handiwork, as was a youthful Jesse
H. Jones: "American literature," Jones wrote, "does not contain
so shameful a case of disreputable conduct as the action of Mark
Twain in his attack."

The American Missionary Board also felt compelled to defend
itself against the charges of exorbitant claims. When Judson
Smith, the corresponding secretary for the American Board of
Commissioners for Foreign Missions, wrote a lengthy letter to
Clemens and then released its contents to the New York *Tribune,*
Clemens dashed off a reply, refusing to retract his statements or to
issue an apology. Three days later he composed another letter to
the editor of the *Tribune* on the Ament matter (W. S. Ament was
the missionary who bore the brunt of the attack in "To the Person
Sitting in Darkness") but apparently decided not to publish it.
On March 10, he wrote a lengthy private letter to Smith suggesting
that Ament "has the unwisest set of friends, and about the un-
kindest, that ever a man in trouble had. They will not let
his case rest, although they surely know that it has not a leg
to stand on." When Ament himself contemplated suing Mark
Twain and the Peking Missionary Board cabled a demand for
retraction—"Peking Missionary Association demand public retrac-
tion of Twain's gross libel against Ament; utterly false"—Colonel
Harvey allowed Clemens to reply with "To My Missionary
Critics" in the April *North American Review,* enlivening that
journal in ways that must have made at least one of its former

editors, Henry Adams, wonder at the loss of decorum. (And, indeed, it was in the *North American Review* that Mark Twain lifted his new voice for the public in the succeeding year—with "Does the Race of Man Love a Lord?" and "In Defense of General Funston.")

The inharmonious notes of criticism were almost completely drowned out by a chorus of praise and encouragement. Poultney Bigelow wrote Clemens, "It was soothing to see Bangs make an ass of himself," and an editorial in the New York *Evening Post* commented on the "magnificent silence which Mark Twain has received from the Imperialist press. . . . And when we assert that nothing has been said in reply to his *North American* article, we do it in full knowledge of the fact John Kendrick Bangs has three columns in rejoinder in *Harper's Weekly.*"

The primary catalyst that provoked Mark Twain's assault on the Christian missionaries was an article describing the indemnities demanded by them for damages and deaths which the "heathen" Chinese had inflicted upon Christian converts. The article quoted W. S. Ament announcing that he also collected "fines" which amounted to thirteen times the amount of the actual damages. The fines were to be used, the story explained, for the propagation of the Gospel. Ament claimed further that his exorbitant demands were moderate compared to payments to Catholics—who demanded, in addition to cash payments, a head for each of the 680 Catholics killed in the Boxer uprising.

From caustic irony at the vindictive and mercenary actions of the missionaries, Mark Twain proceeded to a slashing assault in "To the Person Sitting in Darkness" against what he called the "Blessings-of-Civilization Trust." While proclaiming their dedication to the advancement of Civilization, the Western imperialist powers—the United States, England, Germany, Russia, and France —had each actually exploited and ravaged with a "banner of the Prince of Peace in one hand and its loot-basket and its butcher-knife in the other." It was a mordant assault on the sanctimonious hypocrisy of the missionaries, and "To My Missionary Critics" contained little in the way of apology for the tenor of the earlier

"To the Person Sitting in Darkness." Quite the contrary, the second article assembled wire-service evidence, marked as "Exhibits," to document the accuracy of Mark Twain's earlier charges. When Judson Smith of the American Board of Foreign Missions pointed out that the "thirteen times" of the original news story was a typographical error for "1/3rd," Mark Twain mused:

> Then what does *one third* extra stand for? Will he give that one third a name? Is it Modified Theft and Extortion? Is that it? The girl who was rebuked for having borne an illegitimate baby excused herself by saying, "But it is such a *little* one."
>
> When the "thirteen-times-extra" was alleged, it stood for theft and extortion, in Dr. Smith's eyes, and he was shocked. But when Dr. Ament showed that he had taken only a *third* extra, instead of thirteenfold, Dr. Smith was relieved, content, happy. I declare I cannot imagine why.

While allowing the missionaries the virtues of courage, patience, and self-sacrifice, Mark Twain's diagnosis that "sometimes the headpiece of that kind of man can be of an inferior sort, and error of judgment can result" was not intended to ameliorate the conflict.

With candid self-appraisal that was startling, Clemens made it completely clear how aware he was that the praise and commendation were integral to his pursuit of his opponents. On the margin of one of the impressive sheaf of clippings he collected, saved, underlined, and circled (a New York *Herald* of February 18, 1901), Clemens wrote:

> Broadly speaking corn-pone stands for self-approval. Self-approval is acquired mainly from the approval of others. Conformity is the result. Corn-pone is confor[mity]. Sometimes it has a sordid business interest back of it and is calculated; but mainly it is unconscious and not calculated.

It was the "text" for his essay "Corn-Pone Opinions," where Mark Twain maintains that "a man is not independent, and cannot afford views which might interfere with his bread and butter. . . . He must train with the majority; in matters of large moment, like politics and religion, he must think and feel with the bulk of his neighbors."

Obviously, Clemens found his role as professional after-dinner iconoclast as exhilarating as it was demanding. "I have done very little work," he told Rudolf Lindau, because he had got into "hot water with the clergy and the other goody-goody people, but I am enjoying it more than I have ever enjoyed hot water before." Later in the year he was so dedicated to his new position that he would respond to a request for a speech, "in the *daytime?*—and on a peaceful, courteous, social, non-political occasion? It is too ghastly."

 viii

In June of 1901 the Clemens family—except for Clara, who continued in spite of her parents' attitude to study voice in New York City for part of the summer—moved into a rustic cottage at the edge of Lake Saranac, New York. They christened the house "The Lair," and away from the temptations of notoriety Clemens pitched into frantic literary work in a plank-floored tent that he raised on the grounds of his cottage.

Someone at *The Century Magazine* mailed him a collection of newspaper articles on lynchings in the United States. Among them was an editorial from the New York *Evening Post* (June 8) commending Sheriff Joseph Merrill of Carroll County, Georgia, for holding off a lynch mob; another praised Sheriff Beloat of Mount Carmel, Illinois, for identical heroism; a third catalogues lynchings by fire in Colorado, Kansas, Indiana, and Texas; others describe lynchings in Arkansas and Missouri. Mark Twain wrote Frank Bliss of the American Publishing Company, "The thing I am full of, now, is a large subscription book to be called 'History

of Lynching in America'—or 'Rise and Progress of Lynching'—or some such title." He asked Bliss to hire someone to collect newspaper stories of lynchings, including several that Clemens remembered from his own childhood. As a part of his scheme, he wrote "The United States of Lyncherdom" on August 25, which he planned to use either as the introduction to the proposed book or to publish in the *North American Review* "as an advertisement *for* the book." Three days later he canceled the plan for the anthology of lynchings, "for I shouldn't have even half a friend left, down there [in the South], after it issued."

That same month he had interrupted his writing to join a boatload of Henry Rogers' cronies for a trip off the New England coast. Mark Twain was made the "Official Logger" of the cruise, and his log bears some resemblance to a burlesque detective story. On the first day the men discover that an umbrella is missing. A search—many searches, in fact—boardings by authorities, even a "spectre" of an umbrella all hint at a farcical spoof of Sherlock Holmes. Finally, with a number of less than subtle comic hints about Henry Rogers' kleptomania, the cruise and the log ended on August 17.

After returning to The Lair, Twain produced his 25,000-word novelette, *A Double-Barrelled Detective Story,* in six days, together with "a grist of writing . . . but not for publication soon, if ever." *A Double-Barrelled Detective Story* was at least double-barreled, if not a veritable Gatling gun of ideas, modes of writing, and crossed purposes. It opened with an episode reminiscent of a lynching—a husband persecuting his pregnant wife by having bloodhounds rip the clothes from her while she is tied to a tree. She later bears a son "marked" with a bloodhound's sense of smell. Archy, the son, swears vengeance on his father—"We are Southerners; and by our custom and nature there is but one atonement"—but pursues the wrong man, a cousin of his father, for over a year.

The action then settles down in Hope Canyon, California, a mining town. There a second story line opens. The evil Flint

Buckner has abused young Fetlock Jones, and the boy plans to
murder the offender. Sherlock Holmes, Fetlock's uncle, suddenly
appears in camp, making fanciful, and always illogical, deductions
on the basis of absurd evidence. Jones kills Buckner, and Holmes,
misreading every clue, names Sandy Hillyer as the murderer.
Archy reveals that Jones is the true assassin and finally encounters
the man he had wrongfully pursued—who happens to walk by
providentially during Buckner's funeral. The cousin, insane, be-
lieves that it was Sherlock Holmes who had pursued him rather
than Archy, and his pathetic story incites the miners to form a
lynch mob. Sheriff Jack Fairfax arrives and saves the great detec-
tive. Jones is allowed to escape, and Flint Buckner is revealed to
have been Archy's real father.

The extravagant mixture of literary parody, melodrama, and
low burlesque has only one redeeming factor. In *A Double-Bar-
relled Detective Story* Mark Twain managed for the last time to
complete a substantial work of fiction which embodies elements of
the major themes of his career. The Southern "code" of revenge,
the Western mining camp and its special argot, the lynch mob and
the courageous spokesman for reason and order, these were the
raw materials of the story. That they failed to cohere in this final
attempt at exploiting them is important. The raw materials on
which Mark Twain had established his reputation were no longer
malleable. The memories could no longer be shaped. Except for
unfinished fragments, the whole range of creative sources implied
by the *Detective Story*—the South, the mining camps, the boyhood
detective adventures of Hucks and Toms—were no longer usable
ones. No matter how often he tried to return to it, the tank of
inspiration had gone dry for the last time.

Later attempts were obsessive ones, but they were all unfin-
ished: "Tom Sawyer's Conspiracy," the "Mysterious Stranger"
fragments, and similar manuscripts would present the central
materials again but never in a completed unit. A brief comment
by Archy—"How blind and unreasoning and arbitrary are some of
the laws of nature—most of them, in fact!"—would become the

major focus of Mark Twain's writing and almost the exclusive subject in works of non-fiction.

Following his habit of salvaging any useful material, he managed to insert into *A Double-Barrelled Detective Story* at least a snippet from the summer's concern with the lynching book. In phraseology reminiscent of Colonel Sherburn in *Huckleberry Finn,* Sheriff Fairfax tells the lynch mob:

> "If there's anything I do particularly despise, it's a lynching mob; I've never seen one that had a man in it. . . . The sheriff that lets a mob take a prisoner away from him is the lowest-down coward there is. By the statistics there was a hundred and eighty-two of them drawing sneak pay in America last year."

The day after finishing the *Detective Story,* he wrote Bliss that "the lynching-book still haunts me," and on September 10, he used his ideas as a part of a lengthy sermon to Twichell.

ix

Even though the cottage on the shores of Lake Saranac was so conducive to literary activity that Clemens claimed "nothing can move us out but dynamite," the Clemens family was approaching, although unknowingly, its own disintegration.

The most significant events of the latter half of 1901, both emotional and financial, involved the Hartford house in which the family had spent their "best" years, in which their children were raised, and around which clustered the friends of the past who kept asking them to return to their own elegant, private version of the nineteenth century. On August 27, 1901, Clemens wrote to Franklin Whitmore, the real-estate agent who managed the Clemens business interests in Hartford, that he was willing at least to entertain offers for the Hartford mansion: "I doubt if Mrs. Clemens can ever bring herself to sell, but . . . there has never

been a time when I wouldn't have sold the house for anything it would fetch if the family had been willing." Only a week later he would reply with a lie to one of Twichell's frequent pleas that the family return to Nook Farm: "We've *got* to stick to New York until Jean's doctors give us leave to quit. The Hartford house . . . has cost us $16,000 in the past ten years." Jean was well enough, of course, to risk being as far away from Dr. Helmer as the Adirondacks all summer; and, having leased a home at Riverdale-on-the-Hudson for the first of October, Clemens gave Whitmore specific instructions about selling the Hartford house, even at a loss: "Our Hartford house, stables and grounds (unfurnished) cost $110,000 cash. . . . The land is worth what it cost, $31,000. Do you think you could sell the whole $111,000 worth for $60,000?" Olivia apparently knew nothing of these plans and decisions. Late in 1901 Clemens would tell Whitmore that she would not consider selling, or at any rate advertising, the house "before she *knew* there was some other place that she preferred"; but Clemens urged that offers be reported to him rather than to her, even though the house was owned by her and had been kept from his creditors in 1894 by the claim that it was built from her private income.

Clemens' subterfuge is surprising, but in a sense it is a part of that new "independence" which had domestic as well as literary and sociological overtones. He was torn by conflicting loyalties, traditions, and expectations. In addition to redefining his public role, he was tentatively exploring the limits of his obligations to and dependence on his wife and daughters, living and dead. Perhaps it is unfair to invest a major import in his willingness to sell the Hartford home; but it is also possible that he was beginning to feel excessively penalized by the demands and the emotional and financial expense of his ceremonial behavior and hoped that he might be able to sacrifice its major shrine.

There is no more pathetic indication of the abiding influence of the dead daughter and the desire to return to the days when she was alive than her parents' attempts to communicate with Susy through spiritualism. On May 17, 1900, Mrs. Clemens had taken a

brooch of Susy's to an English medium, Mrs. Thompson, at 87
Sloane Street. In a trance, Mrs. Thompson "contacted" Susy and
answered questions placed to her. She identified Susy as an Ameri-
can, a writer, and a world traveler. As the concluding message in
the transcript that survives, Susy told her mother that she did not
want her own manuscript, presumably her biography of her
father, incorporated in a volume: "Someone belonging to her is
writing a book, and I don't want him to put it in." Mrs. Myers,
who wrote the transcript of the session, was unconvinced that
there was "recognition" but suggested another attempt. A year
later, in March 1901, both parents consulted a Mrs. Koller, and
the spiritualist's failure to reach Susy was emblematic of the
family's failure to recover the equilibrium and security of the
years she symbolized.

The truth is that the Hartford house now served only one func-
tion for the Clemenses: It was a memorial to Susy, and like their
observance of her birthdays and death anniversaries, it was pecu-
liarly unhealthy. Clemens had known from the time of his visit to
Hartford for the funeral of Charles Dudley Warner in 1900 that
he would never live in the dwelling again. Even aboard the
Kanawha with Rogers as August 18, 1901 (the day Susy died in
1896) approached, Clemens wrote Olivia, "I am with you in spirit
every hour, now, and I know how you are feeling as these sad
anniversaries dawn and drag their course and decay. . . . I know
what you are suffering." Clara, twenty-seven years old, was be-
latedly moving toward a degree of independence from her family—
despite her father's demand that she be met by chaperones when
she arrived in New York City at 10:00 P.M. Jean's illness was of
course both functional and severe. As for Mrs. Clemens, a young
girl at Lake Saranac that summer of 1901 reminisced in later
years:

> Mrs. Clemens was a semi-invalid for years and
> . . . I could never see anything wrong with her
> that everybody should "baby" her so much. I
> asked my mother what was wrong with Mrs.

> Clemens. She said she thought Mrs. Clemens was
> "enjoying poor health." That was an expression
> my mother always used when a person had a
> minor ailment and made the most of it to get at-
> tention. Mrs. Clemens sure received the atten-
> tion.

However accurate the charge of "enjoying poor health," Samuel
Clemens' family had always managed, partly from his choice,
partly through illness, partly through introversion, to be a
strangely self-contained, inward-turning unit. Olivia entertained,
but within a limited circle—a small coterie of very close friends,
neighbors, and relatives appeared at her table. The three daugh-
ters were shielded from public schools and were trained by a suc-
cession of tutors. Mark Twain the public figure on the one hand
was shrewdly aware of his need—through lectures, testimonial
dinners, speeches, and interviews, as well as books—to maintain
close contact with his audience. Until late 1900 and 1901, how-
ever, he guarded his family from the public pressures and the
professional and social affairs which were his obligation.

But gradually (starting probably with the assignment of his
copyrights to Olivia in the wake of the bankruptcy) the members
of the family began to share some of his public responsibilities.
Even Jean, who learned to type in late 1900, was given some sense
of participation by copying manuscripts and taking dictation. On
August 2, 1901, as Clemens was preparing to leave on the cruise of
the *Kanawha,* he wrote a list of financial instructions to Olivia:
"Send a check . . . to Miss K. I. Harrison for twenty thousand
dollars. . . . The Chicago & Alton paid a dividend of $200 July
2d. . . . The U.S. Steel pf. will pay one of $175 four days hence.
Those coupons . . . were due yesterday—$1,000." The appear-
ance of Mrs. Clemens in such minute business detail was almost
unprecedented. She even managed to become interested, when on
September 17, 1901, it appeared that some of the old Tennessee
Land that had been in the Clemens family for years might "revert
to us by some mistake in its being sold or something."

After the family moved into Riverdale-on-the-Hudson in the autumn of 1901, their quiescent social life became almost frenzied. "During a single week . . . [they] entertained guests at no less than seventeen out of their twenty-one meals, and for three out of the seven nights—not an unusual week." It is impossible to know whether Mrs. Clemens enjoyed or approved these changes in her fairly sequestered domestic existence, even with a corps of cooks, maids, and butlers assisting her. The clipping of bond coupons, the constant entertaining, the restlessness of Clara, even the sale of the Hartford house, which Olivia could not bear to discuss, all were aggravations, indisputably. She would be driven to the breaking point, but not until the late summer of 1902.

It is extremely important to take from these domestic events of 1900 and 1901 only as much knowledge as they contain. There were no visible signs of antagonism within the family. Indeed, the warm and devoted letters that Clemens was writing his family betray no tensions or frustrations; only the almost constant absences which produced the letters are indicative of his restlessness. Almost compulsively Clemens absented himself from his succession of temporary "homes," rarely accompanied by members of his family.

A curious note, mildly disturbing and perhaps in some ways prophetic, closed the year 1901. At the end of the notebook for that year Clemens wrote a brief outline for a story about the McWilliamses, a name he had used for relating his own family's experiences as fiction since the 1870s:

> Divorce of the McWilliamses on account of his dream-wife and family. He can't conceal, because he talks in his sleep and she lies awake to listen. She wants to prosecute him for bigamy; in his distress he says it wasn't a *real* marriage—she is more outraged than ever; he must consent to a divorce and make an honest woman of dream-wife.

Whatever this unusual story line means, it contemplates, however metaphorically, an "estrangement" that Clemens could never allow to rise closer to the surface than this.

x

The "season" of 1901–1902 was, if possible, even more hectic for Clemens than the preceding one; literary, political, and financial projects occupied his attention almost ceaselessly.

Plasmon was booming in England in 1901, according to Mac-Alister; Clemens responded with delight to the cheering news that "your sales had climbed up to seven or eight tons a month." The American branch of the company was providing less comforting news. It had been organized under the direction of Henry A. Butters, a California investor, and his son-in-law, Dr. Channing H. Cook, with wealthy magnate and prominent mining engineer John Hays Hammond providing the bulk of the financing. The company had managed to print a letterhead—The American Plasmon Syndicate, Ltd., 18-20 West 34th Street, New York, Cable Address: Plasmonia. Dr. Cook wrote Clemens of the enormous sales campaign, including printed posters, which was being planned. MacAlister was dubious about the American officers, but Clemens first reassured him, with what was in the light of the entangled lawsuits about to be filed a magnificent irony, "this American Plasmon is in *first-rate hands.*"

MacAlister continued to mail the £350 quarterly dividend checks to Clemens regularly and continued to tell his friend that the company in London could discover nothing about the progress of the American branch, expressing his concern about the operations in the United States. But Clemens, typically undaunted, subscribed for $25,000 of the American Plasmon stock early in 1902 and was jolted later in the year when Howard E. Wright, the new general manager, placed a $5,000 call on the shares Clemens had bought on margin and refused to allow him a delay in meet-

ing the call. At last Clemens began to get edgy about his American investment and especially so because the English Plasmon was selling not only as powder but also as cookies, cocoa, and chocolate at a rate of £4,000 a month. Clemens declined an offer to sell his profitable British shares, and the contrast with the inactive American company was soon to prove too much for him.

His publishing agreements, too, recaptured his attention when he managed to stir up new difficulties and antagonisms between Frank Bliss and Harper's for competing editions of his works and to involve himself with the sale of his collected sets to the Newbegin Company—resulting in an autumnal storm accompanied by threats of lawsuits. Each of the organizations had been advertising a set of Mark Twain's works (the Newbegin Company was marketing one of the more expensive of the American Publishing Company's subscription editions) ; each was claiming it offered the "best" or the "most" of Mark Twain's works for sale, and each attempted to secure the author's endorsement for its claim. He did his best to avoid entangling himself in the controversy; but, as he told MacAlister on August 27, 1901, the Newbegin edition would assure him of $16,000 a year for the following four years, no minor temptation. Finally, Clemens' temper gave way, and he told Frank Bliss, "Come! With the Harpers to convince the public that 16 of my books are no good, and you to convince the public that the other six are no good, my reputation is in a fair way to land in Sheol in six months! But you musn't expect *me* to join the conspiracy."

In 1902, remembering that Harper's exclusive right to his material was due to expire shortly, Clemens began a little gentlemanly blackmail on that firm. On February 4 and 15, he wrote Frank Bliss asking him to find someone who would buy up the Newbegin marketing agreement for the collected edition "at what seems to be a tall figure" so that Clemens could "go to Harper and say you now have command of the books and are offered $250,000. for 5 years' use of them." Bliss did find a marketer for the edition, Robert Collier, who offered to guarantee a sale of 35,000 sets at a dollar per set profit to be divided between Clemens and the

American Publishing Company. Bliss decided to refuse the offer, but, meanwhile, Clemens tried to play his bluff. On February 26, he told Harvey, "I have an offer for the Newbegin contract (which I now control) of $250,000 guaranty for 5 years. . . . I cannot know if you would care to duplicate it, but you will tell me as to that." Harvey called the bluff, even though it was not until the following October that he reminded Clemens that Harper's would not "consent to the sale of the Bliss subscription edition volumes at a lower price than is provided in the contract." In his notebook Clemens plotted new contracts, clauses, and codicils with enthusiasm, in preparation for the coming negotiations.

Most of the literary projects of the season were as abortive and frustrating as the financial ones. Mark Twain continued to exploit the jeremiad strain in his voice, a strain that was becoming too strident for some magazines to print. Having become an active participant in The Acorns, a reform league bent on ousting Croker and the Tammany Hall Ring from New York municipal government, he composed his "Edmund Burke on Croker and Tammany" and told Colonel Harvey, "If you are going to issue the North American several days *before Election Day* (Nov. 5) I'd like to have a few pages." Since the *Review* was not scheduled to appear propitiously, the campaign speech was published in *Harper's Weekly* for October 19 and was subsequently issued as a pamphlet by the Order of The Acorns. And when the reform candidates were indeed elected, Mark Twain filled pages of his notebook with victory speeches and no small measure of self-congratulation. A sample: "Who won it? Modesty almost forbids." He offered a short item to the "Contributor's Club" of the *Atlantic,* provided it could be printed anonymously to protect his exclusive contract with Harper & Brothers. Toward the end of the year he wrote a "letter" to Jules Hart, assaulting the Infant's Home the city of New York ran on Blackwell's Island, which had, according to Hart, a mortality rate of 90 percent. The letter, dated December 17, 1901, and first published in *A Pen Warmed-up in Hell,* was obviously intended for publication, for Twain followed it with another suggesting alterations which would make the text

"decent enough" for print, though its attack on "Christian" charity was vitriolic and violent. Finally, Hart apparently declined to print the essay, and Twain agreed that "to publish the letter would do harm, not good."

Mark Twain's attempt to duplicate his New Year's greeting to the twentieth century was a manuscript called "The Stupendous Procession"—consigned to the "unpublished" file as too acetic for publication. Indeed, the pattern developing was for him to write bitterly sarcastic pieces on current topics, consign them to his growing collection of unusable manuscripts (perhaps because his "corn-pone" instinct told him they would not meet with approval), and attend another banquet or speechmaking event. Howells had good reason for lamenting, "I hate to have him eating so many dinners, and writing so few books."

xi

In spite of the smoldering tensions in it, the Clemens family loved the house at Riverdale (later known as "Wave Hill" and occupied by Arturo Toscanini and Sir Gladwyn Jebb, British ambassador to the United Nations). It was an enormous fieldstone, three-story mansion with impressive wooded grounds, just inside the New York city limits. A broad porch with Doric columns graced the front, and the scope of the interior is indicated by the dining room, which measured sixty by thirty feet. Howells, who somehow thought that they were living "more unpretentiously than they used, and I think with a notion of economy," accurately described Riverdale as "your baronial hall." He further told Thomas Bailey Aldrich when he called at Riverdale that he saw Clemens' "Hudson and his palisades, and some of the steamboats that he delights in."

Mrs. Clemens continued to be plagued with gout—so much so that her husband found her a "gout-regime" diet, compliments of Dr. James Ross Clemens, a distant cousin. In spite of her ailment, she managed the continuing social affairs at Riverdale in an

impressive fashion. Her diary lists a steady stream of lunch guests, dinner guests, and overnight guests that spring of 1902—a list that included the young novelist Marie van Vorst, a friend of Jean's who visited at least four times and stayed overnight on March 9 and 16. It is impossible to date the following note, or even to supply its context; but presumably something occurred during one of those spring visits to provoke one of Clemens' ill-tempered letters. Possibly it was two short and fairly inchoate poems which Miss van Vorst offered her host as a New Year's present for 1902. But the provocation could have been even more innocuous than that, and the letter may have been a condemnation of the human race rather than a personal attack. At any rate, it was perhaps in early 1902 (Miss van Vorst apparently disappeared from the family's circle of friends after that) that the following letter went from Olivia Clemens to her husband:

> Youth darling, have you forgotten your promise to me? You said that I was constantly in your mind and that you knew what I would like and you *would not* publish what I would disapprove. Did you think I would approve the letter to Marie van Vorst?
>
> I am absolutely wretched to-day on account of your state of mind—your state of intellect—why don't you let the better side of you work? Your pressent attitude will do more harm than good. You go too far, much too far in all you say, and if you write in the same way as you have in this letter people forget the cause for it and remember only the hateful manner in which it was said. Do darling change your mental attitude, *try to chang it.* The trouble is you don't want to. When you asked me to try Mental Science I tried it and I keep trying it. Where is the mind that wrote the Prince & P. Jeanne d'Arc, The Yankee, &c. &c. &c. Bring it back! You can if you will—if you wish to. Think of the side I know; the sweet, dear, tender side—that I love so. Why not show this

more to the world. Does it help the world to al-
ways rail at it? There is great and noble Work
being done. Why not sometimes recognize that?
You always dwell on the evil until those who live
beside you are crushed to the earth and you seem
almost like a monamaniac. Oh I love you so and
wish you would listen and take heed.

The very least that can be made of this letter, whenever it was
written and whatever incident provoked it, is that it suggests all
too clearly Olivia's emotional state when she composed it. The
almost irrational tone, the plea citing injuries to the family, the
cataloguing of the medieval books which had pleased Mark
Twain's genteel audience, all of these suggest a high degree of
hysteria. (Her spelling, however, was no better when she was
calm.) The strains and burdens of her life in 1902 were causing
her, clearly, to recognize the loss of control over a family of which
"she always was: boss."

Her husband's hectic activity continued. With all the family but
Clara he spent a week at the end of January in Elmira, New York,
at the home of Sue Crane; he made another long trip with
Rogers on the *Kanawha*—this time to the Caribbean—from March
13 to April 9, sending reports and letters back to his family. And
he took off alone by train to receive an honorary degree from the
University of Missouri and his final nostalgic and disillusioning
look at Hannibal in early June of 1902—another solitary trip. In
many ways it was the most poignant trip he was ever to make. The
first stop, in late May, was at the Planter's Hotel in St. Louis,
where he was escorted by Horace Bixby, the pilot who had taught
him the Mississippi River in 1857. Then for five days he returned
to Hannibal, visiting the few remaining friends from his youth
and touring the scenes he had immortalized. He ate dinner with
Laura Hawkins, his first sweetheart, whom he identified in a letter
to Olivia only as a "schoolmate 62 years ago." He passed out
diplomas at the high-school graduation, spoke at all the Sunday
schools, and took a long ride with his childhood friend John
Briggs to Holliday's Hill and along the river.

On June 4, he received his doctor of laws degree at Columbia and returned to St. Louis for ceremonies opening the grounds for a World's Fair and dedicating a *Mark Twain* steamboat. But Hannibal and those five days engulfed in a past which meant more to him emotionally and artistically than anything else in his life must have been the most touching part of the entire trip. What he felt is preserved in only a few matter-of-fact letters to his wife and a jumble of abortive notebook entries attempting to revive Tom and Huck for fictional use. He was to try, in a long and frustrating spell of work, to write of the boys' return to St. Petersburg fifty years after their original adventures and to allow Howells to read part of his manuscript. But the material would simply not flow from his pen; and it is a measure of the finality of his resignation that the abortive "Fifty Years Later" manuscript is one of the very few that, in his entire life, Mark Twain actually may have destroyed. Surely the old home that now seemed so small to him, the children who were now old and faltering, and the locales of his youth which were now overgrown or modernized overwhelmed him with a realization of the distance he had traveled since Hannibal and of the loss, now total, of a past that existed only in his acute memory—a memory whose romance was tarnished by the stark reality he confronted in 1902. When he left Missouri he left Hannibal forever; he was never again to be able to complete a work on Huck and Tom.

At the same time, the domestic crisis deepened. Mrs. Clemens' agitation might have been increased by the decision to shop for real estate, even though the Hartford house was still unsold. Riverdale was selling for $150,000, although said to be worth only $135,000, and they felt they could not afford the house. They were looking in the vicinity of Tarrytown; and while Clemens was off on his junket to the Caribbean with Rogers, Olivia decided, after qualms of indecision, to buy a house from Flora McDonald Casey for $45,000. She was to be troubled all year by the possible folly of purchasing the property before the Hartford house was disposed of, but the primary instinct at work was her need to have a

"home." Ironically, the family was never to occupy the Tarrytown house she had chosen.

Their Hartford property was becoming a domestic albatross. It was put on the market for $75,000; but in late May, Clemens told Whitmore that Rogers had advised, "Sell the house, and sell it now; even if you have to let it go at $40,000." On June 10, Clemens authorized Whitmore to reduce the price to $35,000; on October 18, $30,000. In August, at the strong recommendation of Rogers, the nervous owner resisted an offer from Sidney A. Witherbee to purchase the house with $50,000 of bonds in the Kansas City, Mexico and Orient railroad as partial collateral. By late November, when a search of deeds disclosed that Franklin Chamberlin had sold the Clemenses much of the land on which the house rested with clauses forbidding all building or improving on those parts, Clemens proposed in total desperation auctioning the house to the highest bidder. Whether or not the house was as overwhelming a mental burden to his wife as Clemens made it appear, the real-estate speculations and uncertainties contributed to her "nervous state."

Clara was an even more urgent problem in 1902. She had announced her intention never to marry, but she was visiting altogether too much with the young pianist Ossip Gabrilowitsch, in the United States on a tour, to please her parents. In 1901 she and Ossip saw a great deal of each other; and as his engagements ended, Clara recalled that "true love was wielding her wand of harmony and we yielded without struggle to the super command." Her father opposed marriage, but the ornamental diction of Clara's mature recollection is the language of seduction. Whatever the "super command" was, Clara decided to obey it some more in 1902. Almost without warning so far as extant documents show, she departed for Paris, where Ossip was, on April 22. She was accompanied by a chaperone, Frida Ashforth, who, according to Clara, "was not entirely left out of the fun Gabrilowitsch and I had together." It is possible only to speculate about her parents' attitude toward such liberated behavior (though they canceled their plan to spend the summer of 1902 in Venice, where they

would presumably chaperone their daughter). Significantly, however, between Clara's departure and her reappearance in New York on August 12, there are no extant letters between parents and daughter, no notebook entries referring to Clara or to Gabrilowitsch, no reports to old friends like Howells or Twichell on "singing lessons," no indications whatever that there was a Clemens daughter named Clara. The only exception is Mrs. Clemens' report to Mrs. Whitmore that Clara and Mrs. Ashforth were in Europe studying languages: "We shall all be very thankful," Olivia said, "when it is over and she says she will never do it again."

There was, however, a curiously hysterical article by Mark Twain in *Harper's Weekly* for July 5, 1902 (p. 732), called "Why Not Abolish It?" The "it" of the title was the "age of consent" clause which limited prosecution of seducers. In the article, Mark Twain said that a daughter under "the age of consent" cannot "help commit a tremendous and desolating crime against herself and her family; but she is privileged to do it if she is twenty." "Why," he continued, "should there be an age at which a member [of a family] . . . may help a criminal to destroy that far more valuable asset, the family's honor." This cluster of facts—despite the absence of concrete evidence—suggests that Clara's behavior was at least not beneficial to her mother's health.

That health continued to deteriorate. On May 16, Clemens reported to Rogers that "Mrs. Clemens had a bad time with her heart last night, and for a while could only breathe when sitting up." He recorded in his notebook at about this time the prophecy of great wealth which "Cheiro" the palmist had made regarding him, and then wrote an enigmatic note, "His *other* prophecy of '95." According to Olivia's maid Katy Leary, the other prophecy was of the death of Olivia.

Clemens' concern over Olivia's health led him to rent a cottage in York Harbor, Maine, for the summer, where she was transported on Henry Rogers' yacht in late June. On board the yacht, Jean suffered a massive seizure, and another followed in Maine on July 6, one of the few which Clemens himself witnessed: "I have

seen it only three times before, in all these five fiendish years. It comes near to killing Mrs. Clemens every time, and there is not much left of her for a day or two afterward. Every three weeks it comes. It will break her down yet." Clemens' concern for the effect on Mrs. Clemens was not paralleled, at least in this statement, by a concern for Jean herself. And on August 7, just five days before Olivia's major collapse, the harassed head of the family told Rogers that "Mrs. Clemens's five years of constant anxiety and periodical shocks and frights on Jean's account are bringing a break down":

> In order to be able to breathe, she had to sit upright in bed last night from 9 o'clock almost all the time until 4 this morning. This is becoming a nightly experience.

When Olivia's devastating attack came, at seven in the morning of August 12 (the same day that Clara's boat docked in New York), it was abrupt and alarming. She suddenly "said she was dying" and had the seizure from which she was never to recover. Dr. Lambert was at the York Harbor home in thirty minutes; Clara arrived that evening and was admitted to her mother's bedside immediately. Medical attendance doubled; an osteopath and a physician were called in. A few weeks later Dr. Helmer came up from New York to administer a "severe treatment." Drs. Allen and Putnam arrived, ministered, and departed. Dr. Hawkes's name was recorded (he was to be threatened with a lawsuit for charging three dollars a visit to Mrs. Clemens instead of his usual one dollar), and there was an anonymous physician whom Clara excused before he ever arrived. Nurses came and went almost anonymously: Clara fired one, Clemens fired another a few days later. Clara's emerging domination was apparent later in the fall when she also began hiring and firing cooks as well.

Soon after Clara's return, her position in the house was firmly established. Clemens told Rogers, "Clara does all the generalship . . . and is doing it like an expert—same as her mother." Clemens was allowed, for about six weeks, to see and help nurse Olivia. He

told James Ross Clemens on August 22, "To-day, for the first time since Livy was taken sick, I am released for a while from my sick room watch." He blamed the "heart attack" on "overwork—day and night devoted to the children and me." He blamed it on Jean's illness. Twichell replied to one of his letters, "what you tell us of Jean reveals, we conjecture, the cause of Livy's breakdown." He blamed it on her anxieties over having purchased the Casey property in Tarrytown. Even after he was banished from the house to his "room in the house of a friend and neighbor, a fisherman and boatman" named Millard Sewall, first by the doctor and then by the nurse, Miss Gourangé, Clemens apparently did not realize that "heart attack" might be a misdiagnosis or that his own presence was a significant contributing factor in his wife's illness.

But by October 13, a new diagnosis had been made. As Clemens told a young Scotswoman, Muriel Pears, with whom he communicated frequently:

> It is nervous prostration. We thought it was heart disease, and for 4 weeks we had but little hope. But she will get well—they all say it. If we only *could* get home to Riverdale! That would be the right medicine for her.

An undated clipping from the New York *American* (which suggests how intrusively the privacy of the family was invaded) put it more bluntly when the writer said that Olivia would regain "the strength that a well-preserved woman of sixty may expect." While the family awaited the solution to the logistical problem of transporting that "well-preserved" woman back to Riverdale, its total complexion was far from healthy.

xii

Jean, like her father, was banished from her mother's presence at York Harbor—and immediately ceased to have epileptic attacks. Clemens marveled; the improvement in Jean was "miraculous," he told Rogers. She was in fact free from all traces of the disease

for four months. Clara's health, however, deteriorated, and she did not recover quickly enough to suit her father. Clemens told Whitmore in November 1902, "I am a little troubled about Clara, whose anxieties are telling on her." Although there can be no doubt about the sincerity of Clemens' own distress and terror at Olivia's condition, he was still able to write a number of incongruously long and flippant articles and letters and to indulge in some unusual business propositions between midsummer and early fall, almost as a safety valve for his concern. It is evident that the Clemens family was strung together like a number of other Victorian families by tensions and interrelationships as taut as the limits of sanity and decorum could stretch them. Clemens himself responded, in characteristic fashion, with some of the weakest jinglings of his jester's bells. Clara exhausted herself with hard work, contrition, and penance. Jean responded to the stress by her four-month stretch without a "faint." Olivia, who was obviously no longer merely "enjoying poor health," managed by her nervous prostration to pull her family together, to gather them to her vicinity and even to her bedside—when doctors permitted—and to restore her authority and control over the fate of the entire group.

Most of Mark Twain's writing in 1902 was fragmentary, abortive, or simply mediocre. "Does the Race of Man Love a Lord?" and "In Defense of General Funston" had appeared in the April and May issues of the *North American Review,* blending with mitigated success the reformer's zeal and the determinist's fatalism. Mankind did, of course, love a lord—or any conspicuous representation of aristocracy that satisfied its need for self-esteem; and Funston was only obeying the instincts trained into him when he used trickery to capture Aguinaldo in the American involvement in the Philippines.

Stirred by his reading of Jonathan Edwards' *On the Freedom of the Will,* he composed the Socratic dialogue "If I Could Be There," with distinct foreshadowings and overtones of both the method and the philosophy of *What Is Man?* He filled his notebooks with possible story lines in 1902; and after returning from the emotion-packed trip to Hannibal, he added a few pages to his

"Tom Sawyer's Conspiracy" manuscript. Interesting other fables and fantasies, all of which would end up—except for "The Five Boons of Life"—in the ominously burgeoning posthumous file, were "The Bees," "The Victims," and a group of related manuscripts of burlesque futuristic history known as the Eddypus manuscripts (the latter two published in *Mark Twain's Fables of Man*). Among the fantasies and dream worlds he constructed in 1902, most were pessimistic, gloomy, bitter. In the Tom Sawyer and Huck Finn materials, he attempted to recapture the bittersweet recollections of unfettered and hedonistic youth which proved to be impossible to resurrect or transcribe. Most of his published writing reflected his belief that topical and contemporaneous materials—including "The Belated Russian Passport" and his scheme for ante-mortem obituaries published in *Harper's Weekly,* the New York *World,* and offered under the title "Amended Obituaries" to *Lloyd's Weekly* of London—were the proper ones for current publication. *Harper's Weekly* was now becoming his major periodical outlet, a journal of standards distinctly inferior to those of the *North American Review* but one willing to accept the frivolous and prodigal misuse of his talents, time, and literary capabilities.

Perhaps it was his recognition of the public's response to the missionary assault in 1900 that changed Mark Twain's literary focus. It is indisputable that, obeying whatever motives prompted him, he wrote humorous material, fantasies, and fables that he almost always suppressed and "editorials" that were almost always offered for publication. As he told Frederick Duneka of Harper & Brothers with good intentions that he never adopted, "I mean to *stop* rushing things off before they've had a chance to get to the waste basket where they belong."

During the summer he and Howells (who was staying only a few miles away at Kittery Point) "used to sit at a corner of the veranda farthest away from Mrs. Clemens's window, where we could read our manuscripts to each other, and tell our stories, and laugh our hearts out without disturbing her." Mark Twain wrote a comic attack on the practices of the Western Union and a public

letter to the Denver *Post* and the New York *Tribune,* accusing General Funston of persuading the officials of the Denver Public Library to remove *Huckleberry Finn* from its shelves. He asked Whitmore to dig through the manuscripts in Hartford and send him the text of "Captain Stormfield's Visit to Heaven" from the safe, with the intention of adding to that long-uncompleted work.

Perhaps the most emblematic work of the entire period, in the context of Olivia's illness, is the long and pathetic poem "In Dim and Fitful Visions . . ." which Mark Twain composed one week after Olivia's attack in August, taking large segments from an 1898 poem, "Broken Idols." He worked alternately on the funereal poem and "Tom Sawyer's Conspiracy." There is, on the back of one of the manuscript pages of the "Conspiracy" (p. 91), the plaintive note:

> These lines were written to beguile me through
> the heavy hours of the anniversary of our Dark
> Day, and not for print. But I have always meant
> to say some day a modest public word in memory
> of our lost Susy. . . .

The poem itself is a blank-verse reminiscence by a mother whose daughter has died; but the mother is insane (in both the 1898 and the 1902 versions) and believes that she has lost four daughters— Susy in four identifiable phases of her childhood. We can excuse the raggedness of the lines, because Mark Twain was no poet. Perhaps we can understand the mawkishness and banality of the "our Dark Day" brand of sentimentality; the funereal mode was an immensely compelling one for Mark Twain, and in serious moments he almost always descended into the lachrymose voice that he mocked when Emmeline Grangerford used it. But it is difficult to explain the parents' ghoulish attraction to Susy's memory, with what unquestionably could have been only a vicious effect on Clara and Jean. The annual day of remorse on August 18, the public parading of grief which lost its effectiveness by its clockwork regularity, the saving of the "pressed plant from Susy's grave" (which still remains in the Mark Twain Papers) are less

than mature reactions and responses to death, even by Victorian standards. But such behavior was a part of the perversely involuted loyalties which kept the Clemens family together while it estranged its members from one another.

xiii

When he came to move Olivia from York Harbor to Riverdale on October 15, Clemens fretted about the method of the transportation: asking for the *Kanawha,* then canceling the yacht and deciding on a train, arranging for a special car and special engines. Apparently what impressed Clemens most about the mode he finally decided on was the expense. He boasted to Rogers that the nine-hour ride cost $340, and he repeated the figure twice in his notebooks. In June, his own round-trip, drawing-compartment ticket all the way to Missouri had cost only $46.25.

With Mrs. Clemens settled back into the closest thing she had to a home, the family resumed more normal activity. Despite Olivia's temporary improvement, Clemens was restless and frustrated by his continuing banishment from her sickroom. And despite personal anxiety, he accepted the public honor of marching, on October 25, in the procession at Princeton which installed Woodrow Wilson. His bread-and-butter letter to the Huttons, with whom he stayed for several days, mentioned an even more total exclusion from family affairs. He hated

> the stillness and solitude of this [house]. Clara being one of the nurses, I get hardly a glimpse of her, some days. Of Jean also I get glimpses only: she stays up on the third floor and works at wood-carving, or outside prowling in the fresh air.

He went to Elmira in November for the wedding of Julia Langdon to Edward Loomis, reporting back to Olivia the scene there and at his sixty-seventh birthday dinner which George Harvey, of Harper & Brothers, had planned for him. Above his description of

the events he wrote, "Clara dear, this is to your mother, but you must not risk showing it to her without reading it first yourself."

Clara's function as censor extended itself as the daughter assumed some of her mother's editorial duties. Although Clemens told Frederick Duneka, "I have no editor—no censor," Clara had read and complained about parts of "Was It Heaven? or Hell?" which was to appear in the Christmas issue of *Harper's*. Although the original version of the story came from Howells, a number of touches derived from Mrs. Clemens' sickroom and from Susy's death, no doubt making these parts seem too personal to Clara.

The other major literary work at the end of 1902 also had its medical and biographical side. The articles about Christian Science which were published in the *North American Review* in December 1902 and in January, February, and April 1903 were possible outgrowths of Mrs. Clemens' "nervous prostration" (though Mark Twain had begun to write about Mrs. Eddy in Vienna in 1898). When revising the earlier portions of the Christian Science material, Clemens was willing to mention publicly, in one of the footnotes to the book, his wife's "miraculous" cure of paralysis at the age of seventeen by what he called a "quack." And he developed what Albert Bigelow Paine has called an "eclectic theory of medicine." His idea was that physicians, surgeons, allopaths, and homeopaths should each minister to certain kinds of illnesses; most relevant, however, was his ambiguous relegation of "nervous prostration to the Christian Scientist." His description of the benefits and positive merits of the new sect must have struck close to the sickroom from which he was excluded.

> How much of the pain and disease in the world is created by the imaginations of the sufferers, and then kept alive by those same imaginations? Four-fifths? Not anything short of that, I should think. Can Christian Science banish that four-fifths? I think so.

Perhaps Mrs. Clemens' improvement that winter persuaded him to hope that her illness resided entirely in her imagination.

However biographical his interest in Christian Science, the articles provided Mark Twain with another dispute with which to divert himself. The publicity over the articles put him in correspondence with William D. McCrakan of the Christian Science Publication Committee for the State of New York, who published a rebuttal to Mark Twain's assault in the March 1903 *Review*. The author even contemplated the possibility of having McCrakan collaborate on the *Christian Science* volume, "if your article shall turn out to be very brief . . . but not otherwise, for there is not going to be much room to spare." The scheme grew until Mark Twain was suggesting to Percy Spaulding of Chatto & Windus, his English publisher, that McCrakan "can have half of the book to himself." The proposal for a published debate over the new religion never developed, however, because Harper & Brothers were not interested in publishing the book at all.

Frederick Duneka of Harper & Brothers had first told Clemens that he hoped the book, containing both authors' contributions, could be ready in the spring; and Mark Twain went to unusual lengths to have his own share ready. "Jean was his typist, but he was not willing to have her copy any part of it, fearing 'it might damage her soul.' " Apparently Duneka even advertised the book; publisher Albert Brandt, having read "that the publishers had withdrawn the book, refunding to intending buyers the money that had been sent in payment for advance orders," offered on April 14, 1903, to publish it himself. A few days later Clemens replied to a prospective customer's query about *Christian Science*'s fate:

> The Harpers considered the publication inexpedient, as it might injure the house with the Christian Scientists. . . .
>
> The form agreed upon with Mr. Duneka was carefully chosen—and of course departed from. It was, "too late, now, for a spring book, therefore *postponed until autumn*." This was to save my face, and was my suggestion: I did not want

> the fact exposed that a book of mine had been
> (in effect) declined.
>
> The situation is not barren of humor: I had
> been doing my very best to show in print that
> the Xn Scientist cult was become a power in the
> land—well, here was proof: it had scared the
> biggest publisher in the Union!

He also sent the letter to Frank Bliss, who wrote its author that the
American Publishing Company would issue the volume in the fall
of 1903. But the articles in the *North American Review* produced
a disappointingly small response, and the book did not appear until
1907. Meanwhile, Mark Twain continued to smolder in resent-
ment at having a book of his declined.

When it did finally appear, *Christian Science* was a peculiar
volume by any standards. It attracted, as might be expected, letters
from only the wildest adherents to and opponents of the religion.
The author's own resentment of its lengthy "suppression" suggests
that he considered it an important piece of writing. He was
insistent in his claim that it was not philosophical principles but
only Mrs. Eddy whom he was attacking. "Mother" Eddy was
susceptible to the broadest of his talents at burlesque. Her gram-
mar, her theories, and her establishment of the machinery calcu-
lated to propagate her church elicit Mark Twain's special mixture
of high satire and low burlesque. The bulk of the volume was
given over to an analysis of inept and undecipherable language, to
textual criticism of the successive editions of *Science and Health*,
and to an account of Mrs. Eddy's fine "business-talent" controlling
the establishment she had founded.

Underlying the humor was an uneasy sense of the power of
Christian Science, its appeal to the masses, and its potential for
immense popularity. Prophetically, Mark Twain suggested that
Science and Health would secure perpetual copyright because of
the influence of the sect—a prediction that became virtually true
in 1970 when copyright was extended on the volume for seventy-
five additional years. His fear of the power was merely the surface
expression of Mark Twain's real concern about Christian Science,

however; at a level too deep for comedy, he indisputably saw the
relationship of Mrs. Eddy's new science of healing to the illnesses
of his own family, a topic he could no longer mock. The sick
whose maladies lay in their imaginations were not subjects for
humorous copy, and the women of his own household were too
obviously among the potential recruits to the redeeming possibil-
ities of Christian Science (to which Clara would become a con-
vert) for the values of the theory to amuse the humorist.

Mark Twain's mixture of burlesque, satire, and fearsome seri-
ousness is understandable. Mrs. Eddy, in spite of her business
instincts, her vanity, and her semi-literate prose, had a solution to
the "pains" which Olivia and Clara suffered. Unlike a conscience-
stricken and guilt-ridden husband and father, she knew how to
heal the ills that originated in his family's minds. And Mark
Twain's attack on her and his insistence on the publication of the
book became the artistic measure of his own frustration and
anguish about his wife's health.

xiv

Although still forbidden to see him in late 1902 and early 1903,
Olivia was able to read occasional letters and notes from her hus-
band, to read books, even to discuss with Clara and the nurse an
extensive addition to the Tarrytown property which "she is
determined to build." She had a severe attack in November 1902,
news of which Clara first kept from her father and then reported
to him only when he made plans to leave Riverdale for a trip to
Hartford. He told Whitmore, "Henceforth she will not need to
ask me; I shall not go out of town any more until her mother is
on her feet." On December 6 he told a Mrs. Godwin that he hoped
to see Olivia for a moment that day, but the visit was canceled,
perhaps for fear he might tell his wife about a steady series of
epileptic "faints" Jean had begun having. Then when a severe
chill Jean suffered in late December developed into pneumonia,

he was further forbidden, again for fear of his making revelatory comments which would cause Mrs. Clemens to have a relapse.

Eventually he saw his wife on December 30 and 31 for five minutes each day. Although little can be made of it explicitly, one cannot fail to be impressed by the prevailing awareness that Clemens could not be trusted to keep from telling Olivia news that might endanger her life. Even he commented to Twichell on his perverse impulse: "For the first time in months I heard her break into one of her girlish old-time laughs. With a word I could freeze the blood in her veins!"

Clara, enacting the plot of "Was It Heaven? or Hell?" bore the main brunt of the winter's illnesses. To avoid overexciting her mother Clara was compelled to invent fictional occupations for her bedridden younger sister. Clemens was as fascinated by the dramatic possibilities of Clara's role as he was distressed by the health of Jean and her mother; and he wrote several lengthy accounts of the dialogues between Clara and her mother. Even Twichell commented that the account of Clara's lying to Olivia was "all ready for the printer as it is; *any* change must mar it." A sample of Clara's facility:

> Clara does not go to her Monday lesson in New York today (her mother having seemed not so well through the night) , but forgets that fact and enters her mother's room (where she has no business to be) toward train-time *dressed in a wrapper.*
> LIVY. Why, Clara, aren't you going to your lesson?
> CLARA (almost caught) . Yes.
> L. In that costume?
> CL. Oh no.
> L. Well, you can't make your train; it's impossible.
> CL. I know, but I'm going to take the other one.
> L. Indeed *that* won't do—you'll be ever so much too late for your lesson.

CL. No, the lesson-time has been put an hour
later.
L. (satisfied, then suddenly). But, Clara, that
train and the late lesson together will make you
late to Mrs. Hapgood's luncheon.
CL. No, the train leaves fifteen minutes earlier
than it used to.

Long letters to Twichell and Sue Crane, the autobiographical
version of the same dialogue, and Twichell's astute comment that
the material was "ready for the printer" suggest the obsessive
literary fascination the elaborate deception had for Clemens. It
was a great game, a Tom Sawyer prank which had literary possibil-
ities even while real tragedy threatened. The ruse and the agile
lying which Clemens saw as publishable material and in which he
delighted were the kind of adventure to thrill one of his boy
heroes. But it would be grossly incorrect to suppose that his con-
version of serious experience into literary material betrayed light-
heartedness toward Olivia's illness.

Olivia would never become well enough to be told the truth
about that winter's prevarications or to assume an active role in
the management of the household. Jean, even though she re-
covered from her pneumonia, was to be plagued with illnesses and
increasingly severe convulsions although she would continue to
serve her father occasionally as a typist. Clara's own health was
fragile, but she was determined to pursue her singing career.
Therefore, in November 1902 a new member was added to the
household. Isabel V. Lyon arrived from Hartford and began
taking over arrangements of the family's social schedule, writing
letters for Clemens, and keeping books for him. Clara's reaction to
this new arrangement was volatile and ambivalent, an early indi-
cation of future conflicts. On January 3, 1903, Miss Lyon wrote in
her diary:

> This morning as I sat writing in the drawing
> room the closed door cautiously opened and in
> nestled S.L.C.'s head, followed by himself in
> nightshirt, blanket gown, bare legs and black felt

> slippers. We settled some business drawing checks
> etc. and then C.C. appeared (charming C.C.)
> telling him to go up stairs and get into his
> clothes. He refused. She was firm. He was for dic-
> tating letters. She was firm. So off he trotted, not
> to get into his clothes, but to go to bed again.
> Appearing at the landing a few minutes later he
> called, "Is Clara gone?" I said "no"—and he
> said "Then I'll go back to bed." We chuckled
> much. He is delightful.

Miss Lyon had already announced to Whitmore that she loved
"the duties here, now that Mr. Clemens uses me how and when he
will." She was, nevertheless, a complex new factor in the Clemens
family's life, as were Clara's domineering and prudish image and
Olivia's seclusion. The fragile equilibrium had been upset in
several ways and would never be quite re-established again.

 Isabel Lyon told Whitmore on New Year's Day that both Jean
and Olivia were improving rapidly; Clemens even thought his
wife "looks better than she did before she was taken ill." Miss
Lyon reported improvement again on the thirteenth, and on the
sixteenth she wrote Whitmore that Clemens instructed her to

> Tell Whitmore that we are assured that Mrs.
> Clemens will be able to travel by June 1st, and
> the Doctor has ordered that she go to some suit-
> able climate in Europe, to get clear away from
> American climate and worries of house keeping.

Jean was so enervated by her pneumonia—she looked, Clemens
said, "like an escaped survivor of a forest fire"—that her father
packed her off with a nurse to Old Point Comfort, a coastal resort
in Virginia, "until she is wholly restored and can show herself to
her mother without making trouble." His own visits to Olivia
were extended to fifteen minutes a day, but at the end of January
he was once more banished from the invalid's room altogether. On
February 9, 1903—their thirty-third wedding anniversary—he was
allowed to see Olivia for five minutes.

 In March, in spite of his earlier promise not to leave the house

until his wife was on her feet, Clemens attended dinners in New York with regularity—three between the nineteenth and the twenty-eighth; then Olivia's anxiety over his bronchitis "kept me here shut up these past days." During that troubled spring he was recurrently granted and then forbidden admission to Olivia's room and he still saw strangely little of his daughters: "a daily glimpse of them at 7:30 P.M."

Bronchitis put him in bed for five weeks in April and May, and when he "stole down stairs" halfway through his illness he was "ordered back again by his daughter and the nurse." His teeth bothered him; Jean and Clara contracted measles and a quarantine was imposed. Clemens sent a steady procession of notes into Clara's sickroom (none survives addressed to Jean, however). They were illustrated with his comic pictures of Jean, of Olivia, and of Clara herself and were expressions of endearment so solicitous that they might almost have been written to a small child rather than to an adult. "Benny, dear"—as he addressed her in most of the facetious jottings—had ample evidence of his affection, however constraining it might seem to be to her.

Olivia appeared to improve. She was up and sunning on a terrace at Riverdale and was moved into a downstairs bedroom in May. She was even willing to allow Clemens to leave the house overnight, a privilege she had refused for a month "lest her anxieties give her a nervous setback."

In spite of the imposing catalogue of ailments, improvements, and relapses, Clemens managed to remain in generally high spirits. Clara was functioning as censor—editing even letters to Howells and Whitmore, if her father's teasing references to her removing his profanity are to be believed. The tone of the humor was reminiscent of Clemens' teasing of Olivia and maintained the playful attitude the family expected of him.

Among causes for celebration that spring was the sale of the Hartford house. Clemens told Whitmore in January, "if our fortunes reach the high altitude they promise to reach this year, I shall not sell the Hartford house at all, but establish a midnight mission in it." A week later, on January 13, Olivia gave her per-

mission to sell the residence "for any thing you can get for it."
And Miss Lyon told the real-estate agent on March 7:

> Mr. Clemens wishes me to say to you, "Do not
> forget to sell the property at some price, between
> now and the first of May. If it is not sold by that
> time it would be well to tear the house down,
> and let the ground stand, so reducing expenses."

Finally, Clemens wrote Whitmore his own letter the following
month: "For the Lord Jesus H. Christ's sake *sell or rent that God
damned house.* I would rather go to hell than own it 50 days
longer." By good luck, Whitmore made the deadline with weeks to
spare. On May 2, Clemens accepted Richard M. Bissell's offer of
$28,000 (in a letter to Whitmore) and on May 11 signed the deed.
Olivia began writing instructions to Whitmore about which fur-
nishings were to be included with the house, which were to be sold
separately, and which were to be shipped to Susan Crane in
Elmira. She was especially solicitous about all the seaweed in
Susy's room, which was to be stored rather than left for Bissell.
The Clemenses had the mantelpiece removed and replaced and
offered to give a bust of Henry Ward Beecher to Mrs. Hooker and
a statue of Mercury to Mrs. Whitmore. By June 16 the obsessive
activity of closing the Hartford establishment and being com-
pletely freed from its emotional and financial ties had a salutary
effect: "Mrs. Clemens is cheerful and is very much her old self." It
is interesting that Olivia managed to overcome her prostration as
effectively as she did that spring and that the sale of the Hartford
mansion should have been the catalyst for her brief recovery. It is
probably true that Clemens himself believed that the best way to
keep his wife's pulse down was to keep her mind occupied, *"di-
verted . . . from unhealthy channels and compelled . . . to
travel in healthy ones,"* as he put it in *Christian Science.*

Olivia "had happy memories of Florence, and believed if
she could be there again her health would improve." If the symp-
toms were that easy to eradicate, then of course the family would
make the arduous journey (though Clara was apparently hoping
that California might be the destination instead) .

The knowledge that Olivia's illness was neurasthenia, unques-
tionably aggravated by the presences of Clemens and Jean, seems
not to have bothered the family nearly as much as one would
anticipate. The notes Clemens composed for Olivia during his
banishment from her presence through the long winter of 1902–
1903 reflect an interdependence and mutual love strong enough to
withstand the strain both of separation and of whatever form of
psychological distress Clemens caused. Howells remembered his
visit to Riverdale in the spring of 1903 and Clemens' characteristic
solicitude for Olivia:

> One sunny afternoon we sat on the grass before
> the mansion, after his wife had begun to get well
> enough for removal, and we looked up toward a
> balcony where by-and-by that lovely presence
> made itself visible, as if it had stooped there from
> a cloud. A hand frailly waved a handkerchief;
> Clemens ran over the lawn toward it, calling ten-
> derly: "What? What?" as if it might be an asking
> for him instead of the greeting it really was for
> me.

The husband undoubtedly felt himself responsible for Olivia's
illness and accepted his exile as a part of the penalty for his guilt.
Quite possibly, in a social caste in which hysteria and hypochon-
dria were almost fashionable, Clemens was prepared to accept
Olivia's condition without the impatience one might expect from
him.

More puzzling is Olivia's isolation from her husband and Jean.
During his wife's final illness Clemens wrote in his notebook:

> Men and women—even man and wife are foreign-
> ers. Each has reserves that the other cannot enter
> into, nor understand. These have the effect of
> frontiers.

There were undoubtedly frontiers and reserves between Olivia
and Samuel Clemens, but they were minimal. Susy's death, the
around-the-world lecture tour of the mid-1890s, and the financial

dilemmas the family faced in the last years of the nineteenth century were as physically and emotionally exhausting to Olivia as Jean's attacks were, and perhaps both Clemens and his wife quite reasonably believed those traumas were his fault.

At least this much can be said of the Clemens marriage: It united two vastly incongruous personalities who achieved a deep love and mutual understanding in spite of their differences. The documents which survive—the notes, letters, reminiscences—are nevertheless dangerous documents from which to generalize. They show the public and affectionate facets of the marriage without suggesting those reserves and antagonisms from which the Clemenses were no more immune than other husbands and wives. To both Olivia and Clara, Clemens' letters are voluminous, affectionate, loving—but we need to remember that the record is so enormous exactly because Clemens was so frequently absent from his family. And the picture of the husband and father, denied Olivia's bedside and catching only brief glimpses of his daughters in the winter of 1902–1903, is one of an absentee head of the house who could be best appreciated and loved at a respectful distance. The love notes to Olivia during her illness and the playful and lighthearted illustrated letters to Clara during her siege of measles were not merely the "public" version of Mark Twain as a husband and father; in addition, they were the epistolary barriers between strong-willed and aggressive personalities. And it must be more than coincidence that when Olivia improved so dramatically in the summer of 1903, the family's antagonisms and tensions all reappeared.

XV

There were several substantial legal and financial diversions in 1903 to keep Clemens' mind occupied with other matters than his family. He finally exploded, with vitriolic threats of litigation, against the American branch of Plasmon. To John Simon Bergheim, an officer of the English syndicate who had briefly taken

over the directorship of the American branch in 1903, Clemens
wrote an indignant letter about his lack of information regarding
company affairs:

> I . . . know that you could pay a 50% dividend
> today if you wanted to. I am warned from sources
> which I respect, that the Company is crooked,
> and has private schemes which will not bear the
> light. The Company's deliberately dishonest
> course toward me for two years, is good circum-
> stantial evidence that the warning was well
> founded.
>
> I want every detail of the business that I was
> entitled to have while a director, and which the
> Company for its own reasons has withheld from
> me. In addition, I want every report, and every
> document of any kind that any other stock
> holder has received during these two years.

Calls on his American stock of $10,000 in February and $9,500
three months later were the final straws. In his notebook Clemens
listed the various checks he had written for the American Plasmon
stock and the endorsements, various proposals for the restitution
of his money ("I won't accept stock," "Compounding felony"),
and the names of the managers of the company. The treasurer of
the company, endorser of one of the checks Clemens wrote and
Clemens' champion in the impending Plasmon fight, was Ralph
W. Ashcroft. Later, in 1904, when actual litigation was in prog-
ress, Ashcroft was to explain the intricacies of the Plasmon situa-
tion. It turned out that Clemens had not purchased his $25,000
worth of shares from the pool of Founders' Shares of the American
branch (each of which earned a bonus share for each share pur-
chased); instead, Henry Butters had transferred $25,000 of his
own investment to Clemens without including the corresponding
free shares.

While Plasmon simmered, Harper & Brothers' "suppression" of
Christian Science produced another time-consuming debate.
Clemens intended to impose on that firm some highly restrictive

condition for publication of his book—"the original price of the book cannot be reduced without my consent in writing. . . . Bliss shall be allowed to add the book to his collection." As the frustrated author told Rogers, "the Bliss-Collier-Harper matter" as he called it was a "cussed business . . . full of complications." On April 25, 1903, Frederick Duneka complained that the American Publishing Company was selling its twenty-two-volume set at a reduced price "in violation of the American Publishing Company's contract with us," and on the same day Bliss wrote him that Harper & Brothers was suing the American Publishing Company for $8,000 and had a sheriff searching for the plates used to publish the subscription editions. On the envelope of Bliss's letter, Clemens wrote with relish, "War declared." But—for the present—his own sympathies were with Bliss. And Duneka received a bitter condemnation:

> Yes, the collected set is being offered at $36.50, but it is not Bliss that is responsible, it is I. He is to keep within the requirements of the Harper contract, and leave the rest to me. . . .
>
> It ought to be quite easy for the Harpers and me to arrange a just and fair Harper-Bliss contract, in place of the existing contract. A new contract could be made profitable, both to Harpers and to me, whereas the existing one is not largely profitable to Harpers, and is probably only profitable to me at the expence of the collected edition.

It was enough to halt the immediate sources of friction. On April 28 Clemens wrote Bliss, "War suspended. Truce proclaimed. The sheriff will find some other way to amuse himself. Go ahead. There is nothing in your way now."

Robert Collier wrote Clemens on May 4, inquiring about the possibility of publishing an inexpensive set, visited Riverdale on May 11, and wrote again on May 28 with a specific royalty offer for collected-edition sets: $80,000 for the succeeding two years, with the right to cancel the contract in October 1905. But, as Clemens

recorded in his notebook, "the old Harper contracts had full command of the situation—I was a Harper slave and couldn't get free. I had to accept whatever terms the Harper corporation were willing to grant." Sometime during these lengthy deliberations of 1903 Clemens wrote a savage attack on the Harper contracts and organization. In part it read:

> The rights which you possess were procured by crime and must carry the stain of it until by an act of justice it is removed and my unoffending wife and children honorably dealt with. They are now criminally and dishonorably treated. Not a cent goes from my books to the Harper pocket that is not stolen money, for it results from what was distinctly a highway robbery perpetrated upon me 8 years ago.

In May, Duneka arrived on a peace mission to Riverdale and "said he was willing, and the Colonel would be willing, to destroy the existing contracts and start fresh."

Now that Harper's was prepared to negotiate, Clemens shifted his attack to Frank and Walter Bliss of the American Publishing Company. That organization was understandably reluctant to participate in those parts of the proposed reorganization which authorized the Collier editions, since the Blisses saw no advantage to themselves in such an arrangement. Clemens planned a flanking movement to circumvent them.

He had Miss Lyon write Whitmore, asking "if you could arrange to have him meet all the Directors of the American Publishing Co. (except the Blisses) at your house—either singly or together." The meeting arranged, Clemens went to Hartford on June 3, 1903, met the three directors and succeeded in persuading at least one of them, Ward Jacobs, that the American Publishing Company's subscription-set agreement

> means $15,000 to me, salaries to the Blisses, and not a penny for the Company.
> A contract with Collier means $10,000 a year sure, (with prospects beyond)

> It also includes release from Harper law-suits.
> The Blisses, who are to-day running the busi-
> ness in the Bliss interest *solely,* will never do
> these things, but you 3 directors can get together
> and do them.

Jacobs and Frank Bliss went to Riverdale on June 25 to receive
Clemens' offer to buy all rights to his books controlled by the
company for a $50,000 cash payment. This proposal was in effect
an "offer" for the American Publishing Company to go out of
business, since the depleted company no longer controlled any
other significant assets. When it was sensibly declined, Clemens
asked to be allowed to confront a meeting of stockholders with his
proposal to limit the American Publishing Company's rights in
the Hillcrest Edition, to voluntarily reduce his own share of the
royalties, and to insure that his Harper & Brothers volumes were
published in different color bindings so that they would not give
the appearance of a collected set. He also turned his memory back-
ward to all the injustices he had ever suffered or imagined he had
suffered when Frank Bliss replied to the offer with a letter that
questioned the $50,000 sum as adequate for "abandoning a busi-
ness which has taken years to lead up to this point, neglecting other
lines of business for the sake of developing yours." "As Regards
the Company's Benevolences," Clemens titled his formal diatribe,
and in it he opened wounds originally inflicted as far back as 1869.
And he salted his notebook with vindictive slashes at the American
Publishing Company as well.

xvi

While negotiations and litigation over his Plasmon investment
and his publishing contracts were hanging fire, Mrs. Clemens was
doing so well that she and her husband decided to make a trip to
Elmira in July, leaving Clara and Jean in Riverdale. Clemens told
the Huttons:

> We carried Mrs. Clemens down the hill at 8:30
> in the morning, at Riverdale; lifted her into the
> launch, hoisted launch and all on board Mr. Rog-
> ers's yacht, out in the river; steamed down to the
> DL & W dock at Hoboken, carried the madam
> aboard the 10 A.M. train and came through to El-
> mira in the suffocating heat, arriving at 4.40. . . .

Not only was she well enough to withstand such juggling, but
Clemens could even report to Twichell that "in the matter of
superintending everything and everybody [she] has resumed busi-
ness at the old stand." Her "business" included editing an inter-
view that Edward Bok was preparing for the *Ladies' Home
Journal*. Clemens warned Bok to "save bloodshed" by submitting
proof to Olivia before publishing.

But Clara, at Riverdale, was about to cause additional anxiety.
She had a carbuncle and wrote asking her father (also subject to
the infection) for a prescription. Clemens showed the letter to
Olivia, whose response was startling:

> How I wish you were here so that I could see to
> you. I feel that I could do it better than any-
> one. . . .
>
> Oh darling how can I have you suffer with a
> carbuncle? I have telegraphed and hope to get
> better news in the morning. Have the doctor
> come every day and *do be careful to keep up
> your strength*. My dear darling I do wish I could
> help you. Oh *don't* have a bad one.

Clara admonished her father for showing the letter to Olivia, and
he was properly penitent: "It was heedless in me to send your
letter to her—but I never once thought." With Olivia in such a
panic over a boil, it was judiciously decided not to tell her at all
about Clara's tonsils. "Why, dear me," Clemens wrote his daugh-
ter, "it almost gave *me* a collapse to read about the surgical
butcheries you were undergoing and contemplating." Olivia, he
reported, was taking short rides with Miss Margaret Shery, her

nurse, and was preparing to sleep outdoors to cure her insomnia.

She would most certainly have suffered a relapse had she known about Clara's summer activities. Apparently without her parents' knowledge, the daughter had resurrected the singing career of which they both disapproved. Once Jean had joined her parents in Elmira, Clara was scheduled to be chaperoned by the Richard Watson Gilders. And on August 4 Gilder wrote Clemens a letter full of mysteries:

> I took your daughter to Four Brooks Farm, Tyringham, Friday night [31 July]. I told her on the way up that her agent had cancelled all her other New England engagements. When she got to Tyringham Mrs. Gilder took this matter in hand and, assuming a ferocious air, forbade the young lady to go wandering around into strange New England places when she ought to be taking care of herself quietly at Four Brooks Farm. She thought it was not safe for a person who had been going through all she has, mentally and physically, lately to be let loose in that manner. I think she was right. I told Clara there were moments when young people should allow older people to take their consciences in their hands and act for them.

There is no record elsewhere of any "New England engagements" for Clara that summer; indeed, it seems impossible that she could have been singing at all so soon after "surgical butcheries" on her tonsils. It remains at least a strong possibility that there were no throat operations that summer at all. Clara may have invented a summer of surgery in order to schedule a New England tour, however naïve the idea that her parents would not hear about it. Still, the conjecture about her devious plans receives some corroboration from a 1907 letter in which Clemens mentions that Clara has "had a tonsil cut out," implying that they had not been removed in the summer of 1903. Clara's "agent" that summer is unknown. And although her mother's illness and her own assumption of

responsibility might have produced mental and physical strain, Gilder's phrasing—that it was not safe for Clara "to be let loose"— has either a sinister connotation or was a strangely inept choice of language.

It is likely that Clara's parents so sternly disapproved of her singing career because it separated her from them; quite probably they also believed that the scheduled concerts and recitals inflicted severe nervous strain on their daughter. Clara established a pattern of arranging appearances and then canceling them—over and over again—at the last moment because of a sore throat or a similar illness. Her "career," we can surmise, was to Clara a symbol of her independence from her family, and it developed an importance to her out of proportion to her success or her capabilities. Perhaps a woman of almost thirty required a chaperone in New England in 1903; perhaps being "let loose" was simply a poor selection of words; perhaps the lack of conscience which Gilder attributed to Clara was mere rhetoric. But much more probable is that Clara, free from her family's restricting influence and supervision, was trying so desperately to establish her career that even a friend of the family could recognize behavior that was not normal. In any event, Clemens went to Tyringham and put Clara on the train that carried her to her mother on August 12.

While Olivia and her two daughters rested near Elmira at Quarry Farm (Olivia for the last time in her life), the head of the family was in New York engaged in further negotiations with his various publishers. On August 4, 1903, he summoned Bliss to New York, and a fruitless discussion followed. On August 11 another telegram brought Bliss to the Grosvenor Hotel—and again on the nineteenth, the twenty-eighth, and September 3. Finally on September 15, Bliss (who was aware that he could receive several profitable concessions because Clemens was "getting things fixed now to satisfy himself and . . . hereafter he will be clear of the Hartford connection"), Duneka, and Rogers gathered in Rogers' office and hammered out the details of a contract (written up and signed by all the principals on October 23) which made Harper & Brothers the exclusive publishers of Mark Twain's

work, guaranteed a $25,000 minimum annual income, and ful-
filled Cheiro's prophecy of great wealth with, as Clemens put it,
"but a month and nine days to spare."

Meanwhile, the plans for the trip to Italy were changing. After
booking passage for himself and six women—Olivia, Clara, Jean,
the maid Katy Leary, Isabel Lyon, and Miss Shery the nurse—on
the *Lahn,* Clemens decided in midsummer to change his reserva-
tions to the *Princess Irene,* which left New York on October 24,
two weeks earlier than the *Lahn.* (Miss Lyon and her mother had
to keep their reservations on the later ship because Miss Lyon was
being treated for an eye infection.) Working through George
Gregory Smith, the family found and believed they had leased the
Villa Papiniano, outside Florence near the villa of their friend
retired Cornell professor Willard Fiske. But the arrangements for
the Papiniano and another villa fell through; and in September,
Smith inspected the Miravalle, Lallune, di Quarto, Chiari-Pestel-
lini, Ottoboni, and Montealbano. On October 7 he rented the
Villa di Quarto for 10,000 lire—half the original lease price—and
told the Clemenses, "Take it altogether I know of no place in
Florence where you can be so thoroughly comfortable as at
Quarto." As it was to turn out, Smith could not have been further
from the truth.

On October 5, after a final visit to Susy's grave, the Clemens
family moved from Elmira to New York City, where it spent the
last weeks before departing at the Grosvenor Hotel. The Twich-
ells came on October 19 to say goodbye. Olivia was "getting along
so promisingly that to-day the specialist granted her the privilege
of crossing the sea without her trained nurse. This leaves her in the
hands of a special stewardess and our old Katy." Actually, plans
would be changed again, and Miss Shery would accompany the
family to Italy. Clemens arranged the details of a purchase option
on the Casey house at Tarrytown, which had been rented to
Charles A. Gardiner in May. Harper & Brothers arranged a fare-
well dinner to celebrate the signing of the comprehensive publish-
ing contract and as a goodbye banquet. And on the evening of the

twenty-third the family boarded the *Princess Irene* in high hopes of Olivia's recovery and their continued financial tranquility.

xvii

After a trip marred by insomnia, the family stopped briefly at Naples and then left the boat in Genoa. Smith made reservations for the Clemenses at the Grand Hotel and offered "to drive over to the Quarto with you to instal you in your palace, and introduce you to your landlady. Possession will be given at once."

Edward Caulfield, editor of the English-language *Italian Gazette* which was published for the Anglo-American colony in Florence, agreed with Smith's appraisal of the villa. On November 3 he announced in his paper, "Mr. Clemens has hired the magnificent Villa Reale di Quarto. . . . Since buying the Villa di Quarto the Contessa has lavished both money and faultless taste in refitting and furnishing." Clemens was less impressed, as he explained to Howells:

> It must have been built for fuss & show & irruptions of fashion, not for a home. There are 20 large chambers on the top floor, but they are for servants. Our own floor (ground floor) is cut up into 21 rooms, passages, corridors, &c., & the floor above us is cut up into 22 of the like useless things (the house is 200 feet long) —yet if you were to come I could not find you a comfortable & satisfactory place.

In January 1904 he would describe the Quarto in meticulous and equally contemptuous detail for his autobiography.

The owner, who would remain in a house on the grounds, Countess Rebaudi-Massiglia, was an American whom Isabel Lyon remembered from Philadelphia in the late 1880s, when she was only Mrs. Barney Campan. Miss Lyon and Clemens both instantly disliked the countess and recorded descriptions of her. Clemens wrote,

> She is excitable, malicious, malignant, vengeful,
> unforgiving, selfish, stingy, avaricious, coarse,
> vulgar, profane, obscene, a furious blusterer on
> the outside and at heart a coward. . . . It is good
> to be a real noble, it is good to be a real Ameri-
> can, it is a calamity to be neither the one thing
> nor the other, a politico-social bastard on both
> counts.

Miss Lyon managed slightly more restraint: "Here she remains, although she said she was going to spend the winter in Paris . . . [with] the big Roman steward of the place—and they two live together. . . . Here she remains, a menace to the peace of the Clemens household, with her painted hair, her great coarse voice, her slitlike vicious eyes, her dirty clothes, and her terrible manners."

The countess refused to allow an old friend and neighbor, Mrs. Janet Ross, to prepare the villa for the Clemenses' arrival because "the servants cannot enter the Villa until after Mr. Clemens is in possession." So the family had to stay at the hotel in town until November 9, 1903, and arrived at the villa only to discover that Mrs. Clemens could not be placed in the bedroom chosen for her—a clause in the lease specifically forbade the presence of any sick person in that one room. The countess also locked the gates to the villa capriciously so that Olivia's two Italian doctors—Professor Pietro Grocco and Dr. Giovanni Nesti—could not always enter.

After less than a month in the villa, Clemens asked the professional opinion of a Florentine attorney, Paolo de Plaisant, about a mixup over the stables assigned for the family's use. It turned out that the ones specified in the lease were in the basement of the villa itself, directly under Olivia's bedroom. And Arthur W. Higgs, who had originally been the countess's real-estate agent, was unable to collect his commission from her and apparently included the Clemens name in the lawsuit he filed. The countess's next affronts persuaded Clemens to direct all his zeal and energy toward her demolition.

Countess Massiglia turned off all water to the villa. The family could obtain drinking water from the Roman steward but could not flush the toilets because the empty supply tanks

> were in the upper region of the house. . . . The stench was persistent, and dangerous to health. The windows had to be kept open, no matter what the weather was like.

Then the countess's donkey—or at any rate a donkey which Clemens said was hers, although she denied the ownership—joined the battle. It was Miss Lyon who suffered, by her own account,

> a shock to my nervous system; for the Countess's donkey, a creature that has killed his 2 men, suddenly appeared before me [on February 2, 1904]. . . . I knew that if he could get at me he would kill me. . . . Like one in a nightmare I fled up the long winding hill, but before I reached the top my heart began to fail me. . . . For 5 days I lay like one in a dream, but soon I pulled myself together enough to go unsatisfactorily about my work.

Clemens, too, reported the donkey attack as causing "a sudden standstill" in his writing. "My secretary's life was about frightened out of her—since which time she has lain half-conscious in her bed at home, and the doctors cannot foretell what the outcome will be." Beset by this vindictive treatment, Clemens began to prepare legal counterattacks against the countess.

He told Rogers, "I got the weightiest lawyer in Italy, and the game was called. . . . I am backing some peasant-suits against her—2 civil and one criminal—and when those are through I have some more up my sleeve." First, there was the threat of a lawsuit against the telephone company which, on the countess's orders, had stopped the service to the Clemenses' telephone. Next, both Miss Lyon and Poggiali Gerdinando—a peasant whose thumb had been bitten off by the donkey several weeks before Miss Lyon's

encounter—were encouraged to file lawsuits against the countess; and if Miss Lyon's suit was successful, then, Smith suggested, Clemens could sue the countess for the loss of his secretary's services. There was also a suit of obscure dimensions involving a laundress and an attempt to have the villa condemned when Clemens learned "that the house-sewage goes into cesspools *under the house*—almost under Mrs. C.'s room!"

The countess retaliated by having Miss Lyon and her mother evicted from an outlying cottage on the villa grounds; they took up residence with a priest who was becoming a close friend of Jean Clemens and the entire family, Don Raffaello Stiattisi, who would keep the family informed as the various Massiglia lawsuits dragged into 1905 and 1906.

Other stresses than the countess contributed to the strain of Clemens' life in Florence. Someone, Caulfield announced in the December 29, 1903, issue of the *Italian Gazette*, "last week sent us some doggerel purporting to come from 'Mark Twain' and *signed with his name*. . . . We have consulted with Mr. Clemens himself, and acting on his advice we have put the matter in the hands of the police." More important, every attempt that Clemens made to get restitution of his $25,000 from Plasmon met with a counteroffer for him to purchase more stock; so Clemens appointed John B. Stanchfield, an Elmira attorney for the Langdon family, to handle the matter for him while he was in Florence. On January 29, 1904, Stanchfield received Clemens' reply to one such offer:

> I thought it over, and decided against it. . . .
> There is only one proper thing for Butters to do, and that is, to make restitution unconditionally; either of all he stole from me or enough of it to leave him a fair commission on his theft. But I am not going to add any cash to the $32,-500 I have already sunk there.
> As soon as I get back we will pull Butters into Court, and I guess we can jail him. We will try, anyhow. And I will add that libel, and see if he

> has grit enough to prosecute me—which he will
> if he is as much of an ass as he is a thief. *I* think
> he *is*.

Clemens did commit the libel. In *A Horse's Tale,* one of the talking horses comments to another, "I recognized your master. He is a bad sort. Trap-robber, horse-thief, squaw-man, renegade—Hank Butters—I know him very well." That was his second attempt, though; at the same time that he was writing to Stanchfield, the satirist was at work on his brief sketch "Sold to Satan." After deciding to sell his soul to Satan, the narrator "sent word to the local agent, Mr. Henry A. Butters, through his subordinate, Mr. Howard E. Wright"; for some reason, he canceled the names of the Plasmon partners and substituted "Mr. Blank."

According to Clemens in a 1908 recollection, Butters "escaped to California, and there he had to remain."

> He dearly wanted to live in New York, but he
> had to forego that delight, and has chafed and
> lamented in exile for six years. He knew he
> would retire to the penitentiary if he ventured
> into this State, and so he stayed out of it.

In addition, according to the recollection, Butters "commissioned his legal serf in New York to bring against me a libel suit—and he placed the damages at fifty thousand dollars!" Butters died in October 1908, before the suit came to trial.

Other schemes whirred in Clemens' head but with less disastrous results than American Plasmon. He proposed to MacAlister the formation of a stock company—in which they would split half the shares without putting up any money—to market "a specific I've invented . . . a relief for itching piles—and very prompt—in effect, instantaneous." In the winter of 1903, Clemens expressed his intense desire to invest in "Lysoform—if the Bergheims are going to manage it," and later that month he told Rogers of his intention to put $10,000 into that company's stock. Three months later he was "too poor to buy into that new company (the anti-

septic soap one)" but was pursuing a grand plot "to kill Great Britain's coal trade with Italy, France and Germany by furnishing a very cheap and competent and exhaustless fuel drawn from Tuscan sources."

<div align="center">xviii</div>

Mark Twain's literary activity increased in Florence, too. Earlier in 1903 he had produced "Instructions in Art" accompanied by his own primitively spirited sketches. And he found time in Elmira to compose *A Dog's Tale,* a painfully sentimental anti-vivisectionist fable composed at the urging of his daughter Jean and published in the Christmas 1903 issue of *Harper's Weekly.* And he added to the fragmentary "Eddypus" material that he had written earlier.

In December 1903, though, he worked furiously and was able to report to Rogers that he had written $7,500 worth of material. To Duneka he was even more specific:

> Yes, I've written the Midsummer Story ("You've Been a Dam Fool, Mary. You Always Was,") and the next-Xmas Story ("The $30,000 Bequest"), and Mrs. Clemens is editing the hell-fire out of them. The typewriter will take hold, next.
>
> Two weeks ago I wrote a pretty pison article about "Major General Wood, M.D.," and took great pains with it, and worked at it several days and got it to suit me exactly—then pigeonholed it with a sigh. . . .
>
> I am writing "Italian With Grammar," and will send it to the Colonel if it reads to suit me when I get it done.

Neither the attack on General Wood nor the Midsummer Story was published in Mark Twain's life; on February 26, 1904, Duneka told Clemens, "We are greatly interested in your article

on 'You've Been a Damfool, Mary' &c but are scared to death of the title." Two articles on the Italian language appeared in 1904, "Italian Without a Master" in the January *Harper's Weekly* and "Italian With Grammar" in the August *Harper's*.

A letter to Duneka on January 8, 1904, suggested issuing "St. Joan of Arc," which Mark Twain had written years earlier, to capitalize on the proposed beatification that he thought would "start up a run of magazining concerning Joan." Duneka responded on February 4 that he would hold up the "St. Joan" until a more propitious occasion (as a Catholic, Duneka may have felt squeamish at making literary profit of the beatification ceremony).

Also in January, Clemens notified Duneka that he had written "Sold to Satan" and revised it twice, omitting the references to Butters and Wright and canceling a passage about "real estate agents in New York who collect their commission a year before they accomplish the sale"—a reference to George W. Reeves's handling of the sale of the Tarrytown property in 1903.

The intrusion of these biographical references in his fiction underscores that his literature—always as autobiographical as fiction could get and remain fiction—was losing even the slight veneer of imaginative prose. Mark Twain's literary voice, no matter how skillfully he manipulated it for literary purposes, never completely disguised his own articulation. He was a literary ventriloquist whose own lips were moving more and more visibly during each performance. His interest in his own subjective version of reality even led him to reply to a request by an old boatman to visit the Villa di Quarto and recollect the old days, "Let them come here Thursday. But my interest in the subject is dead." And then, as a second thought, "No answer." Introspective autobiography had now become more congenial, and in Florence he found the method of transcription appropriate to the voice.

To Howells he wrote jubilantly, on January 16, 1904:

> I've struck it! And I will give it away—to you.
> You will never know how much enjoyment you

> have lost until you get to dictating your auto-
> biography. . . .
> Try it, & you will see. But with a long-hand
> scribe, not with a stenographer. . . .
> Miss Lyons does the scribing, & is an inspira-
> tion, because she takes so much interest in it.

Miss "Lyons" recorded the discovery in her diary, too, as one of
significance:

> About January 14, Mr. Clemens began to dictate
> to me. His idea of *writing* an autobiography had
> never proved successful, for to his mind auto-
> biography is like narrative and should be spoken.
> At Mrs. Clemens's suggestion we tried, and Mr.
> Clemens found that he could do it to a charm.
> In fact he loves the work. But we have had to
> stop, for he has been ill, Mrs. Clemens has been
> very ill, and I too have taken a weary turn in
> bed.

Not until the end of March, when Miss Lyon had recovered from
her encounter with the donkey, could Clemens record, "Began
dictating again, after an interval of 2 months."

Predictably, many of the autobiographical dictations of 1904
were caustic in tone and temper—about the villa and the countess.
Others were faulty in unity and coherence or too literally chrono-
logical in sequence. Mark Twain still had to discover the exact
modulations necessary to avoid the awkwardnesses of "I remember
two incidents of that Sunday visit [to John Hay] particularly well,
and I think I shall use them presently to illustrate something
which I intend to say." But he was at least moving toward the
mastery of the 1906 dictations which constitute the major portions
of the autobiography.

In the last substantial work of fiction completed and published
during his lifetime, *The $30,000 Bequest,* there were also auto-
biographical allusions and overtones. The wife, named Electra but
called "Aleck," is a hard-headed, conservative investor who begins
her speculations with an imaginary fortune in coal (Olivia's own

fortune was from coal) as well as an orthodox Christian such as
Olivia had been, whom the dreamer husband heedlessly injures
with "untimely and ill-chosen playfulness" about Christian mis-
sionaries. The couple's two daughters lose suitors who have not
reached the station the parents think proper. The enormous paper
fortune that the Fosters accumulate from the promise of a bequest
of $30,000 wreaks its damage: "Vast wealth, acquired by sudden and
unwholesome means, is a snare. It did us no good, transient were
its feverish pleasures; yet for its sake we threw away our sweet and
simple and happy life—let others take warning by us."

That passage might almost serve as the epigraph for the
Clemenses' marriage and life together. The vast wealth tainted by
speculation, the injuries, real and imagined, inflicted on the wife
by the insensitive husband, the pride and ostentation and vanity
that resulted in rejected suitors for the sheltered and frustrated
daughters, all contrasted with a "sweet and simple and happy life."
Such a way of living existed only in the Clemenses' imaginations;
but, measuring their life against that illusory ideal, they suffered
because they were less than perfect. When they blamed themselves
for unavoidable catastrophes—such as the infant Langdon's and
Susy's deaths, for fluctuations in income, even for simply aging—
they destroyed themselves. As long as Olivia was alive and could
impose her domestic standards on her family, the members man-
aged, bound together sometimes by only the slenderest of threads,
to maintain a sense of unity.

Indeed, Clemens was even able to convince himself, in spite of
the statement to the contrary in *The $30,000 Bequest,* that the
energy, viciousness, and malevolence he expended on his financial
affairs were spent in the interest of his family. His notion that
Harper & Brothers was robbing his "unoffending" wife and chil-
dren was one of the self-justifications. And, once he reached
Florence, he threw himself into that burst of literary activity so that
he would fulfill his part of the Harper contract and allow Olivia
"to feel entirely easy about the expenses." Later in 1904 he could
announce with pride:

> Even after we arrived here she was not willing to
> spend money freely, because our expenses were
> $1650 a month—hardly $500 a month short of
> Riverdale; but I said I would earn $10,000 by
> magazine work if she would throw away every
> penny of it on whatever she chose, and please
> me . . . and when I showed her that I had
> earned $11,000-odd, she never again refused to
> buy whatever she wanted.

The truth is, of course, that he enjoyed the battles in which he
indulged for profit's sake. He would have suspected his publishers
and he would have filed lawsuits against every offending party he
could find, even if he lacked a family. Both suspicion and an
almost blinding lust for fortune were a part of his nature; he
speculated, suffered, and sued as instinctively as he wrote.

xix

In spite of all he could do to ease her mind in Florence, Mrs.
Clemens did not prosper. A few days after the family's arrival she
burned herself with carbolic acid—"it was an accident, and not her
fault," Clemens for some reason felt compelled to assure Rogers.
Furthermore, the fog and rain made it impossible for her to spend
time outdoors. The "breathless" spells began again, but in early
December 1903 she felt well enough to send Miss Shery back to
the United States. Shortly after, a major relapse occurred:

> There was a splendid sunshiny day—almost the
> only one we have seen since we entered this
> house—and Livy was taken from her bed and con-
> veyed in her wheel-chair into the garden to enjoy
> the balmy air and the pink cloud of the roses;
> and she was out too long, and caught cold, and
> was fatigued, for she is but a shadow and very
> feeble; and tonsilitis added itself to her other
> ailments; with night-sweats and a high tempera-

> ture for two days and nights. And by conse-
> quence she is now back where she was 8 or 9
> months ago, and is discouraged, and depressed.

A few days later Clemens told Rogers that Olivia's mind was "wandering at intervals."

Perhaps in sheer frustration Clemens fired Professor Grocco and Dr. Nesti (he disapproved of their unavailability and of their *"resumption of electricity"* in treating Mrs. Clemens) ; and on the recommendation of American physician W. Allen Starr, he hired Dr. G. W. Kirch, an Austrian physician who served the Anglo-American community of Florence. Kirch, who believed that Mrs. Clemens needed only one or two visits a week, was ordered to attend her daily and to minister to Miss Lyon and Mrs. Lyon—even to make an inspection of the cesspools under the house in preparation for the condemnation proceedings against the villa. Clemens and he were to file lawsuits and countersuits over Kirch's bill and to threaten litigation as late as 1906. Clemens recorded in his notebook in May 1904, "Asked Dr. Kirch for his 3-months' bill, and got it: $900! It is robbery. . . . The man is a hog." But "I have got to keep Kirch. We dare not change doctors—Livy is too frail." And in addition, Olivia had "come to have a splendid confidence in Dr. Kirch."

Her frailty, and his concern for her, appear not to have impeded the social activities of the rest of the family. Thursday afternoons were the Clemenses' "at home" day, and every indication is that all of them were kept busy. Frederick Duneka told Clemens on February 4, 1904, "I note by the newspapers that you are tea-ing and dining with all the great ones." Clara was taking voice lessons—possibly her family had decided to stop resisting her plans as long as her parents could oversee and supervise her training. More probably, while her mother was critically ill, Clara was able to manage her father—not to defy but to outargue him. One of her letters to Clemens during the Florence residency suggests exactly how well she managed his behavior. Suggesting an itinerary for his day, she added, "Now be calm, father, and discuss this with me by note or any way that you like, but don't bother Mother about it."

At any rate, Clara sang on March 21 at the Alfieri Theater and appeared at the Sala Filarmonica on the evenings of April 8 and 15, 1904. Caulfield noted in the *Italian Gazette,* "Miss Clemens possesses a very sympathetic contralto voce of considerable extension and of a remarkably sweet and touching quality." The singer's father agreed; he labeled the April 8 concert "a triumph. Livy woke up and sent for her to tell her all about it at near midnight." Thereupon Olivia immediately had an "awful attack —for more than an hour. Livy struggled for breath. Clara was in there. Jean and I listened at the door." The immediate conjunction of Clara's public triumph and her mother's near fatal attack— like the seizure the day Clara returned to the United States in 1902—cannot be ignored, although certainly no absolute relationship between the events can be established.

Clemens, too, appeared in public on many occasions. He gave a reading of "Italian Without Grammar" as a curtain-raiser for a performance of "Cousin Kate" for the Florentine British Relief Fund. According to Caulfield in his gossipy *Gazette:*

> The great humorist looked as full of vitality as ever though it was plain that he was labouring under a stress of emotion, and at times he nervously tore the paper he was holding in his hands. At the end of his talk, with a break in his voice, he bade his hearers goodnight, and everyone admired his generous courage when it was known that he had left Mrs. Clemens at home seriously ill.

Indeed, the public appearance occurred in the same week that Clemens reported to Rogers, "The past week has been awful—she has had bad nights, and been obliged to sit up in bed for hours, in order to get her breath. . . . Three nights ago her pulse went up to *192,* and nothing but a subcutaneous injection of brandy brought her back to life." From the time of Clara's concert, her mother's condition deteriorated precipitately—and Mrs. Clemens wished to be certain that everyone knew how ill she was. Clemens wrote Sue Crane, Olivia's stepsister, that spring of 1904:

> I find for sure—and I have suspected it before
> —that Livy *does not like* to have me *diminish the
> gravity of her case* by writing home letters which
> bring back cheerful off-hand remarks. . . . She
> said this morning, with asperity, "I suppose they
> think I am frolicking around Florence!"

In April, Clemens and Jean were once more forbidden to see
Olivia; and according to the recollection of William Lyon Phelps,
who came to the at-home of April 14, Clemens "was 68 years old,
but looked older. . . . During this hour's interview, Mark
smoked three cigars; there was a constant twitching in his right
cheek and his right eye seemed inflamed."

When Clemens was permitted to make a two-minute visit to
Olivia's room in mid-May, he told Gilder that he saw "blue lips,
the pallor of the dead, and that pathetic something in the eye
which betrays the secret of a waning hope." Nevertheless, the
following day, according to the *Gazette* of May 17, "Mr. S. L.
Clemens was the honored guest of the Ponte Vecchio Club at the
usual Saturday dinner last week. . . . 'Mark Twain' . . . pro-
ceeded to tell an excellent story of how he drove an unwilling man
into matrimony"—the story he was to write in several contra-
dictory versions as "Wapping Alice."

During the spring, Clemens began looking for another villa, af-
ter discovering from Dr. Starr that Olivia could be moved to an
altitude as high as two thousand feet without danger to her breath-
ing. Flooded with rental offers, he leased the Villa Collarini for the
coming year. As he told Muriel Pears:

> We have taken a furnished villa for the summer
> months in the hills 20 miles from here—to move
> the madam to it? No—to make her *think* such a
> thing may happen, and so keep her courage from
> perishing. We went through all the motions: ex-
> amined the house searchingly, took it, paid for it,
> and privately bade it good-bye, no member of
> this beleaguered family ever seriously expecting
> to see it again.

On June 4 he looked at two other villas, and on June 5 he and
Jean found one to purchase. When he returned to the di Quarto
and told Olivia of the find, "her eyes danced with pleasure"—for
"she said she wanted a *home*—a home of her own; that she was
tired and wanted rest, and could not rest and be in comfort and
peace while she was homeless."

At nine o'clock that same evening, Clemens "went to the piano
and sang the old songs, the quaint negro hymns," and then went to
his room to await his evening visit to Olivia's bedside. And at nine-
twenty, as Katy Leary attempted to revive her with an oxygen
mask, Olivia Clemens died.

Katy remembered the scene:

> Mr. Clemens ran right up to the bed and took
> her in his arms like he always did and held her
> for the longest time, and then he laid her back
> and he said, "How beautiful she is—how young
> and sweet—and look, she's smiling!"
>
> It was a pitiful thing to see her there dead, and
> him looking at her. Oh, he cried all that time,
> and Clara and Jean, they put their arms around
> their father's neck and they cried, the three of
> them as though their hearts would break.

A year later Miss Lyon recalled the identical scene:

> Today is the anniversary of the great tragedy of
> this family. . . . I can see Mr. Clemens' face
> when I flew to his room and told him to go to
> Mrs. Clemens's room. "Is it an alarm?" he said—
> but I didn't know, they only told me to run and
> get him.

What makes these accounts important is that Clemens' own ver-
sion differs, not substantially but emotionally, from the other two.
By his own report to Howells, "Last night at 9.20 I entered Mrs.
Clemens's room to say the usual good-night—& she was dead! tho'
no one knew it." Indeed, he claimed it was he who held her in his
arms and discovered that she had died.

The variations would be unimportant except that the survivors all participated in peculiarly ritualistic and macabre behavior during the first few days after Olivia's death. According to the newspaper accounts preserved in the Mark Twain Papers, Clemens spent the night kneeling beside Olivia's coffin. And before the sheets on the deathbed were cold—if Katy Leary's grisly account is correct—Clara climbed into the bed in her mother's place. Then Clara went to her room and lay "motionless and wordless" for at least four days, not emerging until June 19. Jean "had an attack—the first in 13 months," and never again was to be free from seizures for so long a period. But in these first days, while Clara's grief expressed itself in silent isolation, Jean became "the executive head and manager" of the family.

Clemens' own grief, although indisputably as sincere, was expressed in surprisingly formal terms. His letters to Howells, Rogers, and Gilder are examples of the false and inflated rhetoric he ridiculed elsewhere. He converted a passage in his letter to Twichell to use as the conclusion of *The Mysterious Stranger*; and another, "I am a man without a country. Wherever Livy was, that was my country," became with minor alterations the last line of *Eve's Diary*, "Wheresoever she was, *there* was Eden."

Other outpourings of his compulsive pen in those days were too contrived, too polished, too ceremonial for the modern reader to view without discomfort:

> The ruined household undivided sail.

> I was richer than any other person in the world, and now I am that pauper without peer.

> Why am I required to linger here?

Even after his return to the United States, Clemens confused his sincere grief by expressing it in contrived literary modes, with convoluted word order and alliteration and elegant literary allusions. To an old, but not close, friend of his wife's, Clemens wrote:

> . . . A whisper of commendation from you was more to her than a paean of praise from another.

She stood in just this relation to no other friend,
indeed to no other person. To her you were a
being apart, and lifted above the common hu-
man level. You planted a seed once which blos-
somed and gave out a grateful fragrance for her
all the months while her life continued. It was a
letter in praise of Susy's little play. It was never
out of reach of her hand for sixteen years till she
died. It is in a little locked box wherein she kept
her precious things—things which have now been
sacred these eight years. It was always by her,
it was familiar with her tears, it was by her when
her tears were dried and she sank to rest in the
Great Peace.

She was beautiful and benignant in death, and
I knew how Sir Ector felt and thought when he
uttered his moving lament over his dead brother:

"Ah, Launcelot, there thou liest, . . . thou
wert the courtliest knight that ever bore shield;
and thou wert the truest friend to thy lover that
ever bestrode horse; and thou wert the truest
lover for a sinful man that ever loved woman;
and thou wert the kindest man that ever strake
with sword: and thou wert the goodliest person
that ever came among press of knights; and thou
wert the meekest man and the gentlest that ever
sat in hall with ladies. . . ."

It is not surprising that Clemens felt it important to place himself
in the room when Olivia died; it is distressing that he declaimed
his grief in such platitudinous forms of expression; it is positively
ludicrous to attempt to contemplate Olivia Clemens as having
"ever strake with sword." Silence would have been more convinc-
ing. A single sentence in a letter to Howells rang with a loneliness
and desolation that was indisputably sincere: "If I could only see a
dog that I knew in the old times! & could put my arms around his
neck & tell him all, everything, & ease my heart."

Public performances of grief included a fall from a chair nearly

out a window of the villa, which Clemens assumed would have
been interpreted as a suicide. They included the admonition to
Olivia's brother to save every scrap of her sacred writings. They
even included shipping a pair of horses that Olivia had bought for
Jean and Clara—"she paid the whole out of her own Elmira
money"—to the United States because they were "the most pre-
cious horses in the world, now."

<div align="center">xx</div>

The Clemens family booked passage on the *Prince Oscar* and left
the Villa di Quarto on June 20, stopping for four days at the Hôtel
de Ville in Florence. Jean "was sick" on the twentieth. On the
twenty-fourth, they moved to Rome for two days while Clara—in
"bad shape"—rested and Jean took snapshots of tourist sights. On
the twenty-sixth Jean had another bad day, and on the twenty-
seventh the family moved to Naples to board the ship. "Unless the
strain is soon removed from Clara," Clemens reported to Olivia's
brother, "she will go down with a crash and her present two-thirds
nervous breakdown will take on an additional third and be com-
plete." Clemens had been forbidden to see Clara during their last
days at the villa in a curious revival of the proscription against
visits to his wife. The ban on his mysteriously unsettling presence
would continue for most of the following year.

The family boarded ship on June 28, but not before Clemens
created one ultimate clumsily inappropriate action for a grieving
widower: He clashed with Dr. Kirch over the final bill for services
to Olivia. Clemens showed Kirch's bill to Dr. W. W. Baldwin, who
pronounced himself "distressed, horrified and inexpressably sur-
prised." Kirch and Clemens met at Haskard & Company, Bankers,
in the Piazza degli Antinori, just before the household departed;
and Clemens told Kirch he would not pay the final bill.

Then, as the *Prince Oscar* was preparing to leave, Clemens dis-
covered that the death certificate and consular papers were miss-
ing. Although the truth was that the Hamburg-American

Steamship Company had forwarded these documents to New York
by an earlier ship, Clemens became obsessed with the conviction
that Kirch had somehow deliberately suppressed them. He ob-
tained duplicates, unnecessarily, from Francis B. Keene, the U.S.
consul in Florence, and wrote an analysis of his grievances against
Kirch:

> Ten dollars a visit (50 francs) —6,700 francs for
> medical attendance 3 months and 28 days. Em-
> balming, 600 fr. Total, 7,300 francs. I paid him
> 5,100 fr. and invited him to sue for the rest. He is
> afraid to sue, but I think he suppressed the cer-
> tificates for spite, and kept still about it.

After his return Clemens would make an appeal to Frank Mason,
American consul at Vienna: "If my poor dear lost incomparable
wife had been thrust ignominiously ashore at Naples—think of
that," he said in a nine-page statement of charges he decided not
to send.

With the body securely on board, the *Prince Oscar* sailed. (The
two most precious horses in the world were on another, slower
boat.) Clara went to her stateroom, where, according to Miss
Lyon, she was "driven frantic by the cockroaches." Jean was
apparently satisfactory, but Miss Lyon herself spent three days
suffering from what she called "one of my strange nervous head-
aches." The *Prince Oscar* docked in New York on the evening of
July 12, with a special directive from President Roosevelt and the
entire Cabinet to allow the family immediate passage through
customs. The Clemenses went to the Wolcott Hotel, and Isabel
Lyon, her mother, and the Italian housemaid Teresa Cherubini,
who had come with the group, went to the St. Denis.

Leaving Miss Lyon in New York to supervise the unloading of
the less essential baggage, the Clemenses went with Edward
Loomis, Charles Langdon, and Joe Twichell to Elmira. Twichell
delivered a brief service in the Langdon parlor; and at the grave-
side, according to her biographer, Clara "gave a cry which stabbed
everyone's heart, and tried to jump into the grave with her

mother." When the coffin was lowered, more was laid to rest than Olivia Clemens' remains: The remainder of the family, for all practical purposes, no longer existed. The two daughters would henceforth spend minimal time with their surviving parent. Clara was apparently unable to endure the presence of her father —perhaps because she blamed him for her mother's death. Clemens was unable to endure the presence of Jean—perhaps because he blamed her epilepsy for his wife's death. Both girls would reside as often in "rest homes," sanitariums, and asylums as they did with their father.

And what had Samuel Clemens lost? A wife of thirty-four years, to be sure; a literary arbiter of taste whose advice he followed to his benefit more often than to his detriment; and a touchstone to gentility and propriety which Clemens persuaded himself he would otherwise never have known. Several years after Olivia's death, Joe Twichell confided to Isabel Lyon about

> how much Mrs. Clemens had done toward re-
> modelling Mr. Clemens. The Hooker girls of
> Hartford had been quite shocked when Mrs.
> Clemens became engaged to him. But Mrs. Clem-
> ens knew what she was about. . . . Of course
> there couldn't ever be anybody who could train
> him so that he wouldn't drop a little back to
> his wildnesses, and his strengths. But Mrs. Clem-
> ens did more than anyone else in the world could
> do. Mr. Twichell said that Mr. Clemens was so
> grateful to Mrs. Clemens, and so humbled be-
> cause she married him. She was his Great Guid-
> ing Star.

What stands out in Miss Lyon's transcription of Twichell's re-marks is the depiction of Samuel Clemens as "so humbled." Of course, it was true, and somehow the impression that he never allowed himself to forget his humility becomes clearer and clearer. Livy and Susy and Clara were Langdons; only Jean was a Clemens. And it was Jean who asked the least of her father and understood him best. The others in the family, much like the Hooker girls of

Hartford as well as Samuel Clemens himself, never forgot the debt
of gratitude that was his obligation.

Still, Olivia Clemens, with all her neuroses, her "enjoying poor
health," and her undoubted responsibility for stunting and warp-
ing the emotional lives of her daughters, was, as Samuel Clemens
instinctively knew when he asked her to marry him, a powerfully
effective and positive force in his life. Whatever direction his life
and writing might have taken had he not married Olivia, it would
have been less productive than it was under her direction and
guidance. Indeed, the value of her vigilant and iron-willed control
over her husband is nowhere more dramatically shown than in the
last six years of his life when, without her, he wandered aimlessly,
wrote fragmentarily, and offended almost all his friends and loved
ones.

Dragging the skeletons out of the Clemenses' closets would serve
little purpose in itself, however, were it not true that the financial
and literary enterprises of the husband and father were inter-
twined with his domestic trials and torments. The Langdons
belonged to the affluent class, and wealth, whether through wild-
cat speculation, literature, or speechmaking, was an instinctive
motivation in Samuel Clemens which marriage into the Langdon
clan merely reinforced. Nothing more explicitly typifies what
Clemens thought the Langdons expected of him than the insecu-
rity implicit in his reiterated insistence to Olivia's brother that she
was never spared any expense in Florence as she was dying.
Clemens did unquestionably create a "muse" by elevating his wife
into a sort of literary and critical idol. But Olivia created a "hus-
band," too, in that strangely loving but competitive marriage.
Whatever was repressed or distorted by the pair to fit their created
images of themselves, it was preferable to a Samuel Clemens
without any wife at all.

II. GÖTTERDÄMMERUNG

(Summer 1904 to Summer 1907)

Mark Twain "saved himself in the end, and came back from the edge of insanity, and found as much peace as any man may find in his last years, and brought his talent into fruition and made it whole again."
—Bernard DeVoto, *Mark Twain at Work*,
p. 130.

i

Isabel Lyon had been hired originally as a private secretary for Olivia Clemens. When Mrs. Whitmore recommended Miss Lyon in the summer of 1902, Olivia replied, "Yes, I am going to want just such a person in the Autumn. . . . I should probably want her to begin her work about the 1st of Oct." As it turned out, ailing Mrs. Clemens was unable to utilize Miss Lyon, but the secretary soon became indispensable to Clemens himself. Clara wrote Mrs. Whitmore after Miss Lyon had been at work for about two months:

> I want to tell you how thankful we are that you told us about Miss Lyon for she is really a treasure and enormous comfort.
> She not only is sweet and attractive, entirely lacking any disagreeable qualities but she is also a pleasure for she has a cheerful manner and way which are particularly welcome in a house at time of illness and consequent depression.

And after Mrs. Clemens' death, Miss Lyon's agreeable qualities made her employer increasingly dependent on her.

Though she answered Clemens' correspondence, took some

93

longhand dictation, and managed to oversee much of the typing of his manuscripts, her duties far transcended the purely secretarial. She kept the family books and bank accounts, she became in December 1905 a co-tenant of Clemens' safety-deposit box, she was a round-the-clock card player (who beat Clemens more often than she lost), and by mid-1905 she was the chief operator of a massively elaborate player piano called the orchestrelle, which became an important diversion for Clemens: "I am satisfied that the machine and the sixty pieces of music which we bought with it are worth the twenty-six hundred dollars they cost," Clemens told Clara; "that is, if Miss Lyon survives. She plays for me every night—sometimes two and three hours on a stretch." All this for her $50 monthly salary, room, board, and clothes; and the salary was never increased during her seven years with the Clemens family (Josephine Hobby, Clemens' stenographer, earned $100 monthly for a few hours' work five days a week).

But Miss Lyon apparently considered the conditions of her job acceptable. Her personal diary was filled with exultation in her work that bordered on ecstasy: "All my days are hallowed by Mr. Clemens's wonderful presence"; "Some day the penalty for such perfect living will come"; "It is too terribly perishably beautiful"; "You want to cry in pain over the beauty of this living." And on at least one occasion in the year after Olivia's death, Miss Lyon's lyricism acquired a calculating tone. In April 1905 she mused to herself, "I've known of several men who have married several times—they couldn't live without the companionship and sympathy of a woman, and I like the thought of it."

Miss Lyon functioned in fact enough like Olivia Clemens in the five years following Olivia's death that Clemens himself noted the comparison. When Jean protested one of the family's decisions, blaming Isabel Lyon for it, Clemens replied:

> Jean dear, if your mother were here she would
> know how to think for you and plan for you and
> take care of you better than I do; but we have
> lost her, and a man has no competency in these
> matters. I have to have somebody in whom I have

> confidence to attend to every detail of my daily
> affairs for me except my literary work. I attend
> to not one of them myself; I give the instructions
> and see that they are obeyed. I give Miss Lyon
> instructions—she does nothing of her own ini-
> tiative. . . . She does all my matters well, and
> although they are often delicate and difficult she
> makes no enemies, either for herself or me. . . .
> The servants in the house are her friends, they
> all have confidence in her: and not many people
> can win and keep a servant's friendship and es-
> teem—one of your mother's highest talents. All
> Tuxedo likes Miss Lyon—the hackmen, the aris-
> tocrats and all.

Moreover, Isabel functioned much like Olivia in directing some of Clemens' literary affairs. As he reported in the months following his wife's death, Miss Lyon was taking over the function of fireside critic of his manuscripts: "I think the Diary [Eve's] is finished, Miss Lyon thinks not"; "Miss Lyon voted against the revision [of *Adam's Diary*], but she wouldn't vote against it now"; "Miss Lyon likes it [*A Horse's Tale*] nearly as much as I do."

She apparently began to screen Clemens from troublesome literary requests. On the margin of a letter from Matthew Gaffney requesting a literary contribution, she noted peremptorily, "wrote him that in course of time his letter will be placed before Mr. Clemens who has been ill."

Finally, like his wife and Clara, Miss Lyon was an excitable, nervous, emotional woman. She functioned efficiently in periods of calm, but when her tranquility was disturbed, she suffered "strange nervous headaches," which Clemens would later claim were alcoholic in origin. For the present, and for five years after Olivia's death, Miss Lyon was an integral member of the family— and probably its sanest member. After her father's death, Clara was to claim:

> I . . . stuck to her and persuaded both my father
> and mother at different times to keep her when

they wanted her dismissed. My mother never
liked her, in fact used to speak of her as untruth-
ful, insincere and even dishonest. My father too
wanted her dismissed when we returned from
Italy before I went into the Sanitarium, but I
thought no one could look after him as well as
she for I was deceived by all her "talk."

I do of course feel most bitterly about her be-
cause I think her and Mr. Ashcroft's dishonesty
were more than anything the cause of my father's
death and consequently I myself am the cause
for being such a *fool* all these years.

While Clara may have had reason to believe that her own actions
contributed to her father's death through anxiety and tension,
there is not one shred of evidence to substantiate the claim that
Clemens or his wife wanted to dismiss Miss Lyon; and, indeed,
after her mother's death Clara had been in no condition to plead
the cause of anyone.

ii

Isabel Lyon, Teresa Cherubini the maid, and sixteen trunks of
family possessions left New York for Lee, Massachusetts, and
the cottage on the corner of Richard Watson Gilder's "Four
Brooks Farm," where Clara had been taken by Gilder the summer
before. Clemens and his two daughters had decided before leaving
Florence that the retreat would be an ideal place to sequester
themselves on returning to the United States. Miss Lyon arrived
on July 15, while the family was in Elmira at Olivia's funeral
services. The next day, "Santa Clara," as Miss Lyon called her,
"arrived pale weak exhausted. Rodman [Gilder, Richard Wat-
son's son] carried her into the house and upstairs. She is so
broken, dear heart that she is. Rodman stayed all night for I feared
much to be alone with her in that delicately overwrought state."
On July 18, 1904, Clemens and Jean arrived, and on the twenty-
second Clara had to leave: "the strain of living here has been too

great. She cannot stand the sounds in the tiny house." The strong probability is that the sound she could stand the least was her father's voice. Clara entered the sanitarium of Dr. Angenette Parry at 117 East 69th Street in New York City, and her father descended on her almost immediately with the unnerving news that Jean had almost been killed when she collided on horseback with a trolley at Lee the evening of July 31. After notifying every-one that Clara must not be told of the accident, Clemens

> entered my room and, after a brief greeting, handed me a newspaper with the headlines: "It is hoped that Mark Twain's youngest daughter, Jean, may live. Her horse fell on her and crushed her."
>
> I read and reread the sentence, unable to feel anything but a sharp pain in my head. This couldn't be true.

While Clemens remained in New York hunting for a house for the fall, Clara dashed to Lee, where Miss Lyon said that "she was hysterical, and alarmed me much." On August 5, as Miss Lyon succinctly put it, "Last evening Mr. Clemens arrived and this afternoon Santissima went back to N.Y." Clemens told Rogers that although Jean had a torn tendon and ten wounds, she was "much better than Clara."

The rest of the family lived quietly at Lee; they saw the Gilders frequently and had visits with Alice Hegan Rice, whose *Mrs. Wiggs of the Cabbage Patch* had been published three years earlier. Jean, her father, and Miss Lyon played cutthroat euchre, while Clara spent most of September at a rest home in Norfolk, Connecticut, before returning to New York at the end of the month to re-enter Dr. Parry's sanitarium. On August 17, Clemens leased the high-arched, cathedral-vaulted house at 21 Fifth Avenue for three years from James A. Renwick for $3,500 annually, and an extensive remodeling was begun. Clemens managed to compose his article "Concerning Copyright," which appeared in the January 1905 issue of the *North American Review*, but the family dilemmas prevented serious literary activity.

Even after the family moved into New York in November, Clara was forbidden to see or correspond with either her father or Jean. Indeed, she was to have "no communication with any but the trained nurse and the specialist." Twichell sympathized over "poor Clara's long imprisonment," but Clemens told Jean that the nurse assured him that Clara's appetite was improving and she was making progress.

The other members of the household began their move to 21 Fifth Avenue without Clara. Katy Leary unpacked the Hartford furniture, while all wept over items that reminded them of Olivia. Clemens' life was a taxing round of bronchitis, gout (which Miss Lyon treated by painting his foot with iodine), and compulsive card playing. Miss Lyon's diary recorded the unbelievable hours spent playing "500." On December 1, 1904, her routine went like this:

> This afternoon Mr. Clemens was restless and after he talked business with me, and after he played through The Last Rose of Summer and Wagner's Wedding March on the orchestrelle, we sat down to play 500 again. We played until tea time, and then after tea time we played until 6:45. . . . We played 500 until eleven o'clock. Mr. Clemens won 14 games.

Jean, who was lonesome for the outdoor activity at Lee, played occasionally (and undertook the simultaneous study of French, German, and Italian). When Clemens caught bronchitis just before Christmas, the threesome played on a large cigar box resting on the side of his bed. Mrs. Lyon, Isabel's widowed mother, moved to New York from Farmington, Connecticut. Clemens spent the rest of December and most of January in bed, padding around the house occasionally and growing a three-week stubble of beard which Miss Lyon said made him look like Andrew Carnegie. And though he declined formal invitations, Rodman Gilder, the Rogerses, Finley Peter Dunne, and Carnegie broke the isolation of the first months in New York with drop-in visits to 21 Fifth Avenue. The Twichells stayed overnight in mid-January, and Sue

Crane arrived for a week's visit the following month. Colonel Harvey, Howells, and relatives dropped into the house with increasing frequency in late spring.

His literary life, like his social activity, began again as 1905 arrived. After the shelling of strikers at St. Petersburg by the Czar's guards on January 22, he was finally inspired to begin writing. Miss Lyon recorded on January 30:

> This afternoon Mr. Clemens went down to the library where I was writing. . . . I had noticed a roll of MS in his hand—and at tea-time he read to us his latest article—the one on the Russians. I had never heard him read any of his writings before, and he is at his best then. Today he was wonderful. Thrilled with the tremendous interest of the naked Czar's soliloquy. His voice shook with emotion. It is the strongest thing he has ever written, and you reach the power of him only when you can hear him read into his mighty words the soul of the thing as it stands to him.

David A. Munro accepted "A Postscript" for *Harper's Weekly*—a brief further thought on copyright. Elizabeth Jordan took "A Helpless Situation" for *Harper's Bazaar*—thoughts on unsolicited manuscripts sent him for criticism—but told him that "A War Prayer" was "not quite suited to a woman's magazine, in my opinion." Other desultory work for *Harper's Weekly* included a brief reminiscence "From My Unpublished Autobiography," about his use of a typewriter in the mid-1870s; "A Humane Word from Satan," ridiculing John D. Rockefeller's contribution to the American Board of Missionaries; "A Monument to Adam"; "Diogenes and His Lantern"; "John Hay and the Ballads"; and "Overspeeding." These were all little more than spur-of-the-moment records of random and inconsequential thoughts.

Impressed with Miss Lyon's and Colonel Harvey's praise of the Czar's soliloquy (which would appear in the March 1905 *North American Review*), Mark Twain began work on a similar experiment concerning the King of Belgium. "Now," Miss Lyon re-

corded on February 10, "Mr. Clemens is writing another soliloquy, King Leopold's—who is gloating over and excusing to himself the Congo atrocities." When he completed it, his secretary was predictably breathless and "weak with emotion when he finished the bold truthful statements that rolled from Leopold's vicious lips. Horribly, too horribly picturesque it is, and Mr. Clemens will cut out some of it." A day later he contemplated a work to be called "Adam's Soliloquy," and on March 5, 1905, he read Miss Lyon "some bits of manuscript that he has been working on. What is Man. He is so wonderful—so ennobling." Jean disagreed. She "hated it and refused to type any of it." Five days later, Clemens read the "War Prayer," and his secretary was, as always, enraptured.

Both Leopold's and Czar Nicholas II's soliloquies were rhetorically flamboyant, and both required a reader's suspension of disbelief that Mark Twain did not quite manage. Leopold confessed too glibly to the crimes of enslaving, mutilating, and murdering Congolese blacks in his protectorate in order to harvest the annual rubber crop for his own treasury's profit. His lip service to Roman Catholic theology was too ponderous a foil to his inhumane behavior in the Congo—as he kisses a crucifix to avoid damnation for his curses against his exposers. Nicholas' reflections as he stands before a mirror nude—"a carrot," he describes himself—are a tediously long repetition of Hank Morgan's comments in *A Connecticut Yankee in King Arthur's Court* on the necessity of clothing to distinguish rank and caste among men but to disguise intrinsic worth. His musing about the fawning servility of his people, his acceptance of the justice of being assassinated by outraged revolutionaries, and his private thoughts about the logic of training Russian children to be patriotic about the Nation rather than the Throne, all are cumbersome irony. But both soliloquies gained in inflammatory self-condemnation what they lost in sustained and believable artistry. Both monologues exposed a Mark Twain who was too angry at the facts in his indictment to contemplate the method of expressing them.

In late March, Mark Twain began work on "Refuge of the

Clemens and Olivia Clemens at "The Lair." Lake Saranac, 1901

Clemens at Dollis Hill House. London, 1900

Clara Clemens in the garden of the Villa di Quarto. Florence, 1904

Jean Clemens and Gerald Thayer. Dublin, N.H. Summer 1906

Clemens and Thomas Wentworth Higginson at the Copeley Greene house.
Dublin, N.H., 1905

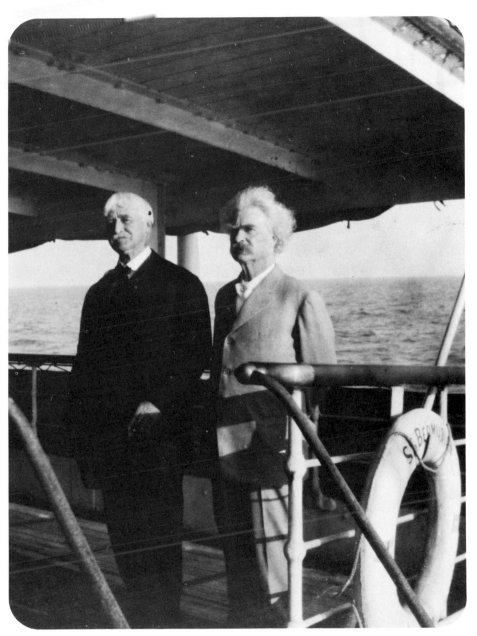

Clemens and Joe Twichell, en route to Bermuda. January 1907

Clemens and Carlotta Wells, followed by Ashcroft, en route to England. 1907

3

Author's League again. . And now Miss Lyon has come up to say some ladies are calling & I must go down & see them. You remember Miss Lyon? You remember how she looks?

The way she looks. Good-bye, I love you very much

SLC

Clemens en route to his bath, with Ashcroft, as caricatured in an English newspaper. London, 1907

(Left) Clemens's caricature of Miss Lyon, in a September 26, 1907, letter to Dorothy Quick (MTP)

Clemens and Louise Paine at Stormfield in the Angel Fish room. 1908

Clemens posing with the pistol used to scare the Stormfield burglars. 1908

Clemens and Henry Rogers. Bermuda, 1908

Clemens's remains, the Brick Church. New York City, April 1910

Derelicts," a long narrative collection of stories about blighted and thwarted people who gather at the home of Admiral Stormfield. The life stories of each of the derelicts is tragic as they "come here to dream their great days over again, and count up the money they used to have, and mourn over this and that and the other disastrous investment, and reason out, for the thousandth time, just how each mistake came to be made, and how each and all of them could have been so easily avoided if they had *only* done so and so. Then they sigh and sorrow over those dreary 'onlies.' " He continued work on this manuscript through mid-April, reading to Jean and Miss Lyon in the evenings and filling the work with autobiographical allusions. He also worked on a sketch about "the universal brotherhood of man—and how it couldn't ever be, not even in heaven –for there are only white angels there."

On March 29, he read his essay on William Dean Howells to the household, and in April he sent the Howells article and the final manuscript of *Christian Science* to Frederick Duneka. But his major interests were torturously paradoxical. His social conscience demanded expression in response to the Czar's cruelty and King Leopold's exploitation of the Congolese blacks. Mark Twain's voice cried out for retribution, for reform, for some moral force to right the injustices he knew, from his daily reading of the newspapers, filled the world. But while his voice called for a "new deal" against oppression and inhumanity, his intellectual premises were becoming more darkly misanthropic and more rigidly deterministic than they had ever been before.

iii

The affairs of the American branch of Plasmon in late 1904 and 1905 would have been enough to motivate Mark Twain to write convincingly of disastrous investments. Ralph W. Ashcroft, twenty-nine years old in 1904 and the son of an English Congregational minister, was the treasurer of the American Plasmon Company (and the prolific writer of trivia-filled letters, over forty of which

to Samuel Clemens survive for 1905 alone). Ashcroft's uncle was a principal investor in the Koy-lo Company and its parent organization, the International Spiral Pin Company, which manufactured "revolutionary" metal and celluloid hairpins. Ashcroft persuaded Clemens and John B. Stanchfield, the Elmira attorney, to purchase $6,000 of stock in the Spiral Pin Company, even though the women in Stanchfield's family experimented with the hairpins and declared them worthless.

More important, Clemens learned from Ashcroft that a plan was afoot to "freeze out" the faction of Plasmon investors which Clemens represented—himself, MacAlister, and the British syndicate. When Plasmon found itself $10,000 in debt in late 1904, John Hays Hammond—alone of the major stockholders—was willing to lend the company the necessary amount. Apparently piqued because Clemens and the Bergheims did not share those costs, Hammond decided to attach the company's assets, declare it bankrupt, and gain complete control when his note came due on September 24, 1904. Ashcroft locked Harold Wheeler, Hammond's agent, out of the Plasmon office and removed deeds, checkbooks, and patents to the safety of 21 Fifth Avenue after an emergency meeting of the Clemens faction of stockholders was held on September 1. That meeting replaced Wheeler as the vice-president and director, and, intemperately aggrieved, Wheeler burst into the Plasmon office in late September with a private armed guard and refused to leave.

In the midst of these flamboyant power plays, offers and counteroffers, and subsidiary lawsuits, the central issue was whether the Clemens faction had taken over the company legally at the September 1 meeting. While awaiting a commissioner's decision, Ashcroft's behavior toward the opposing faction grew even more obnoxious. He printed a grotesquely inadequate burlesque of Byron, *The XXth Century Childe Harold*, as an attack on Wheeler. He composed a clumsy nine-page burlesque legal document, "In the Supreme Court of Fair Play, S. L. Clemens, Presiding Judge." He wrote increasingly insulting—and increasingly lengthy—letters to Hammond, who finally replied with justi-

fication, "Your letters are in many ways offensive, and I would not think of answering them. . . . So will you please desist from sending them."

Ashcroft sent Clemens copies of this glut of writing and was crudely jubilant when the court decreed in favor of the Clemens contingent in the dispute. He proposed that Clemens issue

a neatly engraved and embossed affair (like a wedding invitation), something like this:

With reference to the letter sent you to-day by the Plasmon Company of America, Messrs. S. L. Clemens and R. W. Ashcroft take the liberty of expressing their feelings as follows:

> Embossed
> cut
> of crowing
> rooster

Even Clemens was repelled; on the back of Ashcroft's proposition he had Miss Lyon write, "Mr. Clemens's advice is distinctly to do nothing of the kind. But if you do do it then leave him out entirely."

A few days later Clemens repeated his prohibition in language which should have dampened even Ashcroft's adolescent glee:

Do not put my name in any letters. I think you ought to send none without submitting them to [William Woodward] Baldwin for approval. They are awful letters and will do you great harm.

But Ashcroft, impervious, rushed on with the scheme, producing what he called a "Wireless Snobbigram," engraved with the crowing rooster. He also began setting up galley proof for the publication of his letters to Hammond, with the dreary and irrelevant title "Pudd'nhead Wilson, Jr."

Ashcroft developed other functions—functions, he was later to state and Clemens was not to deny, which he undertook without

compensation of any sort—such as reporting on the hairpin proj-
ect, studying the investment of $16,000 which Clemens had made
in 1901 in the American Mechanical Cashier Company which had
never flourished, and overseeing similar projects. Perhaps the most
fanciful was Ashcroft's attempt to purchase the world rights to a
copper insole worn inside the shoe to cure rheumatism. Ashcroft
mailed a pair of the insoles to John T. Lewis, the aged black
tenant of Susan Crane in Elmira. But Lewis put the insoles in his
shoes upside down and reported to Ashcroft that his legs hurt only
when he walked:

> i am not in much pain now but i am sore and
> tennder when i sit sill i am quite easy but when
> i go to move i am stif and sore and hardly have
> strenth to move. . . . is the soreness any sign of
> geting better or not. i expect it to move slow if at
> all as i have it so long.

On the basis of this ambiguous testimonial, Ashcroft recom-
mended that Clemens and Stanchfield each put $5,000 in the
Insole Company.

However unusual his behavior and his enthusiasms, Ashcroft
was now at least on the threshold of Clemens' inner sanctum. Like
Clemens' nephew Charles L. Webster a quarter-century earlier,
Ashcroft was making himself indispensable by his willingness to
handle a wide range of trivial business detail with promptness,
vigor, and fawning attention to Clemens' whims and desires.

iv

At the suggestion of Abbott Thayer, Jean Clemens and Katy
Leary made a reconnaissance trip in early 1905 to Dublin, New
Hampshire, to inspect the house of artist Henry Copley Greene as
a possible home for the coming summer. After Jean's enthusiastic
report, Clemens promptly rented it. He diverted himself by sug-
gesting nominations to the Academy of Arts and Letters, and at

one meeting in April he showed a spark of his old humor and disposition. As Augustus St. Gaudens told John Hay:

> Clemens made Howells laugh and laugh and shake like jelly with some mild allusion to the "Hell of a fuss that was being made over the corpse of Paul Jones whereas dozens of redheaded girls are being violated, cut up, put in trunks and barrels, left at hotels, at R.R. stations or thrown off docks all over the United States without attracting any ATTENTION but because Paul Jones is alone in *Paris* he takes the PRIZE!" Later referring to a friend who had been interviewed without being aware that he was, he said "it makes one feel like the lady who had been raped up a dark alley, so humiliated."

Such outbursts of good humor were rare that winter.

Clara, continuing to improve, sat up in February 1905, was allowed to receive her mail in late March, and, though she was not to visit her family again until late summer, was astonishingly seen "on the street and they say she looks so well." In April, Clemens authorized Robbins Battell Stoeckel to handle all accounts payable for Clara's upcoming summer stay with Mrs. Bratengeier at Norfolk. On May 1, Katy and Jean left for Dublin; on the fifth Miss Lyon and Teresa followed. Isabel, with an effusiveness that strongly echoed Longfellow, described the area and the Greene cottage:

> The view is wonderful wonderful. Far far distant hills—hoary Monadnock to the South East—and forever the singing sighing breathing pines and hemlocks close to the very windows. And so silent—except for the songs of the pines and the birds. You see a glint of the Lake too. The restfulness of it is beautiful. The house is charming.

She and Jean walked beside the lake and read to each other; Miss Lyon began making pincushions and fussed over the delivery of

the orchestrelle, which was being shipped to Dublin for the summer.

Clemens, as he told Aldrich, was departing on May 18 and would have left New York earlier "but Clara caught an appendicitis" and kept him in town. In spite of her emergency appendectomy on May 10, Clemens was still not allowed to see her, not even after she—and her horse—went to Norfolk in June, where Clara and Jean had "delightful times." The father waited for "a permit from the doctor" while Clara went horseback riding and entertained Joe Twichell, who reported her "looking, and feeling, so well." Jean, with the ever-present Teresa Cherubini, spent two weeks with Clara in July; and Clara wrote Miss Lyon a letter in early June, "clamouring for news, and talking of the concert tours she wants to make next winter," only to discover that her appendectomy had incongruously affected her vocal cords so that she was forbidden to "sing a note for four months."

As soon as she returned to Dublin, Jean had a long talk with Miss Lyon about herself and her sister: "There seems to be a tragic something hanging near. Some fate that is coursing along in their blood, and waiting to drop with a clutch at their hearts." Clemens told MacAlister the same day that "Clara's separation from us is to continue till next winter"; the elder daughter had suffered a relapse: "It is one of those intervals that come in nervous prostration when a whole year's progress vanishes in a week and the patient work must all be done over again," Clemens explained.

Clemens' own activity gained momentum; real-estate dealings provided varying degrees of irritation. Charles A. Gardiner, the purchaser of the Tarrytown property, complained about some adjacent trolley tracks, and Clemens was required to put up $1,500 with a title company to clear the obstruction and to guarantee several quit claims; not until June 1905 was "the Gardiner spirit . . . laid to rest at last." More important, deciding that the heating plant at 21 Fifth Avenue was responsible for his long bout with bronchitis in the winter of 1904–1905, Clemens concluded that it would be "a good idea to bring suit against Mr. Renwick . . . for from ten to twenty thousand dollars damages for last

winter"; John Larkin, Clemens' current New York attorney, advised him to withhold rent payments but finally told him that a new heating plant would be installed to the specifications supplied by John Howells (the architect son of William Dean Howells) without the necessity of a lawsuit.

Larkin also served as Clemens' lawyer for his lingering Italian vendettas, traveling to Florence in 1905 to confer with Sebastiano Cecchi about the suit with the Massiglias and the threatened litigation by Dr. Kirch for his unpaid bill. The countess, on taking back the villa in 1904, had found eight hundred francs' damages which, according to Cecchi, had outraged her; and Raffaello Stiattesi wrote Clemens that the countess was slandering him all over Florence and counseled forgiveness. "Forgive her?" Clemens replied. "Yes, I am quite able to do that, but it would do no good, she would not understand it. The insane seldom understand words or actions that proceed from a moral basis." Later, as Count Carlo Massiglia was about to move to New York as the Italian consul, Miss Lyon noted that

> This afternoon at 3:30 Signor Traverso came in to tell Mr. Clemens about the Massiglia lawsuit. All the misery that Mr. Clemens ever hoped the Countess would get out of this suit she has got, for she has spent a lot of money, the lawyers have taken their time about getting evidence (or taking testimony) and long ago Count Massiglia went to Signor Traverso begging him to ask Mr. Clemens to drop the suit, for it was killing his wife and life at the villa was made impossible for them, for every hand was against them and life had become a Hell. Mr. Clemens listened to Traverso's story, with a keen satisfaction, for the Countess has garnered what she sowed.

Clemens' satisfaction was so keen that he declined to drop the lawsuits until 1906, and even then he instructed Cecchi not to inform the countess of his withdrawal from the legal arena.

Dr. Kirch put up too persistent a fight, to provide any satisfaction to Clemens, by appointing Gustavo Donati his attorney and supplying a defense of his medical fees. Clemens answered in a long letter to Dr. W. Allen Starr, telling Starr that he had not composed it "carelessly, but very carefully; I could not afford to do otherwise, since it will go into my Autobiography just as it stands, along with Dr. Kirch's Statement." Apparently the threat of being included in the Autobiography did not bother Kirch as much as Clemens expected it to, for a few weeks later Clemens found it necessary to write another reply to the statement. But this time he concluded with an offer to pay the disputed 2,200 francs if Kirch would sue and allow Clemens his day in court. Kirch pointed out that his calls to Olivia were lengthy since he was "detained by Mrs. Clemens in conversation, or by what you might call the social part of a medical visit, which in Mrs. Clemens' case, was about as important as a strictly medical visit." In addition Olivia "did not absolutely need a daily visit . . . but Mr. Clemens insisted on my calling every day." Kirch catalogued the ministration to Miss Lyon and the inspection of the drains and sewers as additional functions imposed on him by Clemens and said that he would be delighted to "bring a lawsuit against him, not only now for the collection of my bill, but for damages for slander and blackmail." Unfortunately, though, Clemens had left Italy, and his attorneys could not act for him in the matter, lacking full authority. There was no one to sue. When Kirch's defense was forwarded to the Clemens household, his statements affected Miss Lyon with strangely violent reactions:

> I feel so mentally ill over the harsh statement,
> the false statement that Dr. Kirch has sent to a
> Mr. Barbour who has sent it to Dr. Starr. Mr.
> Clemens told me to read it. Oh, he musn't be
> troubled by the hideousness of it.

Finally, in early 1906, Kirch hired an American attorney, and Dr. Starr advised Clemens to offer a $250 settlement on the disputed

bill. At the suggestion of Larkin, Clemens refused to arbitrate, and the matter apparently died of attrition.

v

The rural atmosphere of Dublin, though it did nothing to calm Samuel Clemens' litigious disposition, did restore Mark Twain's literary equilibrium. He pitched into his writing activity with such fervor that Miss Lyon worried:

> Mr. Clemens spends too much time over his work. Hours and hours and hours he sits writing with a wonderful light in his eyes. The flush of a girl in his cheeks, and oh the lustre of his hair. It is too terribly perishably beautiful. It is no wonder that his tread is that of a spirit's, for the great power of his brain seems to draw him up, and to give him his delicacy of step.

Clemens' own description of the Dublin vicinity, written for distribution to the press, gave the community credit for his "hard and continuous work":

> The summer homes of these refugees are sprinkled, a mile apart, among the forest-clad hills, with access to each other by firm and smooth country roads which are so embowered in dense foliage that it is always twilight in there, and comfortable. The forests are spider-webbed with these good roads, they go everywhere; but for the help of the guide boards, the stranger would not arrive anywhere.
>
> The village—Dublin—is bunched together in its own place, but a good telephone service makes its markets handy to all these outliars. I have spelt it that way to be witty. The village executes orders on the Boston plan—promptness and courtesy.

The summer homes are high-perched, as a rule, and have contenting outlooks. The house we occupy has one. Monadnock, a soaring double hump, rises into the sky at its left elbow—that is to say, it is close at hand. From the base of the long slant of the mountain the valley spreads away to the circling frame of hills, and beyond the frame the billowy sweep of remote great ranges rises to view and flows, fold upon fold, wave upon wave, soft and blue and unworldly, to the horizon fifty miles away. In these October days Monadnock and the valley and its framing hills make an inspiring picture to look at, for they are sumptuously splashed and mottled and betorched from skyline to skyline with the richest dyes the autumn can furnish; and when they lie flaming in the full drench of the mid-afternoon sun the sight affects the spectator physically, it stirs his blood like military music.

In addition, it stirred Mark Twain's writing arm.

He was writing, in late May and through June of 1905 in Dublin, on *Three Thousand Years Among the Microbes* and, as usual, reading the day's collection of manuscript to Jean and Miss Lyon—the latter yet again awed at its power, beauty, and terror. Mark Twain was impressed by his own energy, as he told Clara on June 11: "the best record before was in Florence—5 weeks, ending about the end of January—31,000 words. This is the same output (31,500 words) but the time is considerably shorter." In June he deferred his creative activities long enough to discuss the collection of his letters in a posthumous volume with Clara, with Duneka (who approved the idea), and with Miss Lyon. On June 26, he read his poem "An Invocation to Death" to the cozy group around the fire, and the next day Miss Lyon was "weak with the wonder of that poem" all day long. He also wrote his comic commentary "As Concerns Interpreting the Deity" in June, ridiculing theologians who explain God's ways and intentions.

On June 29, he switched from *Three Thousand Years* to the final version of *The Mysterious Stranger*. He reported to Clara, "I have spent the day reading the book I wrote in Florence. I destroyed 125 pages of it, and expect to go over it again tomorrow and destroy 25 more." Miss Lyon read it on the thirtieth, with consequent emotional exhaustion. Mark Twain continued working on the "wonderful '44' story" in July and gave the manuscript of *No. 44, The Mysterious Stranger* to Miss Lyon to read. She was becoming his testing ground for literary material in a way that Clara may have considered an encroachment on her own privilege and in a consistent enough manner that Witter Bynner was being more than cute when he called her in July "The Lyon of St. Mark." The effusive gasps with which Isabel Lyon greeted each new effort no matter how flawed were neither wholesome nor stimulating for the writer, whose creative spark was sputtering by midsummer. He told Rogers, with irresistible interest in his productivity:

> my output grows smaller daily. It has dwindled
> from high-water mark—32 pages a fortnight ago,
> one day—to 12 day before yesterday, 10 yester-
> day, and 8 to-day.

Clemens wired for Frederick Duneka to come to Dublin to discuss a publication schedule for some of the work of that summer. He suspected that Duneka, a Catholic, might have rejected *King Leopold's Soliloquy* for Harper's, but he concluded "that it is much more likely that Leopold has bought up the Harper silence." The author got furtive joy from an offense to Duneka's religious convictions when the young publisher arrived on July 10 for a brief visit: "Mr. Duneka shrivelled up over the first part of Forty-Four because there is that evil priest Father Adolph in it." Despite their philosophical distance, Duneka was to become, starting that summer, the chief liaison between Clemens and Harper & Brothers. As Miss Lyon was to remember years later, "Mr. Duneka looked after the bulk of Mr. Clemens's Harper affairs with gentle

and tactful help. I say 'gentle' for there were times when he was hard put to it to manage 'Uncle Mark's' savage moods, and his disbelief in the Harper integrity. And those moods could destroy a man's tranquility." (One such mood may have prompted the vitriolic note to Harper's of June 7, 1905: "Please hand to bearer and charge to me, paper copy of your 'Rudiments of Manners;' also paper copy of your 'How to Conceal Mental Vacancy and Seem Intelligent.' ") Duneka's main concern for the present, however, was to obtain material for magazine publication, and on July 12 Clemens began *Eve's Diary* for the Christmas issue of *Harper's Magazine.*

Miss Lyon was dazzled: "Mr. Clemens has made her such a lovable creature and so innocent and so human." On the sixteenth, the writer made suggestions to Duneka about this new diary and the earlier "Extracts from Adam's Diary"—which he revised in the hope that both diaries could be published together; and on the twentieth he mailed the two short pieces to Duneka. Although Duneka agreed to the tandem publication, the books were never published in the format Mark Twain envisioned.

In late July and August Mark Twain lay fallow, resting from his strenuous writing schedule, composing maxims, entertaining and being entertained by the Higginsons, the Thayers, the Pearmains, the Pumpellys, and the Franklin MacVeaghs. He tinkered with *What Is Man?* at the end of August; and he warned George Harvey that he was publishing an anonymous article in *Collier's* ("Christian Citizenship" on September 2, 1905) and was reassured when Harvey could not identify Mark Twain's contribution. "For I have a book which I want to publish anonymously if I can work it off without getting discovered." Duneka made an inquiry for details of the "anonymous" book, but Miss Lyon wrote in reply: "Mr. Clemens will have to think about the anonymous book for a good while, and will not want to publish it without conversing with Mr. Duneka about it."

On September 18, Clemens received a letter from Minnie Maddern Fiske, asking for an anti-bullfight story; perhaps inspired by a

letter from Jean to *Harper's Weekly* ("A Word for the Horses,"
on April 1, 1905) about the evils of check reins and martingales,
she believed that Mark Twain would find the idea congenial. He
thought it fascinating and by September 26 "read 70 pages of the
new story" to Miss Lyon and Jean. On the thirtieth, he informed
Duneka that "it is just finished—15,000 or 16,000 words, I should
say at a rough guess." A week later he revised his estimate to
20,000 words and gave lengthy instructions about illustrating the
volume: "This strong interest is natural, for the heroine is my
daughter, Susy, whom we lost." Finally, on October 5, he "finished
the fifth and last revising of 'A Horse's Tale' "; he was also receiv-
ing correspondence from the Aeolian Company (on October 4)
about the purchase of sheet music and rolls for the cavalry bugle
calls in the story. And before the summer at Dublin ended, Mark
Twain read the saccharine story to an audience with the orches-
trelle playing the bugle calls at appropriate moments. Miss Lyon
almost became uncontrollable in her appreciation and enthusiasm.

It was a summer of literary activity that was mottled at best.
The microbe story began with an ingenious idea: A scientist is
transferred to the bloodstream of a tramp through an error in a
laboratory experiment. There he discovers colonies of microbes
who are content in their belief that God created their world for
their benefit and who exhibit other anthropomorphic quirks of
behavior. But Mark Twain lost interest in his story (in spite of the
central character's nickname, "Huck") and moved to another of
the manuscripts which he could not complete. *No. 44, The Mys-
terious Stranger,* was a jumble of confused motives and ideas, in
those parts written in 1905 as well as the segments composed
earlier. The mysterious stranger creates "Duplicates" to run a
printing shop, performs burlesque miracles, and in general vitiates
the possibilities for effective social satire or philosophical unity
with his pranks. *Eve's Diary,* a eulogy to Olivia, was a sentimental
recounting of the love of Eve for Adam, written with an impres-
sive insight into female psychology. Eve is willing to sacrifice her
prelapsarian innocence for her love of her husband. She recognizes

that she loved Adam "merely because he is *mine* and is *masculine*." When she says, "It is a matter of sex, I think," she says more than Mark Twain had allowed any of his other heroines to say. *A Horse's Tale,* Mark Twain's eulogy to Susy, lacked the grace, sympathy, and perceptiveness of *Eve's Diary*. The macabre story of a young girl's love for her pony "Soldier Boy," *A Horse's Tale* ends when the girl runs into a bullring to protect the horse. Both the girl, Cathy, and Soldier Boy are killed by the bull, and the pathetic tale ends with the bars of the music for "Taps" printed at the end of the page.

In general, it was a summer's work for which the impressive quantity of manuscript was the only justification. Mark Twain had never written with less control and less self-discipline since his days as a Western journalist. The absence of Olivia and the disturbances in his daughters' health were making themselves felt in his creative abilities and output.

<div align="center">vi</div>

Not until August would Clara's doctor give his permission for Clemens to visit her. He left Dublin on August 10, expecting "to stay a week or ten days"; but an attack of gout kept him in Norfolk until the twenty-ninth. Like Twichell, Clemens found his daughter "surprisingly well."

Preceding her father's visit, Clara had made a recovery from her relapse that could almost be called miraculous. In August 1905 she "discharged her trained nurse" and was preparing to re-enter the world. Her father told her that it was good news "that you expect to be at 21 with us in the Fall." Early in September the doctors gave Clara "the right to resume the training of your noble voice." Released from the rest cure, she immediately saw a throat specialist in New York and had what Miss Lyon called "a nasal operation." She moved to 21 Fifth Avenue ahead of the rest of the family and, with Katy Leary's help, began an extensive redecora-

tion of the home. "Miss Clara and I went to Wanamakers Saturday and selected all the covering for the chairs," Katy wrote to Miss Lyon; "she is so happy doing all the things."

At least some of the mixed feelings Clara felt for her father were prompted by his resistance to her development of an independent life. When Clara's concert plans were canceled in June, he told her, "I shan't be sorry if you are with us instead of out on the concert stage singing for strangers." When Thomas Wentworth Higginson's daughter married at the end of the summer, Clemens reported to Clara with an admonitory paternal whine:

> Her poor old father—well, he was a pathetic fig-
> ure to see, after that star had sunk below his
> horizon. A wedding is an awful disaster to a
> family.

Later in the year, he told MacAlister that Clara would not be able to go to London because "there's but a few of us now, and we have to stick together." In an obvious attempt to interest his withdrawn daughter in him, he told her he had appointed

> you and Jean to arrange and publish my "Let-
> ters" some day—I don't want it done by any out-
> sider. Miss Lyon can do the *work,* and do it well
> . . . and take a tenth of the royalty resulting.

Clara's response to the offer is presumably not extant, but a daughter who was attempting to escape from the shadow cast by her father could not have been enthusiastic about the proposition. Another of Clemens' letters of that summer of 1905 probably reflects more accurately the barely hidden antagonism between the two strong-willed adults; father told daughter that he expected her to arrive in New York City to rejoin the family "moccasined, feathered, and in your war paint. (But I have broken my bow and burned my arrows.)" In the imagery of this letter, they have fought like Indians and it is the father who is willing to surrender.

Jean's health was as erratic as Clara's that summer season of

1905. The most athletic of the group, she alone had enjoyed the outdoor activities of Lee during the previous summer, and for at least part of the 1905 vacation she was active in the small community at Dublin. But, almost in proportion to the time her father spent with Clara and away from their summer home, Jean's attacks increased. Two days after he left for his August visit to Norfolk, Jean had three seizures in one day—11:30, 1:20, and 5:30, as Miss Lyon marked them in her diary on August 12. Through the late summer and autumn, additional attacks were entered:

12 September 1905	Jean, Bathroom, 10 A.M.
14 October	Jean, Study, 9:30
20 October	Jean, 10:30, Bed; 5 P.M. Bed —unusually long and severe.
	Jean is in bad shape. Her malady seems to be increasing in violence.
14 November	Jean, 9:30
20 November	Jean 9:30—3 times
26 November	Jean, 3 P.M. 8 P.M. Katie.

The underlined Katie in the entry for November 26 very probably referred to the first of Jean's homicidal attacks on the housekeeper. If so, it was not to be the last attempt Jean reportedly made to kill Katy Leary.

Clemens ignored his own obligations toward Jean when he refused to take her to Boston to visit the Thomas Bailey Aldriches: "I'll have to excuse Jean—she would be too much responsibility for me." And Miss Lyon recorded that "Jean feel[s] the uselessness of the days she is living, doing nothing of value." Finally, in late October 1905, some kind of crisis occurred. Isabel Lyon tore all the pages for this period from her diary, but Clemens told Clara that when the family moved to 21 Fifth Avenue Clara was to have "full and *sole* authority in the house. Require that all complaints be brought to you, none to anyone else. Allow no one but yourself to scold or correct a servant. All this for Jean's sake and to

keep her out of trouble." Two days later he was trying to sympa-
thize with Jean's illness, but it was patently difficult for him:

> Clärchen dear, I wish to learn to make the
> right and just allowance for Jean, and to try to
> keep constantly in mind that she is heavily af-
> flicted by that unearned, undeserved and hellish
> disease, and is not strictly responsible for her dis-
> position and her acts when she is under its in-
> fluence (if there is ever a time when she is really
> free from its influence—which is doubtful) .

With both his daughters suffering from such instability during
1905, it is perhaps understandable that Clemens' humorous inter-
vals were rare and brief.

He kept Isabel Lyon busy with literary copying, letter-answer-
ing, and card- and orchestrelle-playing. Nevertheless, the third
woman of his household had time free for a curious enterprise of
her own. "All the days," she wrote in September, were "sprinkled
with pin cushions. They're pretty little creatures, and best of all
they sell"; a month later she "piled up 172 little pincushions on
the bed today. 172." The pincushions are important because they
became a point of contention in Clemens' later indictment of his
secretary and because they are an indication of the meagerness of
her regular salary, which could be effectively supplemented by
their sale.

Clemens liked Dublin enough that he "secured a house here for
next year, with an option for the 2 years following." The summer
colony, as he told Clara, had formed a club for occasional smoking,
eating, and talking. During an address that Clemens delivered to
the club to benefit a local charity, Thomas Wentworth Higgin-
son's daughter made the mistake of knitting a pair of socks while
she listened. Clemens stopped abruptly in the middle of an anec-
dote, and a painful silence descended in the room until he asked
her what she was doing. When told, he burst out, "I have never
had the pleasure of playing second fiddle to a sock, so I'll stop
speaking! I suggest that you *all* knit more socks and sell them for

your charity. Good afternoon!" Such public displays of petulance and vanity were a new manifestation of his personality which were to become increasingly frequent.

<div align="center">vii</div>

Clemens left Dublin for New York on October 21, followed by Isabel, Jean, and the servants on November 1. Now the family was gathered under one roof in a house decorated by Clara. It was a trip that moved the group from the relative tranquility of summer to the blustery irritations of winter. The new heating system at 21 Fifth Avenue, which Clemens had demanded of the owner, rattled the radiators so violently that Jean and Clara could not sleep in their rooms and had to bunk in the sitting room. Jean continued to have attacks so frequently and so severe that a doctor told Miss Lyon never to remain in a room alone with her or to allow Jean to get between her and the door. Clara, scheduled to sing at a recital on December 1, developed the customary sore throat, took to her bed, and remained there for the balance of the year.

Clemens' social affairs kept him constantly afoot—it was this winter of 1905–1906 that he was nicknamed "the Belle of New York." In late November he dined at the White House. His seventieth birthday was honored with a huge banquet at Delmonico's and again a few days later at the Society of Illustrators. He gave a curtain speech for Sarah Bernhardt's benefit for Russian Jews on December 18, and engaged in a swirl of dinners that kept his days and nights "so full here that there isn't much chance for work or rest." The party at Delmonico's was called "the most notable festival occasion in New York literary history" by Albert Bigelow Paine, one of the guests. To be sure, it included Howells, Colonel Harvey, Brander Matthews, Gilder, Carnegie, and a few other prominent, close, and longtime friends. But among the almost two hundred persons present it also included many of whom no one but the most avid reader of *Harper's* could have heard of and whom Samuel Clemens did not know even as slight

acquaintances. He undoubtedly enjoyed being in the limelight sufficiently to ignore the unfamiliar audience; but Miss Lyon recorded Witter Bynner's report that "Col. Harvey is being much criticized for giving the kind of dinner that he did for Mr. Clemens on his 70th birthday, for it was shameful to sacrifice Mr. Clemens to what is regarded as a great advertisement for Harper." Excluded, and vocal in their complaints, were Robert Reid of *Collier's,* Norman Hapgood, and Moncure Conway. Of the latter, Clemens said testily, "Conway has been dead for 5 years."

Having become interested in the American Congo Reform Association as the result of *King Leopold's Soliloquy,* Clemens gave the association free publication rights to his volume, addressed a meeting on December 21, 1905, and allowed his name to appear on the organization's letterhead in November. His correspondence with Dihdwo Tw̲e̲, Thomas S. Barbour, and E. D. Morel of the English Association attests to his interest, but at the end of the year Isabel Lyon recorded, "The slowness of the Congo movement is troubling Mr. Clemens very much. There is no leadership to it, and he can do no more than he has done."

Similar uninterest marked his literature. Creative lethargy kept him from continuing work on manuscripts in which some sort of literary "trick" originally fascinated him. Technical devices—Eve's keeping a diary, Leopold and the Czar confessing their crimes in overheard monologues, a scientist's description of life among the germs in the bloodstream of a patient—became the only excuse for composition, and Mark Twain found himself unable to submerge the technical device in an elaborate, complex, or even sustained work of art. To the modern reader, all these writings seem tediously overlong, or embarrassingly coy, or shrilly insistent on repeating and enervating a "cute" structural gimmick.

Other literary projects and ideas he frequently greeted with indifference. When Colonel Harvey rejected "Captain Stormfield's Visit to Heaven" for *Harper's*—"His account seems exact, truthful and, as you say, godly—too damn godly for a secular paper like the Magazine"—the author's response was merely bemused.

Clemens's sense of enervation was matched by increasing dete-

rioration of the health of his family. Jean became completely unmanageable in early 1906. On January 5, Miss Lyon, on whose shoulders Clemens was placing most of the burden of caring for his younger daughter, wrote in her diary:

> Jean is not well. Not only has her malady increased, but her whole physical condition is at low ebb. . . . In these last few days a sadness has settled over her, a gentleness that is pitiful, and you long for the masterful young creature whose powerful moods spread consternation, but always back of the moods there are an individuality, a frankness of a very high order.

A week later "a mood of Jean's" stopped Clemens from reading his autobiographical dictations to her and Miss Lyon, who wrote on January 15 that "The reading of the dictated MS. is now forever postponed." On the twenty-second, during an attack, Jean burned her arm on one of the new radiators at 21 Fifth Avenue; and two days later when her father received the illustrations for *A Horse's Tale,* Isabel recalled that

> Jean had been promised that she should see them, and . . . I suggested that they be taken to her room, where she is confined by a burned arm. . . . Along the hall we went—the light shining through his hair like a halo—all eagerness to show the pictures of "Soldier Boy" to Jean. But Jean was only half aware.

Three days later, "a tragic day," Jean's lethargy was fearfully overcome:

> I [Miss Lyon] came in from a shopping expedition for Jean and others, and when I went into her room for tea, she told me that a terrible thing had happened. In a burst of unreasoning rage she struck Katie a terrible blow in the face. The significance of it is what is so terrible, for now she has done what I have seen in her and feared

she would do. She described the wave of passion
that swept over her as being that of an insane
person. She knew she couldn't stop—she had to
strike—and she said that she wanted to kill and
was sorry she hadn't—to her mind it doesn't seem
right not to finish any job you have begun and
she had wanted to kill Katy.

When Jean had three more attacks on February 2, Miss Lyon had
"a very plain talk with Mr. Clemens this morning about Jean's
condition, and told him how on Tuesday I had talked with Dr.
[Edward] Quintard." Clemens' response to the plain talk showed
clearly that he had been insulated from, or had refused to ac-
knowledge, his daughter's condition:

The dreadfulness of it all swept over him as I
knew it would and with that fiercest of all his
looks in his face, he blazed out against the
swindle of life, and the treachery of a God that
can create disease and misery and crime. . . .
Dr. Quintard is going to change her treatment,
and they are going to give up Dr. Starr.

On February 5 it was Miss Lyon and not Samuel Clemens who
took Jean to see Dr. Frederick Peterson, "who is going to take
charge of her case, her pitiful malady, if he feels that he can
benefit her." And Miss Lyon was unable to go with Clemens for a
speech at Barnard College in March because Jean could not be left
alone.

That same month Jean made a brief visit to "Lakewood"
(perhaps for a trial stay at a sanitarium), leaving 21 Fifth Avenue
on the twenty-first and returning on the twenty-seventh "sud-
denly . . . and quite white," to remain with her family under
Miss Lyon's care and supervision until fall.

Clara's throat affliction continued into January. As soon as she
was able, she went back to the Norfolk sanitarium (on January 6),
returned on the ninth, and then went to Atlantic City, where her
father wrote her to remain until she was cured: "Don't hurry

back—*don't.*" On February 28, she attempted to sing: "Some of her notes were very very beautiful," Isabel commented; "but she has the beginning of another cold, and so she was a little nervous." Two days later Clara returned to Atlantic City, making another trip to New York on March 13 to audition for Loudon Charlton, whom she wished to have as her manager. He decided that "she is not yet ready for public appearances, not yet ripe." According to doting Miss Lyon, Clara was depressed:

> At fifteen minutes past midnight Santa stole up to my room. She couldn't sleep, poor dear, for Charlton's verdict was one to keep her awake. So she sat in a dear curled up heap on my couch, and we talked over things and people until now— and it is past 2. I have with me the memory of her darlingness, and especially as she stole down stairs into the black black hall, with 2 little bottles of bromide powder in her dear little hand.

The next day Clara tried out again for Isadore Luckstone. He "gave his verdict and it was that C.C.'s breath is not as it should be." Clara went back to Atlantic City once more on March 17, canceling a reservation for a cabin on board the *Minnetonka,* which was sailing on June 9, 1906, for Europe. She was still taking the bromides Miss Lyon had provided for many months; as late as October 9, 1906, her father wrote that he hoped she was sleeping "well, now, and without the help of drugs."

The strain of managing the ailing household had its effect on Miss Lyon's health, too. She was swallowing bromides and other drugs for her nervous headaches. On May 6 she recorded taking "2 heavy drugs, but they don't effect—a terrible anxiety weighs." Then she canceled from her diary the sentence "When Santa started for the Gilders tonight I told her I'd go for whiskey—but there was no whiskey to quiet me. Foolish for me to think it would—it doesn't."

Even the domestic help did not escape the prevailing plague of

illnesses. Teresa Cherubini, the Italian servant whom the Clemens family had brought to the United States, was "rapidly growing iller with stomach trouble, almost an ulceration of the stomach." She was placed in a hospital, where she apparently remained until September 1906, when Clemens next saw her. He described her as "smitten with death and doesn't know it; no one would imagine it, for she does not look ill. It is very pathetic." He told Clara that Teresa must be shipped back to Italy: "I cannot take the responsibility of letting her stay here against the doctor's advice and warning. If I allowed her to stay I should feel that I was treacherous to her people, who are trusting me and believe me worthy of their trust." Apparently Clemens' morbid diagnosis was incorrect, for Teresa was still with the family as late as 1909.

Surrounded by so many unhealthy members of his household in early 1906, Clemens experienced outbursts of rage and spells of loneliness. While Jean was gone to "Lakewood" he

> went down to the living room and there wasn't anyone there. For a half hour he waited for a human being and none came to stay. C.C. looked in upon him as she passed out of the house, and then a blast of cold and bedeviled loneliness swept over him and made him hate his life.

The same day he called 21 Fifth Avenue a hospital: "I am a patient myself—but I am only a 'temporary,' not a 'permanent,' like the rest of the family." The next day Isabel wrote after a conversation that Clemens hated the dwelling. "He calls it 'The Valley of the Shadow.' " And in April he told the Aldriches, with justification, "I have led a turmoilsome life this winter, and am tired to the bone."

To occupy himself with more congenial matters, he abandoned all household responsibility to Miss Lyon and engaged in a frenzy of outside activities. He attended the Players Club on January 3; dined with Mrs. Ditson and went to a performance of *Tosca* on the eighth; dined with Elizabeth Dodge, with Dr. Quintard, with Twichell; spoke at the anniversary of the founding of Tuskegee

Institute on January 22; went to Washington to lobby for a copyright bill on the twenty-fifth and stayed until the thirtieth. In February he entertained Susan Crane, Witter Bynner, and the Albert Bigelow Paine family, lunched with Maude Adams, Henry Holt, dined with David Munro, the Broughtons, at the Players, and with the Colliers, Hapgoods, and with Miss Lyon at a Press Club banquet. He went to Hartford for the funeral of Patrick McAleer, his old servant, and stayed three days, catching a head cold which could not even slacken the pace of his activities.

March brought speeches at the Majestic Theater for the benefit of the YMCA, at Barnard College, at the Freundschaft Club, dinners somewhere other than 21 Fifth Avenue most evenings. Miss Lyon catalogued the various houses where Clemens left calling cards after dinner: "Mr. Carl Schurz, Mrs. Burden, Norman Hapgood, Prof. Sloane, Mrs. Alexander, Mr. Henry Holt." He went to lunch and a play with Henry Rogers on March 10; he planned his appearance at the Fulton Memorial Association, which he billed as his "farewell appearance"; he hosted a dinner for the Rogerses and Dr. Quintard on the fifteenth. After a siege in bed with a severe cold from the sixteenth through the twenty-third, he lunched with Winifred Holt and had tea with Howells on the twenty-fifth. He had Rodman Gilder and Mr. and Mrs. Albert Vorse to dinner on the twenty-sixth, presided at a meeting to benefit the blind at the Waldorf on the twenty-ninth, and had dinner with Mr. George Brush, a Dublin artist, and his son Barry and Gerald Thayer on the twenty-ninth at the Players. In April the same relentless pace continued: a talk at Smith College on the seventh, followed by an evening at the Gilders; a lunch given by Howells for H. G. Wells on the eighth; attendance at a world's championship billiard match with Rogers on the ninth; dinners for the visiting Russian revolutionaries Gorky and Nerodny on the tenth and eleventh; a St. Andrew's dinner at the Engineers' Club on the nineteenth. When no other diversions came to mind, he would take long subway rides with Isabel Lyon, walk around the streets at the end of the tracks, and then return to Fifth Avenue.

The catalogue of Clemens' social busyness in early 1906 would

be impressive enough for a man of seventy without domestic worries; for one who was confronted with a household riddled with crucial illnesses, it was formidable. The sense of loneliness he felt in March would become increasingly frequent, and his daughters would alleviate it less and less. The hectic schedule of dinners, parties, and lunches would provide him—with Miss Lyon's constant help—the companionship he so desperately needed and found impossible to obtain or accept from his own family.

viii

As his own daughters retreated—both physically and mentally—from his presence, Clemens sought company for his loneliness. Some of the gloom that hovered over 21 Fifth Avenue in the first days of 1906 was relieved by the arrival of a new figure on the scene—Albert Bigelow Paine. Paine visited on January 6 to discuss the possibilities of beginning work on an "authorized" biography of Mark Twain and was immediately commissioned to commence the project. The attentiveness of a biographer sparked Clemens to reminisce about his childhood, and, as a result, the Autobiography was resumed after a lapse of almost two years. Columbia Gramophone cylinders, which he first tried and found unsatisfactory, were supplanted by Miss Josephine Hobby, a part-time stenographer who had worked for *The Century Magazine* for many years. Paine began to put the random conglomeration of Mark Twain manuscripts in order. He began on January 12, wrote Miss Lyon, by "classifying the assembled autobiographical papers and matter for biography this morning. It is satisfying to see him at his task, for he touches it with the hands of one caring for and realizing the value of every scrap." Within a week, her enthusiasm had increased:

> Mr. Paine *is* a "find." He is doing the very thing that I have longed to have some worshipping creature do with Mr. Clemens's papers and letters and clippings and autobiographical matter.

> He is bringing the mass into order, reducing the
> great chaos that I have always longed to be able
> to touch but have never found time for.

Paine shared Miss Lyon's adulation for Mark Twain, and in
January 1906 they began long conversations and discussions about
him. On January 23, when Paine told her that Clemens "was
King—yes—he was far and away the King distinguished above all
the others," the appellation seemed wonderfully felicitous to the
sycophants. Paine was a "comfort to have . . . in the house"; he
was also Clemens' companion at many of the social functions
during that spring, and later that year, when Mrs. Henry Rogers
gave Clemens a billiard table for a birthday present, he became
the constant competitor at the game.

A pattern established itself: "Every day except Sat. and Sun. Mr.
Paine and Miss Hobby come, and every day is a delight and an
inspiration." The arrangement was so satisfactory that Clemens
persuaded a reluctant Miss Hobby to resign her position at *The
Century Magazine* to accompany the rest of the household to
Dublin for the summer. The ties of the court were becoming
stronger and more formal, as Miss Lyon rather desperately re-
corded on March 19:

> Mr. Paine spoke to me about a piece of land 75
> acres with an old farm house on it in Redding,
> Ct. where he recently bought a place—$2,000.00
> is the price—and when I told Mr. Clemens about
> it, he closed in with the idea as a good invest-
> ment, and Mr. Paine has sent off the first $100.00
> to bind the bargain. I didn't think he would
> want it, because I couldn't think he would want
> anything that I want. With an aching heart I
> reached out for that farm for I don't ever want
> to go back to Farmington again.

Although there were some tentative gestures about moving to
another house in New York City that spring, the land suggested by
Paine was to provide Clemens with his final home.

In spite of Paine's attention and interest, Clemens found other companionship in early 1906 which diverted him even more than his prospective biographer. He met the first of a number of surrogates on whom he lavished affection and from whom he demanded unquestioning devotion and frequent companionship. Gertrude Natkin, a fifteen-year-old girl, had caught Clemens' eye one day leaving Carnegie Hall. He began a lengthy correspondence with her- nicknamed "Marjorie," after Marjorie Fleming, a precocious Scottish girl whose writings Clemens admired. He wrote his "Marjorie" more than a dozen letters between February 3 and late April of 1906, repeating over and over that she was an adorable, dear, and "unspoiled" child, inviting her to his YMCA talk on March 4 and to the Fulton speech, telling her, "Don't get any older—I can't have it. Stay always just as you are—youth is the golden time" and calling her his "dream grandchild." It was apparently a more real demand than it might seem, for when Gertrude turned sixteen in early April, Clemens was strangely unhappy:

> So you are 16 today, you dear little rascal! Oh come, this won't do—you mustn't move along so fast, at this rate you will soon be a young lady and next you will be getting married. . . .
> *Sixteen!* Ah what has become of my little girl? I am almost afraid to send a blot [a kiss], but I venture it. Bless your heart, it comes within an ace of being improper! Now, back you go to 14!— then there's no impropriety.

When he was ready to leave for the summer in Dublin, Clemens told Gertrude that he hoped the fall "shall find you a little girl *still*. Cling to your blessed youth—the valuable time of life—don't part with it till you must."

Whatever a psychiatrist might make of the relationships Clemens was to have with young girls for the succeeding four years, even the untrained eye notices several facts in the letters to Gertrude which set the pattern for later friendships. The "un-

spoiled" and prepubescent "maid" attracted Clemens. At sixteen she was too old, susceptible to "spoilage," and growing physically in a way that made the avuncular or grandparental image unwieldy. Possibly it is no mere coincidence that Susy wrote her adulatory biography of her father when she was fourteen, only to become estranged from him later in her life. And it is certainly no coincidence that Laura Wright, his early sweetheart—about whom he dreamed throughout his life as recorded in a multitude of passages in his notebooks, and even alluded to frequently in sentimental and romantic contexts in his fiction—was exactly fifteen when she and Sam Clemens met. The strange emotional mixture in his attitude toward young girls was paternal enough to suggest that they were surrogates for his daughters but implicitly sexual enough to reflect the image of the sweetheart whose memory obsessed him until the end of his life.

ix

Even the social schedule, Paine, and Gertrude Natkin could not exhaust his energies. Clemens discovered a few potential villains on whom he satisfied his fury by writing insulting letters rather than instituting litigation. Seymour Eaton wrote requesting an additional investment in the Booklover's Library stock, and Clemens wrote a characteristic letter which purged his system of animosity toward Eaton:

> I have been persuading myself that you would reform—partially reform, I mean; partially—for I have never known, in the case of any petty thief, of a reform that covered the whole ground, after he had once gotten habituated to the feel of the coin in another man's pocket.

Clemens' International Spiral Pin Company stock paid 6 percent dividends on May 10 and July 30, so that he even risked another $6,500 to purchase $19,500 of additional stock in that organiza-

tion. John Larkin arranged to have the "obstreperous parts of the [heating] system" repaired at 21 Fifth Avenue, obviating the necessity of suing the landlord. Larkin also incorporated the Fentress Land Company in New York, with Clemens as one-quarter owner, in an attempt to retrieve some of the Tennessee land holdings, but more at the encouragement of Samuel E. Moffett, who also owned one-fourth interest, than from Clemens' own prompting.

Both Winthrop Ames and Otis Skinner risked damnation by telling Clara's close friend, Mary Lawton, that she could not act. Clemens interested himself almost hysterically in both cases, writing violent letters, but cooled quickly. Colonel W. D. Mann, editor of a notorious rumor-mongering paper, *Town Topics,* received only restrained sarcasm rather than the threat of a lawsuit when he apparently alluded to Clemens in his gossip column. "We are old, now, and nothing matters much for you and me," Clemens wrote in response to an apology from Mann. "In a little while—ah, such a little while—you will be borrowing a fan and I a halo." Even more startling, the aggrieved author resisted the appeals of the *Evening Post,* the *Herald,* and the London *Times* to publish his reply in their papers.

Even Plasmon could produce only occasional flareups of temper in 1906, as its most vocal adherent grew wearier of the world around him. Clemens managed to write another attack on Butters, in reply to an inquiry if he repented his public assault:

> If you mean, am I sorry I allowed myself, in a moment of passion, to carry my quarrel with Mr. Butters into the newspapers and call him a swindler, I answer yes. It was not the right way. . . . That it happened, was not wholly my fault, but was largely his own, in that he has persistently remained away from this State, and thus has kept out of the penitentiary, where he belongs, and where I was purposing to place him.

It apparently did not matter to Clemens' logic that Butters was a longtime resident of California.

In January of 1906, when he was asked to invest additional money in American Plasmon, Clemens wrote a bitter letter to MacAlister:

> I'll have no money in any new Plasmon Co— not on your life! Not if there's a Hammond or a Butters or a Law (senior) in it. (I believe Hammond is square—when not being used as a convenience by Wheeler and Butters—but Wheeler and Butters are by nature and training rascals.)

Nevertheless, Clemens did put up $2,500, his third of a preferred-stock issue, and advised the British Plasmon syndicate to agree to put up its third rather than dissolve the company and split the $10,000 worth of assets that still remained. Finally, on March 28, 1906, Ashcroft told Isabel Lyon:

> At our Plasmon Board meeting to-day, Mr. Davis was elected president and director, Mr. Baldwin was elected a director, and two of Hammond's nominees were likewise honored. The Wheeler Board is to meet to-morrow, and make the same appointments. Mr. Clemens remains a director and vice-president.

But Clemens was either too tired to enjoy a good fight or too preoccupied with other interests to pursue any matter for very long. His instincts as a reformer atrophied. He told one correspondent who attempted to rekindle his interest in the Congo battle, "Can't really depend on my reforms. So likely to be inspirational and temporary." He allowed himself to be named to advisory boards and executive committees of many self-righteous organizations (including the Society for the Suppression of Unnecessary Noise), but always accepted his post with the clear understanding that he was to be required to do absolutely nothing. When an attempt was made to arouse his indignation over the plight of the Philippine natives, Miss Lyon recorded his exhausted reply: "The woes of the wronged and the unfortunate poison my life and make it so undesirable that pretty often I wish I were 90 instead of 70."

In April of 1906 he withdrew his support of the fund-raising revolutionary Maxim Gorky because the visitor to the United States had violated custom by arriving with a mistress rather than his wife. If there was any cost to Clemens' social conscience, he soothed himself with alibis that sounded shallow and contrived.

The most convincing justification for his abandonment of the revolutionary cause in the face of a violation of moral custom was a volume Mark Twain worked on in the spring of 1906, his "Gospel," *What Is Man?* During March he wrote Miss Lyon a note, telling her to invite Mr. and Mrs. Frank Doubleday for luncheon the following week: "they want me to read my Gospel of Self." The Doubledays apparently approved the philosophy of the Gospel; on May 9 Isabel Lyon wrote:

> I think it was this day that Mr. Clemens gave
> the Gospel MS. to Mr. Frank Doubleday to take
> and start in on the publishing of 250 copies to be
> printed on the DeVinne Press, not to be pub-
> lished in Mr. Clemens's name, not even to be
> copyrighted in his name.

Other literary matters included a reiteration of Mark Twain's wish to have *Adam's* and *Eve's Diary* printed together, but, so far as is known, he voiced no objection when Harper & Brothers issued *Eve's Diary* alone in 1906. When Colonel Harvey wrote to explain a six-month delay in issuing *A Horse's Tale* as a book, Mark Twain wrote in the margin of the colonel's letter, "Let the tale wait, there is no hurry." His indifference was to be shattered by a second, disastrous summer in Dublin.

On May 15, 1906, Jean, Miss Lyon, and Clemens went to Dublin, followed on the nineteenth by Miss Hobby, Paine, and the orchestrelle. Miss Hobby was disturbed at the lack of propriety in sharing a cottage with Paine, and for a while Mrs. Lyon was considered as a possible chaperone. But, said Miss Lyon, "Miss Hobby was impossible in her old-maidish whims":

> Mr. Paine said he had worked with her for 8
> years and never before knew what a dam fool

she is. In her stenographic capacity she is excel-
lent, but as a human companion she is impossible
—a terror.

Clemens settled in to diligent literary work, meanwhile catching a
cold and having his teeth worked on—neither of which improved
his disposition. And very quickly the Upton house they had rented
because the Copley Greene house was not available became
troublesome. It was more isolated from the other residents—"re-
mote from all human beings—and wonderful as the view may be,
the 'human jewel' is more of a necessity than is the view."

Loneliness and isolation might be assuaged by hard work; and
Mark Twain began the summer with another intensive spell of
composition. By May 16 Doubleday was mailing proof of *What Is
Man?* to Dublin and Miss Lyon found proofreading enthralling:
"It is so beautifully printed to begin with, and so absorbingly
interesting that once you begin a galley, you can't stop until
you've read all the batch. And Mr. Clemens does like it so much!
It is his pet book." (Indeed, he liked the "Gospel" so much that
he declined to contribute a chapter to a round-robin novel, *The
Whole Family,* to which Elizabeth Jordan of *Harper's Bazaar*
wanted him to provide a "boyhood" chapter, while Kate Douglas
Wiggin, Howells, Mary E. Wilkins Freeman, and even Henry
James were to provide other segments.) On May 23 Mark Twain
sent Doubleday some additional Gospel to insert in the volume
What is Man? and included a letter outlining his expectations for
the book:

> Your share of the swag is 20% whenever we sell
> a copy—which will not happen for a good while
> yet; nor until the edition is rare and people are
> willing to pay $300. a copy for it. That is the
> price, or we hold on and wait ten years—you and
> my daughters.

On August 25 the author received two copies of *What Is Man?*
from Doubleday, only to discover almost immediately that a line
of type had been inadvertently dropped from the bottom of p. 131

of the text. Instead of raging, the writer was uncharacteristically calm: "Can't it be *written* with a pen and thus added to the 260 copies? I think that would answer quite well." But J. W. Bothwell of the DeVinne Press corrected his 260 copies—not with handwriting—and asked for the return of the two sent to Mark Twain in order to rectify the error in them.

The Socratic dialogue of *What Is Man?*, however much it thrilled Isabel Lyon, was a rigged argument. The Young Man is not merely an idealist; he is also naïve, easily persuadable, and almost a straight man for his opponent in debate. The Old Man, a mechanistic philosopher, is skilled at the full range of rhetorical ploy, illogical persuasion, and of course is the proponent whose side Mark Twain knew would win. His argument, that man is a machine and as exempt from guilt, blame, or praise as any other machine, was familiar. But the mode of presentation was unusual.

Mark Twain's Young Man is gradually enlightened to the truth about conditioning, heredity, and external approval which inviolably control his destiny. The Old Man argues relentlessly, exposing the selfishness of human motivation and the utter inability of man to achieve an altruistic act unless it also satisfies his ego impulses. It is possible, the Old Man suggests, to train ideals upward until general good does not conflict with self-interest. But except for that glimmer of possible hope, man is a determined animal whose inner conflicts result from his attempt to follow a frustrating altruism known to Mark Twain as the Moral Sense.

The principles of the philosophy dated at least as far back in Mark Twain's own writing as *Huckleberry Finn* and *A Connecticut Yankee in King Arthur's Court,* where they achieved an intelligent integration in fiction. In *What Is Man?,* stripped of fictional trappings, they lose effectiveness. Mark Twain convinced himself that the dialogue would cause an immense furor and felt compelled to hide his identity as its author under the mask of anonymity. But the truth is that the ideas were old ones, the mode of writing was dull, and the characters of the two speakers precluded any serious consideration of the philosophical premises.

Indeed, what merits the "Gospel" has arise from values opposite

to the intended ones. As the embodiment of Mark Twain, the Old
Man enunciates with almost monomaniacal insistence his doctrine
of basic innocence. And *What Is Man?* can best be seen as a
monologue with occasional, unnecessary intrusions. As an essay, it
contains several worthwhile insights into the Old Man's mind and
character.

It is the "Conclusion" of the volume that is most significant:
The Old Man has uttered his lengthy speeches in response to the
Young Man's one-sentence questions and has converted his youth-
ful friend to mechanistic determinism by a series of arguments
which are as patently Mark Twain's own as the rhetoric which
contains them. The Young Man remarks that

> it is a desolating doctrine; it is not inspiring, en-
> thusing, uplifting. It takes the glory out of man,
> it takes the pride out of him, it takes the heroism
> out of him, it denies him all personal credit, all
> applause; it not only degrades him to a machine,
> but allows him no control over the machine;
> makes a mere coffee-mill of him, and neither
> permits him to supply the coffee nor turn the
> crank, his sole and piteously humble function
> being to grind coarse or fine, according to his
> make, outside impulses doing all the rest.

But the Old Man denies that pessimism is a necessary consequence
of such a belief; he insists that, even with his code, he is himself
cheerful and happy—because it is his temperament. And he con-
cludes with a much more consoling thought than the one about
training ideals upward. "Is the human race cheerful?" he asks the
Young Man.

> You know it is. Considering what it can stand,
> and be happy, you do me too much honor when
> you think that *I* can place before it a system of
> plain cold facts that can take the cheerfulness out
> of it. Nothing can do that. Everything has been
> tried. Without success.

It was an echo of Philip Traum's revelation in *The Mysterious Stranger* that laughter was the salvation of the human race:

> Will a day come when the race will detect the funniness of these juvenilities and laugh at them —and by laughing at them destroy them? For your race, in its poverty, has one really effective weapon—laughter. Power, money, persuasion, supplication, persecution—these can lift at a colossal humbug—push it a little—weaken it a little, century by century; but only laughter can blow it to rags and atoms at a blast. Against the assault of laughter nothing can stand.

Whether the prescription was in fact useful to the human race as a whole, it was indisputably the salvation for Mark Twain. Cheerfulness and laughter, essential ingredients in his own temperament, would not only continue to ameliorate his cynicism but would also continue to control and motivate the impulse in him to write comic materials.

Clemens sent a few copies of the Gospel anonymously to friends, expecting explosions, but Carnegie's response was typical: "It will startle the ordinary man, but I don't see that it goes much deeper than we were before." Mark Twain was morose at such reactions; Miss Lyon remembered years later that "the disinterested reception was a keen disappointment to Mr. Clemens, and he wanted to burn the 240 volumes left." On the other hand, the Chicago *Tribune* reviewed the Gospel as a volume that belonged on a shelf with Socrates. In a real sense, though, the book was a private exercise, a version of the studied obscurity and anonymity which Henry Adams found equally congenial. Privately printed (even Bothwell, who copyrighted the work in his own name, did not know the identity of the author), given to a few friends, and ignored by most reviewers, it satisfied some urge in Mark Twain other than the prevailing impulse for notoriety and controversy.

Other, briefer works speckled mid-year. The tribute to Howells appeared in the July *Harper's Magazine;* an obituary, "Carl Schurz, Pilot," in the May 26 *Harper's.* Mark Twain wrote his

brief anecdote on the subjective nature of reality, "A Fable," in early June 1906 in Dublin and recounted "The Gorki Incident" of the Russian's impropriety. And he probably did additional work on his "Adam Monument" manuscript in 1906.

x

But the abiding literary interest of the year was the all-encompassing autobiography which Albert Bigelow Paine had revitalized by his appearance on the domestic scene in January of 1906.

If we consider the emotional distress that confronted Mark Twain in 1906—illnesses, erratic impulses, aging, loneliness—we can see how useful the autobiographical dictations were to him. Rejecting most of the external world, he created a preferable one from his own imagination and with his own voice. He could surround himself with loyal, salaried minions and address to them his own memoirs, insulated from truths too harsh to accept or endure.

He claimed he would tell the whole truth about himself, except for the sexual truth: "There were the Rousseau confessions, but I am going to leave that kind alone, for Rousseau had looked after that end." And when the Knickerbocker Publishing Company asked him to proofread his biography for their *National American Biography*, he replied: "Have nothing to do with blowing my own trumpet except when I do it with my own mouth. I do it in autobiography—don't care how degraded I am in that."

Nevertheless, as Paine realized in the first few weeks after their resumption in January 1906, the dictations were decidedly not the "degraded" truth. They "bore only an atmospheric relation to history," Paine noted. To be fair, Mark Twain's memoirs were amazingly accurate, especially when he catalogued the crimes and dishonesties of his enemies; but his recollections were immensely selective. He created his own history and made public only that part of his life which he could filter through his own sensitivity and allow to escape. The result is a testament and a testimonial, an

egocentric attempt to find in his own life an alternative to the real world in which he lived. For several hours a day, with Paine, Isabel, and Miss Hobby as dutiful auditors, he spun and wove a fabric from his own past; he never deviated, however random, associative, or spasmodic his narrative, from his realization that he was the indispensable center of the document and that he required a live audience for the performance.

In his biography *Mr. Clemens and Mark Twain*, Justin Kaplan has called the autobiography an example of "anti-form," but in a very real sense the dictations were as perfectly felicitous and organic a formal mode as Mark Twain could achieve. True, it did not conform to the tight, coherent, traditional unities he had attempted in vain to establish in his fiction. Substituting for them were the theatricality and the self-centered concern of the auto-biographical voice. Nothing could be more apt or more harmonious with the basic nature of a man whose natural modulations always reverberated through his writings, and the effects were all the more impressive because the voice was oral. If, like Whitman, his aim was to put a man, himself, in the nineteenth century, in America, on record, then traditional criticism had every right to be as baffled by the outcome as it had been by *Leaves of Grass*. It was, in fact, the ultimate in form for Mark Twain; plot was at last irrelevant, point of view was inescapably restricted to the author's own vantage point. The unity of the dictations was unimpeachable; as long as a reader could justify his interest in the mind of Mark Twain, no other excuse was necessary. Here was the record, as accurate as stenography, typing, and several revisions and proof-readings could make it, of a major literary talent seeking in the creative act an order and serenity that nothing in his world of 1906 could provide.

Of course there were dangers on which he could founder; but Mark Twain slipped into the banal, maudlin, and acrimonious pitfalls of his form less often than one might expect. And since banality and acrimony were integral parts of his personality, even they had a justifiable place in his official record.

The most important balance Mark Twain had to maintain—

always bearing in mind that "this autobiography of mine is a mirror, and I am looking at myself in it all the time"—was between what he called "history" and "news." News was the contemporaneous event—sometimes a letter, a newspaper clipping, a social engagement—which served as the catalyst for those reminiscences and recollections which were his own "history." As long as he retained the proper equilibrium, he was recording, or at least thought he was recording, the associative processes of his mind, the "mirror" which was all-important to him. If, as happened more and more often in the dictations of 1907, he merely recorded "news," the result was no more than a diary. If he produced only "history," even though it was the most engaging and interesting portion of the dictations, he lost *the thing uppermost in a person's mind* which was his controlling idea.

His earliest comments about writing an autobiography foreshadowed the ultimate, near stream-of-consciousness technique. In 1876 he had announced that the autobiography

> is to appear as it is written, with the whole tale told as truly as I can tell it. . . . I shall not limit myself as to space, and at whatever age I am writing about, even if I am an infant, and an idea comes to me about myself when I am forty, I shall put that in.

But the segments he wrote in 1870, 1877, and 1885 were straightforward and strictly chronological in their arrangement—genealogical information, childhood memories, and an account of his publication of Grant's *Memoirs*. Other spells of work, in the years between 1897 and 1904, still failed to capture the elusive spirit which Mark Twain wanted his autobiography to achieve. And the 1904 dictations to Miss Lyon apparently lost spontaneity because the secretary could transcribe only in longhand. Not until Miss Hobby's rapid shorthand removed the restrictions on Mark Twain's natural pace could the material flow easily and be recorded accurately.

The result might be an associative nightmare. On March 26,

1906, for example, Mark Twain commented on a letter from Calvin Higbie, an old Western friend who was seeking help in trying to place a manuscript with an Eastern publisher. The letter reminded him of his advice to Samuel E. Moffett to work for no salary until an employer of his own accord offered pay. That in turn reminded him of the identical advice to his older brother Orion years earlier; and he produced many days of dictations about Orion's eccentricity, dropped whenever a more urgent matter interested him. Certain subjects held his attention for concentrated periods of time. When what he called "the Harper treacheries" were uppermost in his thoughts in the summer of 1906, he dictated for nine straight days on his suspicions and accusations of earlier publishers (May 21 to June 2, 1906), stopping on the anniversary of Olivia's death to dictate for three days about her and returning to publishing affairs to add the Harper "insults" on July 17.

Until mid-1906, Mark Twain dictated "several thousand words a day," giving samples to Clara and William Dean Howells to judge. Two different sources provided him with the "news" necessary to trigger his memory. One was the biography of her father which Susy had written in 1885 and 1886. In the second month of the dictations, Mark Twain began introducing passages from his daughter's record and then commenting on them, providing details and corroboration. He did not reach the end of Susy's biography until the final dictation for 1906, on December 29, by which time he had exhausted family reminiscences.

The other "source" of inspiration during the early phases of the dictation was the obituary column—or other accounts of the deaths of people he knew and loved. In the first six months the autobiography was as much Mark Twain's "Thanatopsis" as it was his *Leaves of Grass,* with death stalking through its pages almost obsessively. Patrick McAleer, Langdon (Clemens' son), Susy, actor John Malone, old friend John Brown, Emma Nye, Olivia's father, Mrs. Mary Wilkes, Orion, Bill Nye, Olivia, John T. Lewis, Georgia Cayvan, the English merchant Whiteley, Clemens' brother Henry, Isabella Beecher Hooker, Thomas Bailey Aldrich, and Jim

Gillis: The deaths of all, recent and remote, were recorded and made the basis for extended recollections in the autobiography.

The morbidity, the traumatic effect of moving to Dublin, the melancholia of age, the distractions of other work and of the "Harper treacheries" may have been responsible, but whatever the cause, Clemens grew less diligent in the dictations during the summer of 1906 in Dublin. The clocklike regularity of the morning dictations began to pall and week-long gaps began to separate dictations. Except for the extended history of his publishing misadventures and a series of heretical dictations (June 18 to 25) undoubtedly inspired by the proofreading of *What Is Man?*, the summer's output of autobiography was spasmodic and uncohesive.

<p style="text-align:center">xi</p>

There were a number of "Harper treacheries" to distract Clemens and to send him from Dublin to New York or the Fairhaven home of Henry Rogers for consultations. Having decided that Duneka was "slippery beyond imagination," Clemens began

> negotiating with Mr. Rogers by long distance telephone to make a plan for Mr. Clemens to go to N.Y. next week and begin operations against the Harpers. . . . He grows so angry, so indignant, and every day he makes a fresh plan, every day he outlines a fresh attack on those publishers. He said they are all of them scamps, but Mr. Duneka is more fool than knave, the King says.

The first wound was an old one—the suppression of *Christian Science.* Clemens had received several inquiries from admirers about its publication; to one he replied, "nobody but the publishers—Harper—can answer your question. The book has been in their hands for 3 years awaiting publication." Clemens wanted Rogers to retrieve the manuscript from the Harper safe, and he in-

structed Ashcroft to look in the files of *Publishers Weekly* "for 1903 and see if he cannot find some time in April, about the 11th an insulting advertisement withdrawing C.S." Much later in 1906, when Harper & Brothers finally released the volume, Clemens imagined that the company was deliberately failing to produce appropriate advertising. Only a lengthy letter from Major Frederick Leigh, treasurer of the company, explaining the principles of Christmas advertising campaigns, made him "understand the whole situation now and approve of it."

Clemens was even more distressed at the handling of his *Library of Humor*. Duneka had explained that a new edition of the 1888 collection—with only a 3 percent royalty—would be printed to protect Clemens' copyright on the anthology and to forestall probable piracies. In fact, a completely new collection, which bore no resemblance to the old subscription volume, was published and advertised; and on June 4, 1906, Clemens' temper flared higher than on any other occasion that year. To Duneka he wrote (sending Rogers the text of his letter for approval) :

> I find that this "Library of Humor" is not the one which was compiled by me, but is a new book, in whose compilation I have had no part.
>
> Also, I find that this book is being actually "published" and its sale pushed.
>
> Also I find that it is not a cheap book, "with no money in it for either of us," but is cloth-bound and higher priced than my own book. . . .
>
> This astounding violation of a plain and simple agreement is most unsatisfactory to me. . . .
>
> I must ask you—in fact I must require you—to take this book out of print immediately, and destroy the plates.

As an afterthought, Clemens remembered to require "20% royalty on all copies of the book sold between its issue and its suppression." The *Library of Humor* was removed from the market, but not as dramatically as Clemens remembered when, two years later, he wrote an inscription in a presentation copy, claiming it was

unique: "The plates and the rest of the edition were destroyed, by my order."

Clemens also concluded that Harper & Brothers was violating its agreement to advertise his books in each issue of *Harper's Magazine*. He claimed from Duneka "your check for $600, as my books have not been advertised in Harper for Jan. Mar. and June," and was pacified only when Duneka assured the petulant author that "in 3 of those Harpers the advertisement was present, but in the back part of the magazine."

As happened so often with Clemens' suspicions, specific charges and grievances inflated to general distrust and massive overreaction. Probably the delay in publishing *Christian Science* was responsible for Clemens' decision to force a codicil into his Harper contract: "Have to remind Duneka to pay up," he wrote. "When I offer an article you pay for it on the spot and if you don't then the article is mine"; more than that, he noted, "Want expert accountants to go through the Harper books. Looks suspicious to get only $25,000.00 [the guaranteed annual minimum royalty]. Ought to fall short—or go at least 10000 beyond."

Assumptions of contract violations were further aroused by an enticing letter from Samuel McClure, who, on June 8, 1906, offered $1,000 an article for a series of short excerpts from the autobiography for syndication. When Clemens reported the offer to Rogers, it was 50,000 words for $50,000 cash—the magical dollar-a-word rate. And instead of replying to McClure, as he had to other offers since 1903, that his Harper contracts made acceptance impossible, he told his inquirer, "It may be that I can accept your offer, but I can't tell about that yet." Miss Lyon recorded in her diary that for two hours Clemens plotted "a course of action to be followed out in his scheme of breaking away from the Harper Contract and selling 50000 words to McClure for $50,000."

After leaving Dublin to do battle with the Harper hierarchy, Clemens reported gleefully back to Miss Lyon, "Mr. Duneka is frying in the fire which he prepared for himself, and is a very humble and suffering sinner. His sufferings are not going to end just yet." As Clemens lingered in New York, spending nights

aboard the *Kanawha* with Rogers, his fury diminished. Finally, on August 3, 1906, he told Clara the final results of his summer's tantrums:

> Before leaving New York I finally concluded not to syndicate any of my Autobiography, and sent that definite word to McClure. Then Col. Harvey arrived from Europe and we straightened out our snarl in five minutes. He told me of his great plan: to turn the North American Review into a *fortnightly* the 1st of Sept, introduce into it a purely *literary* section, of high class, and in other ways make a great and valuable periodical of it.

He repeated the news to Mary Rogers (Henry Rogers' daughter-in-law) the following day with puzzling enthusiasm, unless Harvey had successfully persuaded him that the revamped *North American Review* was to be Mark Twain's magazine. And indeed the autobiographical dictations did provide copy for twenty-four consecutive issues, but never to the extent of more than ten or eleven pages per issue.

xii

The second summer in Dublin was distracting to all the members of the Clemens household, even those whose interests did not extend to real or imagined publisher's "treacheries." Jean intruded on her father one morning while he was eating breakfast, and Clemens told her not to disturb him. "This last and very unfriendly and unaffectionate statement irritated and hurt me considerably," Jean wrote in her diary. On another occasion Jean said her father "was horrid to me tonight and I hadn't done anything to warrant his saying what he did." Clemens stayed in his bed all the following day in a fit of petulance. And in response to a letter from Miss Lyon about Jean's condition, Dr. Frederick Peterson was "sorry to learn . . . that her mental and nervous im-

provement do not keep pace with the physical change for the better" and sent a prescription for more potent medication.

Jean and Isabel were having difficulties, too. Jean expressed hostility at the effusive secretary's constant references to Clara's abilities:

> We couldn't seem to talk pleasantly. When Miss Lyon talked as only she can of Clara's marvelous grace, subtlety, and wonderful powers— genius—it almost invariably irritates me & last night it did more than ever. . . . After all this piling on of facts to my discredit, it of course wasn't especially consoling to hear that Clara was the one and only person . . . that Miss Lyon could think of as being competent to dance the Smoke dance [at a local entertainment]. I have known for a very long time that to Miss L. Clara is heaven & earth, but I never get sufficiently used to her gushings for them not to bore, and as a rule, even annoy me.

Jean's problems would become even more acute as the summer passed; and even Miss Lyon's earlier lyricism about the New Hampshire countryside vanished: "The loneliness here this year is enough to do one a damage, and the loneliness is not because one is alone, either."

Clemens' temper flared and began to burst like fireworks. He grew irritated with Paine: "I'm afraid, in fact I know," Miss Lyon wrote in her diary of June 13, 1906, "that Mr. Clemens is a little tired of him, but he'll get over that. He must—for Mr. Paine is doing a great work for Mr. Clemens and the children. He is invaluable, for his interest does not slacken in his daily labor." Miss Hobby earned her share of Clemens' wrath. "She invariably corrects Mr. Clemens' writing. . . . Today it passed the limit of his endurance. Through his tightly shut teeth he damned that 'hellfired work' until he was tired; and then he went for 'that idiot!'— 'that devilish woman! I'd like someone to take her out and have her scalped and gutted!' " Miss Lyon found humor in the fact that

Miss Hobby, who had "strained points in her wish for chaperones, won't need one now I think, because the discussion of the Immaculate Conception [for the autobiography] doesn't leave much uncovered. Not if Mr. Clemens is doing the discussing."

Clemens spent some time planning his own funeral; and however facetious his tone in his letter to young playwright Charlotte Teller, there was something distinctly macabre in the diversion. The household kept

> interrupting me every time I try to arrange about my funeral. It is to be in January, a year and seven months from now—January the 4th; if I told you the 6th it was a mistake. . . . Last night I was arranging about lamentations, and was remarking that friends who cried would get a chromo, but I was as rudely stopped, there, as if I had been committing a felony.

Clara, who remained behind at 21 Fifth Avenue rather than accompany the rest of the family to Dublin, "cannot understand how" Miss Lyon could find her father's "presence . . . always restful" to her. "But," insisted Miss Lyon, "it is. If I'm tired or nervous and he comes in to talk over things, or I go to him in his tobaccoed room, I'm rested before I've been with him very long, and then I'm more than rested. I'm refreshed and stimulated."

Other stimulation came when Clemens, Jean, and Isabel went to the Handasyd Cabots for dinner and a music recital, arranged evenings of charades with the Thayers and Brushes, or dined with the Pearmains and the Joe Smiths. Miss Lyon and Paine developed the habit of taking long walks and indulging in philosophical talks through the summer. "He is a rare good man," Isabel said, "and how I have needed him this year." In fact, their relationship apparently blossomed in ways that led Miss Lyon to use astonishing imagery: "I am giving birth to something," she wrote. "The parturition pains are great, and the birth is a slow one—weeks and weeks. I know not what shall be born but it will be greater—greater than I, and the shell of *me* is not worthy to be its mother."

A few days later she recorded that "it is only by fertilization that any best in us can be brought to full flower and fruit"; and a month later she was jubilant because "if I am good—very good—I am to have a strip of land in Redding to build me there a little house. AB will let me use the strip from his own property. Oh I must be good—monotonously good." There is no indication what derelict behavior she was expected to avoid.

Clemens left Dublin on June 26 for his protracted battle with the Harper dynasty. Until his return on July 25, Miss Lyon and Jean filled their time with headaches, seizures, walks, and parties. Shortly after her father arrived in New York, he reported to his secretary that "Clara took the alarm and fled to the sanitarium in 69th street. It was because the tearing up of the avenue made such a pounding racket. I hope she will stay there—for two reasons. Miss Gordon [her nurse] is good company for her, and there's none here; and up there she is close to Luckstone."

After Clemens returned to Dublin a series of parties, charades, and plays (one with young Ethel Barrymore starring) kept the family amused and the animosities and antagonisms from more than smoldering. But shortly the three women of the household were all to suffer major traumas; and perhaps it is symptomatic of Clemens' own edginess that he suddenly began writing long, frequent, and intimate letters to Henry Rogers' daughter-in-law Mary in the summer of 1906. He told her in exact detail about his negotiations with Harper & Brothers, his autobiography—some of which he gave her to read—and the family illnesses. And from her he constantly demanded "butter": praise, flattery, and affection. By contrast, when Clara showed affection, he told Mary bitterly, "it's butter from the butterless! . . . Next, there'll be butter from Jean." And Miss Lyon remembered years later that "In July 1906 Mr. Clemens wrote Howells: 'That miracle has happened again which happened months ago, one of my children has complimented her father.' "

In the midst of the activities at Dublin, Miss Lyon went to New York "to be gone a week and more, and meet Clara there and help her and the architect plan the new house." Isabel and Clara, able

to get along comfortably with each other, traveled to the site of the planned house in Redding with John Howells, the son of William Dean Howells, who was to design the structure. Clemens abandoned Jean to visit the Rogerses in Fairhaven—"Dublin is become an impossible place for him to live in."

In late August all the court regathered around the King, who dictated furiously to Miss Hobby, spoke on the topic "Spontaneous Oratory" to the Dublin Club on September 1, 1906, and engaged in a constant exchange of entertaining with the Smiths, Franklin MacVeaghs, and the Cabots. On September 15 he returned to Fairhaven, but on the nineteenth he was in New York to address the banquet of the Associated Press. When Clara scheduled a "debut" in Norfolk for the twenty-second, Clemens was immensely proud that she had "got things arranged to your mind with Mr. Charlton, and that your outlook is so full of promise, and your heart so full of courage." But his paternal pride was not reciprocated. Clara "dreads to have me present," he told Mary Rogers, "but she hasn't *asked* me not to come, in so many words"; then Clemens "asked her to let me lead her out before her audience. She said, no—'You'll get all the welcome, and I none.'" Clemens attended but was "given a seat in the third row and admonished to keep quiet and not to try to attract attention." After the concert—which he found "a beautiful, and blood-stirring, and spirit-satisfying triumph"—Clemens managed to gain the footlights, where he made a twenty-minute speech; inevitably, an article in the New York *Sun*—on September 24, 1906—devoted the headline of its story and seventy-two of its eighty lines to Clemens' closing remarks and gave Clara's recital only the last eight lines.

She was scheduled to repeat her performance in Hartford and then in Providence, but the specter of her father's renown continued to haunt her. "Clara's manager wanted her to be photographed with me," Clemens told Jean, "but she wouldn't allow it. She told him she wouldn't be publicly connected with me, but is going to stand or fall on her own merits." After a few recitals—at Irvington on October 25 and in the Bowery on November 16—

theatergoing, and the firing of a cook, Clara dashed away from her father and her "career" as winter closed in: "Clara's just gone [28 November]! ordered to the country for two months by the doctor."

Jean's attacks increased in severity while her father was gone from Dublin for Clara's concert and his business engagements. Miss Lyon wrote on September 20, "The seriousness of Jean's disease is increasing, and I am very anxious about her." On the twenty-fourth, Miss Lyon "went to pieces and stayed in a dark room all day—suffering." Four days later, Jean had two attacks:

> Jean's condition being worse I wrote lengthily to Dr. Peterson in Europe. She subconsciously feels my weakness, and all her venomous points are to the fore; for it is absolutely essential that a person who is mentally strong should be with her and should fearlessly direct her.

But Jean's problems and dilemmas were not entirely epileptic in their origin.

As the summer's activities mixed together young people of both sexes constantly, Jean, now twenty-five, began feeling frustrations and anguish which were only incidentally related to her disease. On July 4, 1906, she recorded in her diary:

> Why must I live on aimlessly, with nothing to do, utterly useless, all my life? I who long so for the love and companionship that only a man can give, and that man a husband. The affection of friendship between man & woman does not suffice; & of course the love between two women cannot even be considered in the problem of this hunger. Am I never to know what love means because I am an epileptic and shouldn't marry if I had the chance? I seem never to be attractive to men. Is that also entirely due to my disease? And if a man that I could love loved me would it really be an actual wrong for me to marry him,

> because of the possibility of the children inherit-
> ing my malady? Will I have to go on indefinitely
> leading this empty, cheerless life without aim or
> real interest? Oh! it does not seem as though I
> could. This hunger, this passionate desire is so
> constant, that every time I see a young man that
> I like I begin to hope that he may before long do
> more than like me. Even when they are younger,
> as is generally the case, than I am, I cannot help
> wishing, wishing, wishing, that some day they
> may overlook my age, my stupidities and espe-
> cially my disease—if Dr. Peterson finds that he
> can do nothing real with it.

The tragic self-confession only gained in poignancy as the summer
continued.

Clemens imposed severe restrictions on Jean's participation in
the Dublin festivities, and Clara approved the limitations. Jean,
most understandably, rebelled:

> It seems that a while ago Father offered objec-
> tions to my going up the mountain alone with
> Tom & Clara, too, had written about it. It wasn't
> about my health then but about the propriety of
> it. If those two can't leave me *any* freedom at all
> there will be trouble. Clara has gone wherever
> she wished to with her friends, such as John, etc.,
> & they were young gentlemen, too, & not boys.
> . . . Fortunately the Lioness thinks as I do about
> it, although she would consider it absolutely my
> duty to do as Father wished. . . . I should hate
> to have a fight with Father & yet I am no child
> but older than mother was when she had two
> children!

It turned out that Jean's intuition about Miss Lyon's sense of duty
was correct; it was the secretary who was on September 29 re-
quired to undertake action for "propriety's" sake in Clemens'
stead:

> In the King's name, I had to forbid Gerry Brush
> going with her for a long walk, and then I col-
> lapsed. Jean would not listen to reason. She was
> far too ill to go. . . . In Jean's present condition
> it isn't safe for me to be alone with her. She could
> easily lapse into the violence the doctors fear may
> come in time.

Clemens told Ashcroft that "Miss Lyon is suffering a severe ner-
vous collapse," and Isabel herself recorded that "Dr. Stowell
commands that I go away for a rest cure, but now I think that
won't be necessary." On October 9 Clemens wrote Charlotte
Teller that " 'The Lioness,' as Jean and Clara call her, is about
well again, and refuses to take the rest-vacation she ought to
take." But when he returned to Dublin on October 1, Clemens
finally recognized his own responsibilities to his younger daughter.
He described the Dublin scene for Clara:

> Miss Lyon is still feeble and has to go carefully
> and not overexert herself. . . .
> Jean is strong, hearty, and very sweet and de-
> monstratively affectionate. But it is pretty plain
> that she has to have at her elbow an indisputa-
> ble authority. And so I realize that I must stop
> junketing and stay at my post and not try to dele-
> gate its duties and large responsibilities to an-
> other. I realize it just in time; for I was . . . go-
> ing 'mobiling in the South of France a month or
> two in the spring with Col. Harvey (and possibly
> Mr. Howells.)

He told Aldrich the same day that no authority but his own could
control Jean when she was ill—"and she is always ill, poor child,
these latter months."

Clemens was temporarily reassured a few days later because, he
said:

> Jean seems to be getting along very well, now.
> She is hard at work carving things—*to sell!* At
> first I was shocked, when Miss Lyon told me, for

> I feared that the inspiration was need of money.
> But it isn't that: Jean mourns because she is the
> only member of the family who has no calling,
> and is accomplishing nothing in the world.

Her occupational therapy did not relieve him of the burden of
caring for her, however.

And the continued sexual frustrations were simmering in Jean
in spite of a surface serenity. Just at the time that her father was
writing his pleased letter, Jean was recording intimate thoughts
about Gerry Thayer in her diary:

> What can I do? I have a decided feeling that
> I *love* Gerry and yet I ought not to. I'm much
> too much older than he and to show real affec-
> tion, I ought to force it to become merely a quiet,
> warm affection such as a boy & girl can perfectly
> well have for each other. The hard part of it is
> that the older I grow—the nearer & nearer to old-
> maidhood—I get more & more anxious to marry.
> I know perfectly well that while my illness flour-
> ishes I ought not to think of such a thing, but
> the idea of spending all my older years practi-
> cally by myself—Clara & I won't want to live to-
> gether very much and we aren't especially sym-
> pathetic, anyway—is perfectly hideous. Nancy is
> beginning to have boys devoted to her at sixteen,
> Clara began at twelve, Lioness along about four-
> teen, I believe, & I have had but one person care
> for me & that was wholly improper—that old
> married farmer whom I shouldn't have allowed
> to say a word. I, poor mortal, am crazy to
> have the kind of liberty that only marriage can
> give & not one person that I ever see cares a snap
> for me. I believe that the desire to marry is so
> strong in me that no matter what man, provided
> he was at all nice, were to propose to me & seem
> to be in love, that I should almost at once fall in
> love with him, or at least imagine myself to be in

> that state. Of course father would at once raise
> every objection, no matter whether I were better
> in health, or who the man might be, but if I
> could believe myself in love & loved, I should pay
> no attention to his desires . . . so tremendously
> hungry for love-marriage—makes me fear, almost
> believe, that I shall never have it.

She was obviously involved in an emotional situation which the carving of wooden objects was not likely to ameliorate.

For Clemens, such a responsibility—and such a deprivation of his public life as was required to care for Jean—was exacerbating. Although he spent the following week in almost ceaseless socializing, Miss Lyon sensed that "the King is growing restless here. He wants his playmates and his intellectual associations—mostly the playmates I think though." In response to Miss Lyon's letter of September 28, Dr. Peterson cabled his colleague, Dr. Frederick Hunt. Hunt wrote Miss Lyon, including Dr. Peterson's cable with his letter. The cable, which Isabel took to Clemens on October 11, 1906, was presumably a recommendation that Jean be committed to an institution.

xiii

On October 17, 1906, the Clemens entourage moved back to the quarters at 21 Fifth Avenue which Clara had redecorated—but not to her father's liking. He distressfully catalogued his hatred of the house in his autobiography:

> There was not a window in the whole house,
> either on the Fifth Avenue front or on the long
> Ninth Street side that had ever known what a
> ray of sunshine was like. . . . The entire house
> is in shadow at all seasons of the year except dead
> summertime. . . .
> Nobody thrives in this house. Nobody profits

by our sojurn in it except the doctors. They seem
to be here all the time. We must move out and
find a house with some sunshine in it.

Colonel Harvey's acceptance of the autobiographical dictations for
continuous appearance in the *North American Review* was com-
forting, for it allowed the family to "bank" the autobiography
payments for building a house on the property at Redding, Con-
necticut. Clemens authorized Clara and John Howells to "draw
upon it up to $15,000 to build the house with. Then if you find
you *must,* you can draw out $5,000 or $6,000 more of it." In the
same communication he told Clara that their income from all
sources for 1907 should be $70,000 to $80,000. After Clara, Miss
Lyon, and John Howells got their heads together, there were
shocking repercussions. The cost of the house Clara envisioned was
substantially different from her father's estimates. Howells
blithely assured Clemens that $25,000 or $30,000 would build a
perfectly adequate structure, but rumors of dissension reached the
ears of Alice Pearmain in Dublin, and she suggested to Clemens
that Benjamin Howes might be a suitable substitute architect if
"you thought the price submitted for the plans chosen, was ex-
orbitant." The situation cleared itself up, at least temporarily,
and Howells began planning "Autobiography House," as Miss
Lyon named it.

But Clemens' August 1906 estimate of a $70,000 minimum
income for 1907 dropped precipitously in December. Miss Lyon
wrote in her diary on December 29, 1906:

> This morning Mr. Clemens talked about the fi-
> nances. The coming one will be the last year of
> assured $25,000.00 from the Harpers. Next year
> will begin the 40% of the previous year's income
> from the books—which this year has been $40,-
> 000.00 and the children must begin to realize
> that if they have only $25,000. a year to live on—
> they must manage to live on that. Live on the
> book-income, if they can—and try to keep the
> dividends as a back fund.

Apparently the 40 percent formula developed during the summer negotiations with Harvey; but what is vastly more important about the December call for economy is that Miss Lyon and Clara had entirely different conceptions of Clemens' income. Clara, believing $70,000 to $80,000 was available, was prodigal; Isabel, presuming that the domestic purse had shrunk substantially, and in control of the purse strings herself, began to economize. To further complicate the situation, she made a vow:

> I know that the King must be kept calm, where
> I know how to do it. He mustn't be harassed, he
> mustn't have unnecessary matters brought to him
> to fret over, he must be saved in all ways that
> he can be saved from anxiety—for he has had
> enough of it in his life, and I'm worried since
> once or twice recently he told me of a vertigo
> that surged over him because he was harassed.

Miss Lyon was committed, suicidally as it would turn out, to taking over the management of Clemens' financial affairs, to denying Clara's and Jean's requests for money, and to shielding her "master" from his daughters' complaints. She could not have exposed herself to greater danger, as she was to discover in a few years.

And she made the further mistake, as it was to turn out, of supervising Jean's wanderings from rest home to rest home. On October 22, 1906, Isabel took Jean to inspect a sanitarium at Katonah, New York, and on the twenty-fifth, Jean entered one of the establishments there. Clemens greeted the cable from Dr. Peterson which had suggested Jean's confinement unexpectedly: "There's been a cloud-lift today," he wrote Mary Rogers, "and I've got to jubilate with somebody or expire with satisfaction." The real grief and responsibility he felt in connection with Jean's illness are apparent in the honest relief he expressed in place of customary sentimentality. To Mrs. Henry Rogers, on the day before Jean left for an exile that was to last almost three years, he wrote reassuringly, "I am all right, this morning, in *all* ways, and

your letter comes at a happy time." A day earlier he had written Mary Rogers, "Jean departs day after tomorrow. It will add to the already sufficient solitude of this house. She doesn't go far, yet she will seem a whole light-year distant"; but on the day Jean left, he sent Mary a playful, facetious letter without a mention of his daughter.

Clara visited Katonah and was "much depressed over the place and the great pathos of the situation," according to an entry in Miss Lyon's diary on October 27, 1906. Clemens visited, too, and called it a "pathetic exile and captivity"; but with his paternal responsibilities no longer a problem, two days after Jean moved to Katonah he began enthusiastically planning a trip to Egypt.

On October 27, Clemens announced to Miss Lyon

> that Mr. Leigh Hunt has invited him to go to Egypt for the winter—to spend his days and weeks on the Nile, and to take with him whomsoever he will. It will mean to take with him a stenographer and a biographer. He couldn't take me because I'm needed at this base of action, although he says he wishes to take me. I'm so stunned.

He decided on Ashcroft and Twichell as companions, and on October 30 Ashcroft accepted the stenographer's post. But an annual siege of head colds and bronchitis forced Clemens reluctantly to cancel the trip. He considered Japan as a possibility for the coming spring, but for now he played billiards on the new table Mrs. Rogers had given him for his birthday and hosted almost nightly dinner parties: Rodman Gilder and the Loomises on November 2; the Riggs, Hapgoods, Rodman and Dorothea Gilder on the seventh; a "buck" dinner for Aldrich, Howells, Carnegie, Henry Arthur Jones, and Colonel Harvey on the ninth.

Miss Lyon collapsed from the strain. After a week in bed at 21 Fifth Avenue, she "left for Hartford . . . ordered by the doctor to remain away and rest for two weeks." She went to Hartford on November 24, 1906, resting until December 10. The cause of her

breakdown may have been Charlotte Teller Johnson, the young dramatist who wrote under the name of Charlotte Teller. Clemens had become interested in Charlotte Teller early in 1906 at a meeting to support the Russian revolutionaries, when he discovered that she was writing a play about Joan of Arc. Clemens and Isabel both read the manuscript of that play, of the drama "Mirabeau," and of her novel *The Cage*. Clemens wrote her a number of letters, combining playfulness with serious suggestions about her writing. And until the Clemens household moved back to 21 Fifth Avenue, Miss Lyon shared his admiration for the budding authoress. But Charlotte lived at 3 Fifth Avenue, a rooming house for writers concerned with politics only a few doors away from the Clemens house.

On October 22, 1906, Isabel wrote in her diary, "I told the King some gossip I heard—gossip going around 'The Players'—about other quill drivers of No. 3. Mr. Paine told me. The King repeated the gossip to the one gossiped about." The rumors concerned Clemens and Miss Teller, who remembered that

> Mr. Clemens, much agitated, told me he had heard people were gossiping about his seeing so much of me. . . . When I insisted upon knowing just what the gossip was, he sent for his secretary, Miss Lyons, who said that someone at the Players' Club had asked Mr. Paine (whom I never met,) who this Miss Teller was that Mark Twain was seeing so much of.

Clemens asked Miss Teller to move from the neighborhood, but she refused, pointing out that he was as old as her own grandmother; but Miss Lyon, who said she told her employer only "what I dared" of the gossip, might quite justifiably have felt that her meddling was improper. Perhaps she also reflected about what gossip might say regarding her own proximity to Clemens if it could vilify a woman who lived several houses away. It was a difficult enough situation to explain the secretary's collapse.

During Miss Lyon's absence, the house was too lonesome—"I'm a solitude," Clemens told MacAlister—so he went with Paine to Washington to lobby for a new copyright law in Jean's and Clara's interest, as he explained to Jean. It was there, before Congress, that he made his first public appearance in the dramatic, stark white suit which he had decided would be his year-round clothing on October 8, 1906, when Miss Lyon wrote: "The King is filled with the idea of defying conventionalities, and wearing his suitable white clothing all winter, so he has bidden me order 5 new suits from his tailor."

Although Clemens could not obtain the floor of the House for lobbying, he was allowed to meet the Representatives in the Speaker's room, where he "laid off his dark overcoat and stood there, all in white, certainly a startling figure." Miss Lyon noted, "The papers are full of him, for he went down there with a plenty of white clothes, and people love to see him in them." He appeared before the copyright committee the following day in the same spectacular garb and with the same theatricality, which his speech before the committee did not dispel. His erratically disquieting behavior upstaging all Congress in an anteroom, was equaled by a surprisingly impromptu tone in his opening remarks before the committee for such an important occasion:

> I have read the bill. At least I have read such portions of it as I could understand; and indeed I think no one but a practiced legislator can read the bill and thoroughly understand it, and I am not a practiced legislator. I have had no practice at all in unraveling confused propositions or bills. Not that this is more confused than any other bill. I suppose they are all confused. It is natural that they should be, in a legal paper of that kind, and I understand it. Nobody can understand a legal paper, merely on account of the language that is in it. It is on account of the language that is in it that no one can understand it except an expert.

While the intervening remarks were relevant, the conclusion was more appropriate to the lecture hall than to a Congressional committee room:

> I do seem to have an extraordinary interest in a whole lot of arts and things. The bill is full of those that I have nothing to do with. But that is in line with my generous, liberal nature. I can't help it. I feel toward those same people the same sort of charity of the man who arrived home at 2 o'clock in the morning from the club. He was feeling perfect satisfaction with life—was happy, was comfortable. There was his house weaving and weaving and weaving around. So he watched his chance, and by and by when the steps got in his neighborhood he made a jump and he climbed up on the portico. The house went on weaving. He watched his door, and when it came around his way again he climbed through it. He got to the stairs, went up on all fours. The house was so unsteady he could hardly make his way, but at last he got up and put his foot down on the top step, but his toe hitched on that step, and of course he crumpled all down and rolled all the way down the stairs and fetched up at the bottom with his arm around the newel post, and he said, "God pity a poor sailor out at sea on a night like this."

xiv

Back at 21 Fifth Avenue on December 12, Clemens asked Paine to move into the nearly empty dwelling with him. Miss Lyon was back, more devoted than ever. Clemens "can go away from me," she wrote, "but I shall not go away from him again unless he sends me." She and Paine would continue to nurture their almost idolatrous admiration for the man whose welfare they guarded and protected.

Having canceled trips to France, Egypt, and Japan, Clemens decided to escape the icy winter of New York City and his sunless home with a whirlwind trip to Bermuda, according to Miss Lyon, "if Mr. Twichell can go too and I'm to go as valet and myself. I've written Mr. Twichell, and now we're waiting." The day after Christmas "came Mr. Twichell's letter with Hurra! Hurra!! in it, and the King echoed it—so I rushed up to my telephone to ask Mr. Coe to see about our passage—he got it—and we're to sail on Jan 2nd."

But Clemens' enthusiasm was countered by Clara's distress. When her father attempted, through attorney Samuel M. Gardenhire, to appoint Paine his literary executor in December 1906, Clara annulled the plan and insisted that she be named the literary executor of her father's estate. He complied with her wishes on January 14, 1907, for he told Miss Lyon that he was "in trouble now because last night Clara struck a note—the same note that he struck when he was 20 and said 'What's the use, I'm 20 and haven't got a start in life yet.' " Clara's mood of depression was manifest on New Year's Eve, when a party for sixty people with elaborate charades was marred by her sudden decision not to participate. Miss Lyon had never seen Clemens "so serious—so disappointed" as he was at Clara's behavior. (Nevertheless, he was able to disguise his disappointment; the New York *Herald* reported on April 28, 1907: "It will go down into history that on last New Year's Eve Mark Twain appeared in his Fifth avenue home in a gorgeous white flannel suit, which was the feature of the occasion. In taking a part in the programme of the festivities he appeared as one of the Siamese Twins. His spotless white suit was decorated by a red ribbon linking his leg to the leg of a companion, representing the other twin. It was a remarkable fact that this other man—the lesser half of the Siamese twins—drank most of the champagne of the evening, while Mark Twain drank nothing but water. The merrier the other man grew the more solemn Mark Twain became, and finally as the last moments of the year melted away he broke into oratory and delivered the most powerful temperance address of his life.")

Jean with her usual insight had realized the difficulties that were growing between Clara and her father:

> I can't help feeling that Clara's love for Father is not what it should be. She shows a good deal of irritation and even that she is hurt, by his many little ways that are exasperating until one gets used to them. I know just how they affect her, as I have been all through it, but I do believe that I have passed that undesirable stage of not being truly devoted to him. Of course, Father's rude and ungentlemanly ways often make me angry and I don't in the least refrain from criticizing those things, but with all that I am most fond of him.

Unlike Jean, Clara was incapable of such tolerant acceptance of her father's behavior and personality.

Clemens, Twichell, and Isabel left on the *Bermudian* on January 2 and stayed in Hamilton, Bermuda, until the seventh. Miss Lyon found the island restful and charming; Clemens found it vexatious because he was constantly irritated with Twichell. "Mr. Twichell tires him beyond words," the secretary wrote, "so that the King almost loses patience." Twichell's deafness was a major aggravation to Clemens, as was his constant trivial chatter. As Miss Lyon recorded in a notebook, Twichell was not unique:

> Sometimes he is very much irritated by people. He hates Mr. and Mrs. R. U. Johnson; he grits his teeth at the mention of either of them. I'm afraid he really hates R. W. Gilder, and he can scarcely tolerate Mr. Twichell, who does reminisce over the trivial ones of the earth until the King begins to show a blue flame out of him. . . .

> At luncheon Mr. Twichell said he had only one disappointment on this trip and that was his lack of appetite. (The appetite that he *has* had has been a marvel to me.) I repeated that disappointment to the King who said—"Well if we

had stayed 2 days longer he'd have had a child. He's been on the verge of it several times". . . .

Jan. 9 We were so long docking this morning— a sunken ferryboat barred the way—but Mr. Twichell didn't know the cause of the delay and stepped about to show how it should be managed. "Go out into midstream, turn the Bermudian at a right angle and come in SO!" The King said he'd make ever so much more money if hc'd leave the pulpit and instruct seamen how to pull out from Bermuda and anchor in NY— and when Mr. Twichell's excitement increased, the King said to me, "now look out, he'll have triplets in a minute."

Clemens' appetite caused him as much discomfort as Twichell's did. On board ship he "ate too heartily of baked beans and bacon and cabbage and milk yesterday at luncheon, so he has had indigestion ever since." But the kindness of the Bermudians, the fascination of the tropical fish at Devil's Cave, and the beauty of the crystal-blue waters restored Clemens' spirits.

On his return, he launched into the same relentless social pattern that had marked his earlier winters at 21 Fifth Avenue. He played billiards with Paine and, when the biographer's research took him on a trip to Nevada and California to explore his subject's early years, with Finley Peter Dunne and Franklin Whitmore as substitutes. A day's billiard session lasted sometimes for ten hours. Clemens entertained Helen Keller on January 16 and established a pattern of dining with the Rogerses or the Coes and sleeping over in order to avoid the lonely return to 21 Fifth Avenue in the late night air. He dined at the Robert Colliers and played billiards. He attended a lunch in his honor at the Players' Club on February 2, and played billiards. He had the entire Paine family to 21 Fifth Avenue the next day, and Miss Lyon reported ominously, "Mrs. Paine is jealous of this whole situation."

The mirage of prosperity that Clemens envisioned in late 1906 continued to gleam into 1907—but for less than a month. On

January 12 Jervis Langdon persuaded Clemens to "make an investment for the children—not for himself. . . . It was to be a $5,000.00 in an organ association," the Hope-Jones Organ Company, of which Langdon was the president.

But disquieting news was only four days away. On January 16, 1907, Clemens discovered that the *North American Review* was dropping from 128 to 112 pages per issue "and so Col. Harvey feels that he must cut out some of the Autobiography." This meant that Clemens would have to sell stock to finance the Redding house, and in addition he believed that "Harpers must be near collapsing again or they would not cut out 16 pages of reading matter of a magazine that is only 5 months old." On the twentieth, perhaps sensing Clemens' anxiety,

> Col. Harvey came in and the King's worries are
> at an end over the N. A. Review and its dockings
> of the MS. The plan has been made to pay the
> King $2,000.00 a month until the one hundred
> thousand words have been turned in, and that
> will provide the needed amount to build the
> house.

Feeling secure again, Clemens "signed the contract for the building of the house on my Connecticut farm and specified the cost-limit, and work has been begun."

The fear of an insolvent publisher continued to haunt Clemens even after the building was in progress, nevertheless. In mid-year Harvey "asked Mr. Clemens to wait for the autobiographical monies that are due him; to wait until the first of the year, for funds are low and he must borrow if he pays. It annoyed the King, for it is, as he says, 'doing business through sentimental channels' and he doesn't like it at all."

xv

If the autobiographical dictations were to finance the building of the house at Redding, Clemens had even greater cause for worry.

He managed to do more sustained work on the autobiography in the winter of 1906–1907 than he had since April 1906 (the point at which Paine's edition of the autobiography ends). His speech on simplified spelling was issued by the Simplified Spelling Board, and when he received a copy he dictated on that subject (November 7, 1906). That discussion suggested Susy's idiosyncratic spelling. He moved on to the question of copyright. A description of a minstrel show (November 30, 1906) revived a three-day description of the mesmerist who went to Hannibal when Samuel Clemens was a boy. Susy's description of *A Connecticut Yankee in King Arthur's Court* impelled him to discuss King Leopold, the Czar, and the impending arrival of monarchy in the United States (December 5 to 13, 1906).

But, except for his epic tirade against Bret Harte (February 1 to 4, 1907), the daily stint was getting shorter and shorter. Mark Twain began clutching at mere "news" too frequently, without transmuting it into "history." Possibly he felt that some of the criticism he was receiving over the published "chapters" in the *North American Review* was justified. Mrs. C. E. Paxson, the daughter of the James Lampton who had provided most of the traits for Colonel Beriah Sellers in the novel *The Gilded Age,* complained to Mark Twain that he had represented her father as a "foolish, shiftless man unable to keep his family from starvation" in one of the autobiographical selections published in the *Review.* And John Raymond, son of the actor who had made Colonel Sellers a stage success in the 1870s, called Mark Twain's description of his father "a cowardly attack" on a man dead twenty years.

The inspiration was clearly draining swiftly away, whatever the cause. Earlier manuscripts were appropriated as padding for the autobiography, as when he inserted his description of his first use of the typewriter (on February 27, 1907), his 1900 description of Dollis Hill House (also on February 27), and his manuscript of "Wapping Alice" (on April 9) into the record. By the spring of 1907, his copper-mining stock investments, the trial of Harry Thaw for the murder of Stanford White, and the parties he was attending were his subjects.

Mark Twain would continue working on the autobiography in sporadic fashion until the end of 1909, but in 1907 he devised a new reason for its existence. In January he and Miss Lyon "talked for a long time about the way the auto. should be used to perpetuate the copyright of the books, and he was glad when I told him that C.C. appreciated his plan." By March, that justification was augmented by Mark Twain's own sense of satiety:

> I do not need to stay here any longer, for I have completed the only work that was remaining for me to do in this life and that I could not possibly afford to leave uncompleted—my Autobiography. Although that is not finished, and will not be finished until I die, the object which I had in view in compiling it is accomplished: that object was to distribute it through my existing books and give each of them a new copyright life of twenty-eight years. . . . If I should die to-morrow this mass of literature would be quite sufficient for the object which I had in view in manufacturing it.

As the last substantial effort of his literary career, the autobiography was an amazing achievement in its original intention and its first year of dictation. But Mark Twain's statement about its use to extend his copyrights was the weary valedictory of a man who had not only written himself out but, even worse, had remembered himself out as well.

xvi

Clemens' social calendar blossomed with the spring of 1907. He entertained Gutzon Borglum on February 22 and read a poem at the Shelley-Keats Memorial, though "he took some whiskey, and just enough to bring cobwebs and make him forget the things he planned to say." On March 5, he signed a lease with Mr. William Voss for a summer house at the luxurious private community of

Tuxedo Park, New York. The Whitmores came from Hartford for a three-day visit in March and the Twichells in mid-April. Clemens, Miss Lyon, and a young girl named Paddy Madden dashed to Bermuda and back between March 16 and 21; and as Miss Lyon wrote when the trip was being planned, "We should have but one night there . . . but the King won't care. He will have 5 days away from home."

His dislike of 21 Fifth Avenue was growing into total revulsion because it represented his increasing distress and frustration. On January 27, Isabel Lyon had found him "cursing the loneliness of the house." After Clara departed for a concert tour on February 19 and Paine left for the West on the twenty-second, the depression grew more intense:

> This is too dreadful, this loneliness for the King. The evil month of March is coming galloping along, when he is usually tried beyond some kind of endurance; if it isn't physical, it is social, and I'm afraid for him. I telephone in every direction to get hold of people to come in for billiards, but no one is to be reached. Mr. Dooley is South, Col. Harvey is busy, or skittish, Dr. Rice is busy, the Coes are in Florida, the Benjamins in Lake Placid, the Broughtons en route for some Southern place, and the rest of the world can't play. When I go to his room to tell him that these people are all otherwise employed, he says "It doesn't matter—" but it *does* matter; it matters very much indeed.

Miss Lyon's solution was to have Clemens avoid the house as much as possible.

He went to Hartford to address the thirtieth anniversary meeting of his old Saturday Morning Club in late April, boarded the *Kanawha* on the twenty-fourth to view a naval review at Jamestown, Virginia, until May 1; and, as he told Jean, had

> appointments in the first fortnight of May for Tuxedo—4th; Actor's Fund Fair, New York—6th

and 8th; leave for Annapolis 9th—return in 5
days. Then Tuxedo and *rest*.

He moved to Tuxedo for the summer on May 4, attended the
Actors' Fund Fair even though an ardent Christian Scientist
attempted to have his invitation retracted. Then he went with
Miss Lyon to Annapolis as a guest of the governor of Maryland,
leaving earlier than scheduled because "he was in despair and said
we've got to get away from here." He commuted back and forth
between New York City and Tuxedo and planned and canceled
another lightning trip to Bermuda with Colonel Harvey. Despite
his flights, he liked Tuxedo, "carried away by the loveliness of this
place. He says he has never seen so beautiful a place in all his
travels."

During his springtime engagements he had attended an ex-
tremely important luncheon, as it turned out, given by the staff of
the New York *Times* for visitor C. Moberly Bell, editor of the
London *Times*. Recalling the event later, Miss Lyon spoke the
only word of reproach she was ever to express about Clemens'
behavior:

> Probably in late 1906 Moberly Bell was over
> from England, and Mr. Clemens saw him—
> lunched at some function and Moberly Bell sat
> beside him and asked "When are you coming to
> England?" "When Oxford bestows its degree
> upon me!" and Mr. Clemens told me with satis-
> faction that Moberly Bell said he "would arrange
> *that*," and he did. That red Oxford robe was
> cheapened (for me) because it was asked for!

If indeed Bell was instrumental in the offer from Oxford, the seed
that Clemens casually sowed at that lunch would take only two
weeks to germinate.

The cable from Whitelaw Reid, American ambassador to Great
Britain, offering the Oxford Litt. D., arrived on May 3, 1907, and
Clemens accepted it joyously. He appropriately thanked Moberly
Bell—"Your hand is in it! and you have my best thanks." While

Miss Lyon packed his trunks, Clemens arranged for Ashcroft to accompany him to England. They sailed on the *Minneapolis* on June 8, but Miss Lyon was full of apprehension which was also cryptically critical of Ashcroft. "I do hope Ashcroft will brace up and take care of him," she wrote. "He ought to go with proper protection." And after he landed at Tilbury, she was still concerned: "When the King is on the ocean there is anxiety; but there is more anxiety of another kind when he is on the land." She had every reason for apprehension; the father's behavior was becoming almost as unpredictable as his daughters'.

<center>xvii</center>

Jean became increasingly temperamental in early 1907. On returning to New York from the January trip to Bermuda, Clemens and Isabel had gone to Katonah to visit Jean, "who was in a torrent of impossible moods and distressed her wonderful father until he was ready to weep." She wanted her horse, Scott, which was promptly shipped to her, and then her father brought her a carriage to use. She recorded a romantic interest in one of her physicians at her sanitarium, a Dr. Hibbard, in her diary:

> I don't in the least hope to win him, fond as I am growing of him, but I can't help wishing that if he is engaged I didn't have to be thrown with him so incessantly as I am. . . . That desperate hunger for love does not leave me and doesn't seem to intend [to]. Doubtless for that very reason no one will ever care for me and I shall have to drag my useless, empty life out by itself. Oh! is there no hope whatsoever for me? What can I do! I feel as tho' I must find some means to prove attractive to a person that I can also learn to love.

She was also aware of being neglected in the planning of the new house at Redding:

> Lioness came and brought the drawings of the
> house we are going to build in Redding. It seems
> that at first John (Howells) had planned a very
> small room for me with no fireplace in it and
> with Anna's room placed next to mine in such a
> way that the only way out of her room would be
> through *mine*. Of course neither Clara nor Father
> noticed that dreadful inconvenience, or the small-
> ness of the rooms, but the Lioness did and it has
> been changed.

It was a pathetic indication of Jean's unimportance in the family's
plans for the future.

She was also causing trouble with her dislike of the maids her
father was furnishing her. She was unhappy with Anna Sterritt,
and Clemens finally urged her to try to "call back the gentle spirit
you were born with." Jean recorded her own honest indignation
at the request:

> And then I . . . said that I had often felt that
> it would be a relief to the family to have me out
> of the way, because I often caused trouble by be-
> ing unmanageable when I was ill, etc. I laid no
> blame on Father or Mother and I said that quite
> recently I had begun to have the above feeling
> less because of his & Clara's sweetness. That is
> true, but still, while I know that neither one of
> them would admit being glad to have me away &
> therefore relieved of the presence of an ill per-
> son, I am sure that they must feel so. I don't for
> a minute believe that I was sent out here for any
> such reason, but since it is better for me to be
> here it at the same time must be a relief to them.
> Also, the idea that they miss me is absurd. Clara's
> & my interests are too absolutely different for us
> to be necessary to one another even if we are
> fond of each other & Father can't possibly find
> any entertainment or interest in me. I am sure
> he is fond of me but I don't believe that he any

more than Clara, really misses me. It seems a
heartless thing to say, but now that I am accus-
tomed to this place, I don't really miss either of
them. I far more feel a desire to see Father than
I do to see Clara, which is only right & natural.
I do often have a sort of hunger to get hold of
him & hug him, but if I were to say I missed him
or Clara steadily, I should be lying.

In April, Anna was replaced by Teresa Cherubini, whom Jean
sent back to 21 Fifth Avenue in June. When Teresa returned she
confided in Miss Lyon and "cried bitterly up in my room when
she told me of Jean's unkindnesses." Teresa was replaced by
Blanche; and Jean's father counseled her to try Christian Science.
He said that he appreciated the "good news that Dr. Hunt per-
ceives that your condition is improved"; Hunt had reported on
February 22 that Jean had only one seizure—a mild one—in the
preceding three weeks.

Clemens told his younger daughter that Dr. Quintard was
trying to find the household a summer home in the neighborhood
of Katonah; but he was entertaining offers of summer leases in
Bermuda at the same time. The most effective medicine Jean
could have had was the only one denied her, even when the move
to Tuxedo was made—the presence of her father. Her stratagems
to gain his attention and interest were transparent.

In March, Miss Lyon reported that Jean was "improving, and is
full of plans for the future home in Redding." After her father
was invited to receive the honorary Oxford degree in May and
made preparation for sailing to England, Jean became even more
possessive; her father had to reassure her that he would not "leave
the country before I've seen you. If you were sound and well and
there was *time* for some travel, you and I would go together." A
little later, having visited Katonah, he echoed her misery at his
departure: "It saddened me, too, dearest Jean, to go away from
you, and it has saddened me since to think about it. But I hope
this is the last far journey I shall ever have to take." And in a final
attempt to focus her father's attention on her, "Jean got the King

to promise that he would cable *her* and not Santa, upon his arrival in England." Clemens simply lied outright when he told Rogers in the midst of these pathetic goodbyes, "Jean will never be well, but is contented and happy where she is and does not want to see the city again."

<center>xviii</center>

In the midst of preparing for her spring 1907 concert tour, Clara spent several days in a Katonah sanitarium near Jean's as a patient; indeed, she alternated between Katonah and Atlantic City, traveling almost as if to avoid settling in at 21 Fifth Avenue. On February 19, she began a tour that included stops in North Adams, Elmira, Hartford, Bangor, and Utica. Miss Lyon commented lyrically at Clara's return on March 25 that she was "a made over creature with happiness and success and music running rampantly through her veins"—but not money:

> C.C. has come back from her tour and it has cost at least $2,500.00—a financial loss, but when I talked with him [Clemens] this morning about the chances of proceeding for another 4 weeks, he said, "Pay the bills and tell Ben to go ahead."

Clara left immediately for Atlantic City and then stopped briefly in New York on the way to Katonah on April 2, 1907. On the sixth, she returned from Katonah and left again on the eighth. She dashed between Tuxedo, Redding, and Fifth Avenue, and from June 29 to July 8 took a trip with Miss Lyon to Halifax, Nova Scotia.

Possibly some of her fluttering is explained by the romantic attention she was receiving, and not alone from Ossip Gabrilowitsch. Competing with Ossip was Charles E. Wark, nicknamed "Will." Wark, the most elusive figure in the household biography, became Clara's accompanist some time in the winter of 1906–1907, when he was living at 17 West 8th Street. By February 24

Clemens told Clara, "I like Mr. Wark and his honest blue eyes ever so much. I think you are fortunate to be in his guardianship." In late March, Wark sent Clara and Miss Lyon tickets for a Verdi *Requiem* and took Miss Lyon to a performance of *Martha* a few days later. On April 6, he took both ladies shopping, and on June 1 he visited them at Tuxedo. On June 6, he followed the group to New York City, and on the ninth he and Clara "went off for a holiday up to the Bronx." On both June 17 and 22, he was at Tuxedo with the two women, and Isabel called the group "the trinity of us." By June 28, he was dining at the Tuxedo house "every night"; and when they returned from Halifax, Will met Clara at the train in Boston, while Miss Lyon continued on to New York alone. Possibly there was nothing irregular about Clara's relationship with Wark in early 1907, but by 1908 he would be publicly identified as her fiancé.

Miss Lyon continued to stagger under the burden of her domestic duties in 1907. Clemens told Rogers, "Miss Lyon runs Clara, and Jean, and me, and the servants, and the housekeeping, and the house-building, and the secretary-work, and remains as extraordinarily competent as ever." Her own catalogue was even more specific:

> I have been so busy, for there is this house to look after, and the Tuxedo house to think and plan for, and the Redding house to be after too, and Santa to love and be with when she was here and do for, and Jean to be anxious over and to help if I can, and her doctors to see, and the King's social life to look after—for in these days he is very lonely and reaches out for people —and people he must have, so now I'm planning parties for him.

Once "Santa . . . passed with approval upon the plans," which John Howells presented to her on March 27, 1907, the entire supervision of the building in Redding fell to Miss Lyon.

Clemens refused even to discuss the subject of the new construction:

> He won't allow himself to be informed or con-
> sulted; he will pay the bills and that's all he
> will do, but when the house is finished then he
> will go to it. . . . He doesn't want to see it, or
> hear anything about it.

On May 23, 1907, Miss Lyon, Paine, John Howells and several builders attended an informal ground-breaking for the house ultimately to be called Stormfield—and poured whiskey into the first hole the shovel dug.

Just before departing for England, in appreciation for her services, Clemens deeded to Miss Lyon "a certain tract or parcel of land situate in the town of Redding." On June 13, Miss Lyon traveled to Redding and visited her "dear little house" on the property, to become known in the future as "The Lobster Pot." "Oh, it is so darling," she wrote, "and it is going to be so beautiful." But she took the responsibility of halting work on the main house when she discovered that it was being built on the wrong spot.

As she and Clara traveled constantly, Isabel wrote somewhat raucously:

> We remind ourselves of the waterbugs, for we
> dart from N.Y. to Tuxedo and to Redding and
> to Boston and back again. It isn't going to be a
> sweet and restful summer. But at all events as
> Santa mirthfully says, "it isn't a treadmill."
> Damned if it isn't a treadmill, we've got into
> the habit of shooting the shoots and can't stop it.

House-supervising and traveling were demanding enough, but while Clemens was in England an even more vexing event occurred—one that touched the sensitive area of Isabel's increasing solicitude for her "master."

On May 22, 1907, Clemens had Miss Lyon call on Charlotte Teller, who was indignant about stories that "she was an adventurer and planning to marry Mr. Clemens." Miss Lyon made the mistake of laughing at the suggestion and predicted accurately, "I

think we'll hear from her again." On July 4, the New York *Herald* ran a story claiming that Clemens and Miss Lyon were engaged to marry. She denied the rumor, and on the fifth, Clemens wrote a denial which the *Herald* published: "I have not known, and shall never know, any one who could fill the place of the wife I have lost. I shall never marry again." Later, he and Miss Lyon agreed that Charlotte Teller had undoubtedly initiated the rumor; but he began fastidiously taking chaperones on his rides with Miss Lyon for what she called "protection."

<div align="center">xix</div>

While Isabel, Clara, and Will were "waterbugging" around the whole of New England, Clemens was at the pinnacle of his public career. Paine commented after the Oxford degree that "the great career . . . in a sense now had been completed since he had touched its highest point." There were some newspaper rumors that Mark Twain was a contender for the Nobel Prize for Literature for 1907, but he seems to have taken no notice of them himself. The Oxford degree healed what he called an old sore, perhaps because Howells had received the degree earlier than he had; and almost from the time the *Minneapolis* left the pier in New York Clemens enjoyed himself with the glee of a small boy on his last trip before summer vacation ends. Miss Lyon might be distressed about the proprieties and Clara might cable him to be circumspect, but Clemens—with Ashcroft tagging along, making appointments and collecting enough newspaper clippings to fill two scrapbooks—transcended proprieties with a magnificent combination of humor, eccentricity, vanity, and pathos.

Even before his boat arrived at Tilbury, Clemens had found another girl like Gertrude Natkin to interest himself in. This one, Carlotta Welles, reportedly looked like Susy—and, like Susy, stayed in her room after the novelty of Mark Twain's attentions wore off: "I used to get restless and chafed at times at being expected to sit quietly with him when my inclination was to race around," she

remembered many years later. She managed to escape from him but not before a cartoonist on board the ship drew a caricature of Clemens and her—trailed by ever-present Ashcroft—walking around the promenade deck while all the other passengers read the works of Mark Twain. Carlotta—"Charley," as he called her—received several notes from her self-appointed guardian before he grew disgruntled at her indifference.

When Clemens landed, MacAlister, Bernard Shaw (present to meet his biographer, Professor Archibald Henderson), a regiment of newspaper reporters, and the dock workers all cheered his arrival. By the time Clemens made his way to Brown's Hotel, the lines of friends, acquaintances, admirers, photographers, and interviewers were already waiting. Having promised himself only two public appearances—a dinner hosted by Ambassador Reid and one by the Pilgrims at the Savoy—Clemens promptly violated his rule and threw himself into society on a schedule that Paine later said he could no more resist "than a débutante in her first season." The list of people he encountered at breakfasts, luncheons, teas, and dinners included everyone Clemens had ever known in England and a significant number of those he did not know. He even attended the King's garden party at Windsor for 8,500 guests on June 22, keeping on his hat at the Queen's command.

British journalism took a holiday, reporting little but the antics of Mark Twain from the first day of his arrival, when the conjunction of his landing and the theft of the Ascot Cup provided humorous copy across the entire country. Clemens obliged with some touches of what the press politely called "eccentricity." A few days after settling in at Brown's Hotel, Clemens—who had developed the habit of walking around 21 Fifth Avenue with "just his silk underclothes on"—marched through the lobby, out into the morning traffic on Dover Street, to a public bathhouse for a swim and breakfast. Miss Lyon's fears about Ashcroft's lack of control seemed realized. Clara cabled an admonishment; Paine made light of the incident. And one cartoonist captured the humor of the scene, especially with nattily dressed Ashcroft following along behind Mark Twain in his dressing gown. The London

Times noted that "after his bath Mark Twain returned to his hotel in his three-piece costume of one bathrobe and two slippers, and had the pleasure of making a lot more people open their eyes very wide."

After the Pilgrims' dinner on June 25, Clemens went to Oxford for the bestowing of his degree. The other honorees included Rudyard Kipling, General William Booth, Auguste Rodin, and Camille Saint-Saëns, but the undergraduates at the ceremony, like the rest of England, reserved their loudest cheers for the American humorist. Lord Curzon pronounced the Latin introduction, "Most jocund, pleasant and humorous man, who shakes the sides of all the circuit of the earth with your native joyousness, I, by my authority and that of the entire university, admit you to the honorary degree of Doctor of Letters"; and the ceremony was over.

Clemens made further public appearances at the Oxford pageant, a dinner at the Savage Club, another at the *Punch* offices, and, after repeated attempts to decline the invitation, a trip to Liverpool with Thomas Power O'Connor and a banquet at the Town Hall at which he delivered the most poignant speech of his entire career. As Paine said, when Ashcroft and Clemens boarded the *Minnetonka* for the return journey to the United States on July 13, "the world had nothing more to give him now."

xx

The Liverpool speech was touching in its finality. There was something funereal about the trip to England and about Clemens' own behavior. Miss Lyon had been bothered all year because "the King talks so much about his death in these days—his death—what can that mean to those of us who live only as he lives." And as he watched the Oxford pageant with hundreds of historically costumed characters, he explained that he was especially interested in the spectacle "so that I could get ideas for my funeral procession, which I am planning on a large scale." Many of the private

dinners were in effect personal goodbyes to friends whose comradeship stretched as far back as 1872. But the Liverpool speech closed with the most effective and moving farewell of all.

Borrowing an anecdote from Richard Henry Dana's *Two Years Before the Mast,* he elaborated:

> There was a presumptuous little self-important skipper in a coasting sloop engaged in the dried-apple and kitchen-furniture trade, and he was always hailing every ship that came in sight. He did it just to hear himself talk and to air his small grandeur. One day a majestic Indiaman came plowing by with course on course of canvas towering into the sky, her decks and yards swarming with sailors, her hull burdened to the Plimsoll line with a rich freightage of precious spices, lading the breezes with gracious and mysterious odors of the Orient. It was a noble spectacle, a sublime spectacle! Of course the little skipper popped into the shrouds and squeaked out a hail, "Ship ahoy! What ship is that? And whence and whither?" In a deep and thundering bass the answer came back through the speaking-trumpet, "The *Begum,* of Bengal—142 days out from Canton—homeward bound! What ship is that?" Well, it just crushed that poor little creature's vanity flat, and he squeaked back most humbly, "Only the *Mary Ann,* fourteen hours out from Boston, bound for Kittery Point—with nothing to speak of!" Oh, what an eloquent word that "only," to express the depths of his humbleness! That is just my case. During just one hour in the twenty-four—not more—I pause and reflect in the stillness of the night with the echoes of your English welcome still lingering in my ears, and then I am humble. Then I am properly meek, and for that little while I am only the *Mary Ann,* fourteen hours out, cargoed with vegetables and tinware; but during all the other twenty-three

> hours my vain self-complacency rides high on
> the white crests of your approval, and then I am
> a stately Indiaman, plowing the great seas un-
> der a cloud of canvas and laden with the kind-
> est words that have ever been vouchsafed to any
> wandering alien in this world, I think; then my
> twenty-six fortunate days on this old mother soil
> seem to be multiplied by six, and *I* am the
> *Begum,* of Bengal, 142 days out from Canton—
> homeward bound!

It was an amazing rhetorical *tour de force,* an emotion-packed and
exactly appropriate conclusion—and all the more so because his
audience, appreciating the flourish, burst into applause and cheers
when Clemens said, *"I* am the *Begum,* of Bengal, 142 days out from
Canton." As O'Connor reported in his *T. P.'s Weekly:*

> It seemed like an inopportune cheer, and for a
> moment it upset Mark Twain, and yet it was
> felicitous in opportuneness. Slowly, after a long
> pause, came the last two words—like that curi-
> ous, detached and high note in which a great
> piece of music sometimes suddenly and abruptly
> ends—"Homeward bound."

Dramatic though it was, it was also heartfelt—an honest and self-
effacing analysis developed with forensic ability that had no closer
parallel than Hank Morgan's "last effects" as he died at the con-
clusion of *A Connecticut Yankee in King Arthur's Court* yearning
for a bygone time. Mark Twain was as completely lost to the world
after the triumph of the Oxford degree as if it had indeed been the
funeral he was planning. "Homeward bound" was the perfect
epitaph.

III. THE DERELICT

(Summer 1907 to 1910)

The years they come and the years they go,
 As I drift on the lonely sea,
Recking no more than the winds that blow,
 What is in store for me;
For my shames are over, my soul at peace,
 At peace from the loathsome strife,
And I wait in patience for my release
 From the insult of this world's life.
> —From "The Derelict," *On the Poetry
> of Mark Twain,* ed. Arthur L. Scott

Here lurks no treason, here no envy swells,
Here grow no damned grudges; here are no
 storms,
No noise, but silence and eternal sleep.
> —*Titus Andronicus,* I, i, as transcribed
> by Mark Twain on the first page of
> the Stormfield Guest Book (MTP)

i

In 1907, both before and after the Oxford ceremony, Samuel Clemens and his hovering aides received and preserved more mail than in any other year of his life. The torrent of correspondence was so relentless that, according to one exaggerated newspaper story, a stenographer was kept busy twelve hours a day simply answering letters. Bogus relatives wrote for genealogical information; indigents with tales of woe wrote for money; heads of various organizations wrote requesting his endorsement. Childhood companions and Mississippi boatmen sent their recollections; aspiring authors mailed published poems, novels, plays, and unpublished manuscripts. Invitations to breakfast, lunch, tea, and dinner were constant, as were requests for speeches, lectures, anecdotes, and even Mark Twain's mere presence on platforms.

But although Clemens had loved popularity and the limelight in earlier years, in 1907 he could develop no enthusiasm for any of the enterprises his letter writers offered. To a request to become a member of the American Academy of Political and Social Sciences, he replied, "My membership would be purely ornamental and therefore valueless. Have retired from the activities of life." To an invitation from Brander Matthews to attend a dinner of the

Simplified Spelling Board, he wrote, "Wont go to any banquet not even the Last Supper." S. S. McClure asked him for an article endorsing osteopathy: "For various reasons (and indignations) the subject does not interest me," he answered. Archibald Henderson diagnosed the problem in a letter to Clemens after both men had returned to the United States from England:

> Is it not Goethe who says that when a man becomes truly great, the world does everything it can to prevent him from doing other great things —with its receptions, dinners, and diversions of a thousand different kinds?

Although it is dubious that the avalanche of letters and invitations impeded Clemens from doing "other great things," it did require enormous time and energy from an aging and ailing man who had little of either to spare. In the following year Howells was to say with trenchant accuracy, "but, poor fellow, I thought you went to Redding to get rid of Mark Twain." Even after Stormfield was complete, however, Clemens was unable to escape.

And completing Stormfield was not an easy task. The site was moved a second time, to the crest of a hill, and John Howells wrote a distressed report to Miss Lyon in mid-1907: "When I dined with Miss Clemens [Clara] this week, I could not help seeing that she rather expected to find 'her suite' when the house was finished!" Since everyone appears to have been terrified at the possibility of arousing Clara's anger, a change of plans and bedrooms was made to conform more closely with her expectations. And when Harvey asked for the delay in paying the royalties on autobiographical dictations, Miss Lyon wrote:

> The building of the Redding house is stopped again—or we are trying to stop it. Since his return from England Mr. Clemens has been troubled about living so far away—or worse still having to live alone out there for Santa cannot be with him now, and he musn't be with Jean.

But John Howells reported that the work of H. A. Lounsbury, who was in charge of the heavy labor, and W. W. Sunderland, who was the builder, was too far advanced to permit a halt: "Arresting work at Redding at this time would probably make you liable for between ten and fifteen thousand dollars."

The financial dilemmas were further complicated when the Knickerbocker Trust Company, where Clemens had $51,000 on deposit, suspended payment on October 22. He fumed at the scoundrels who had accepted his deposits knowing that the bank was to fail shortly, and he planned to economize:

> Sell the steel bonds a few at a time to build the Redding house with, for the Autobiography money is in the Knickerbocker, and live on what comes from the Harpers. Clara's expenses this summer have been extremely great. We thought they were heavy other years but this year has exceeded the others, and she has all her plans made for another costly concert tour.

The worry was unjustified, however, because the Knickerbocker ultimately reopened and resumed payments on all accounts.

To relieve Clemens of the tribulations of money matters, Ashcroft had an inspiration in mid-1907: "To prevent piracy in years to come," he suggested, "why not trade-mark now in the name of Samuel L. Clemens such things as the 'Mark Twain Cigar,' tobacco, whiskey, shirt, corset, hair-restorer, etc. etc." Miss Lyon noted on the margin of the letter, "Mr. Clemens likes that idea. How shall he proceed?" By November of 1907, "Mark Twain Whiskey" and "Mark Twain Tobacco" were registered with and published by the office of patents and at least a rudimentary prototype of the Mark Twain Company was about to be born.

ii

As soon as the *Minnetonka* landed in New York from the Oxford trip, Mark Twain moved to Tuxedo Park and began the autobio-

graphical dictations once more. Ashcroft had kept a detailed account of the English activities, called "What Happened." Using "What Happened" to jog his own memory, Mark Twain set feverishly to work capturing his impressions of the events. Isabel declined an invitation by Mrs. Rogers with the explanation, "he has been very much tied up here, trying to finish his dictation of the trip to England. If he stops once . . . he knows he will be unable to resume work again." The enthusiasm carried the dictations—nineteen separate days' worth—into early October 1907. As usual, there were diversions. When he described Whitelaw Reid's party in London, he devoted a day's dictation to vituperation against the American ambassador (August 26). When he received word of the banning of *Huckleberry Finn* in Worcester, Massachusetts, he trotted out his old clichés about the obscenity of the Bible (August 10). And Theodore Roosevelt, a Robert Fulton naval review at Jamestown, Virginia, and collections of jokes and anecdotes (dictations of September 13, September 26, and October 7) soon supplanted memories of Oxford.

Social activities intruded on the literary schedule constantly. The exclusive society of Tuxedo Park entertained its literary visitor almost daily. Usually with Miss Lyon accompanying him, he made the rounds: Mr. and Mrs. Tams, Mr. and Mrs. Davies, Mr. and Mrs. Ogden, Mr. and Mrs. Kane, the Masons, the Mortimers, Mrs. Deacon, the Ronalds, the Sampsons, and the Hoyts were among the names she recorded over and over as guests and hosts until the Tuxedo Park house was vacated on October 24.

His family was less comforting. Clara had apparently sequestered herself at Norfolk as soon as her father returned from England, going to Tuxedo on August 29, looking "beautifuller than she has ever been." But the visit was not a very satisfactory one:

> I don't know how he came to say it, but he said that he didn't get much good out of Clara. When she is in N. Y. he never sees anything of her and when he goes to her rooms he feels like

a stranger making an untimely and unwelcome
visit. Poor King! It is all too true.

A week later Clara distressed her father even more. She decided
that

> she wants to give a concert here [Tuxedo Park]
> for Mary Lawton. The King was upset by the
> suggestion, for as he truly says it would be a "bid-
> ding for reluctant courtesies" to have a concert
> here. If these people were to ask for C.C. to sing
> here that would be one thing—and the King said
> "if she comes here to sing in public, then I must
> leave Tuxedo."

On November 18, 1907, Clara left the Clemens household, "to be
gone a good while, and she will be missed—nobody left but Miss
Lyon and me," Clemens wrote.

Jean, who was willing to join the family circle, was not allowed
to. Clemens went to Katonah to see her on August 12, shortly after
returning from Oxford; and a room for her and another for her
maid were included in the original Stormfield plans. Anna Ster-
ritt, the maid she sent away earlier in 1907, "received a letter from
Miss Jean last week in which she said she would like me to come
back to her this winter. She said she was very much improved in
health as well as temper and that she would treat me better if I
came back." But in October there was presumably a serious re-
lapse; Miss Lyon recorded in her diary:

> Oh, Terrible, Terrible that his children cannot
> come under the spell of his glories, his subtleties,
> his sweetnesses. For this morning there was a
> cruel letter from Jean damning me—finding fault
> with him—with *him*.

Miss Lyon rushed to Katonah for an interview with Dr. Peterson,

> who doesn't want Jean to leave her Sanitarium
> where she is improving but hating the Sanitar-
> ium viciously. I didn't tell the King how he said

that the epileptic temperament rarely improved,
but that it grew worse, and that Jean must never
live with her father again, because her affection
might easily turn into a violent and insane ha-
tred and she could slay, just by the sudden and
terrible and ungovernable revulsion of feeling.

Clemens, who knew only the heartening part of Peterson's report,
wrote Jean a few days later, "I hear that Dr. Peterson is exceed-
ingly well pleased with your year's progress, and certainly I am.
How fortunate it was that fortune put you into his hands. He
expects this improvement to go right along."

Clemens wrote his younger daughter gossipy and innocuous
letters about his activities—thanking her for some copper frogs she
made for his birthday and telling her of a farewell visit to bid the
William Dean Howellses goodbye before their trip to Europe. He
ignored the truth that she wanted desperately to be included in his
life rather than be the recipient of his accounts of it. One letter
told Jean:

When I break into hellfireworks of speech, Miss
Lyon sets down the words in a book. Mr. [Mar-
tin] Littleton says it takes three historians to
record me: a biographer, an autobiographer, and
a naughty biographer—Paine, myself, and Miss
Lyon.

There was no mention of a place in the scheme for a daughter.

Miss Lyon's responsibilities expanded even further. Twichell
had written Clemens jubilantly earlier in 1907, "Miss Lyon! A
daisy—a bouquet of daisies—a bushel of 'em, is she!" And she
continued to earn the compliment. She began the close super-
vision of the construction at Redding, inspecting the work on
September 12, 1907: "the outlines are all up, and it is going to be
beautiful," she wrote. A description of her capabilities at Storm-
field reached print:

Anyone who has ever superintended the build-
ing of a home from a distance will appreciate

> some of the difficulties experienced by Miss Lyon,
> whose duties were divided between New York,
> Redding, and Bermuda! The workmen . . . were
> not slow in learning that the little woman who
> was likely to appear suddenly in their midst
> almost any day, had knowledge, sympathy, tact,
> taste, and executive ability of a high order.
> Under her leadership, they worked amazingly.
> Prosperity came in her train.

In the process, she was supervising Eugene Adams, who was rebuilding her own cottage.

Miss Lyon was also keeping a solicitous and worried eye on her employer. She wrote in September, "I don't know if it is significant of 72 years or if the King has always done it, but he loses track of the hours of the day"; and she commented the same month, "The King slept right through last night without whiskey or other aids," evidently an unusual achievement. A few weeks later she convinced herself that "The King cannot bear to stay alone in this house or any house. If I stay away the night he cannot eat, for it is solitude, and he says that he will not try to ever again."

iii

But there was hardly time for Clemens really to experience loneliness. En route home from England on the *Minnetonka,* he had struck up an acquaintance with Dorothy Quick, another of the small girls who became a member of the Aquarium. Unlike Carlotta Welles, Dorothy seemed to enjoy the company of Mark Twain; her reminiscence of her acquaintance was published in 1961 with the title *Enchantment, A Little Girl's Friendship with Mark Twain* (with no mention of Isabel Lyon or Ralph Ashcroft). As soon as the *Minnetonka* landed, newspapers across the country ran stories of Mark Twain's conquest by the pudgy, serious-faced young girl of eleven, who apparently spent most of the trip being photographed in Mark Twain's lap. As soon as

Clemens and Miss Lyon left for Tuxedo after his boat landed, Isabel arranged for Dorothy to come for a visit, from August 5 to 9. She returned on September 3 to stay until the twelfth. He also began corresponding with Francesca Nunnally—whose real name was Frances but who was nicknamed Francesca for "short," according to Clemens. She had been on the *Minneapolis* on his outbound trip to England and had accompanied him on social calls in London. He wrote her on September 3 and 18; indeed, even though Miss Lyon said that "the King cannot bear to write letters. He looks at a pen with a shudder in these days," he wrote a cascade of letters to his young girls. He promised Dorothy, "I would write you every time I wrote the other children, and I've just finished a letter to Clara."

Ashcroft, who had written many of Clemens' bread-and-butter letters in late July, was becoming a closer member of the family through Clemens' growing confidence in him. Impressed by his ability in England, Clemens dubbed him "Ashcroft the Indelible":

> That name has grown out of an accident of speech. Ashcroft is a young business man and knows how to do everything that I am incapable of doing, and whatever he undertakes to do he does promptly and in the best and most effective way; hence he never fails, and cannot fail. I have long thought of him privately in my mind as Ashcroft the Infallible, but the first time that I tried to utter that phrase I made a mistake in the word and told Miss Lyon to call up Ashcroft the Indelible.

Clemens explained the epithet in an autobiographical dictation which Paine or Clara later canceled from the typescript. "Little Ashcroft," as Isabel called him, stayed at Tuxedo during the first week of October and returned on the thirteenth for games of cutthroat hearts at which Clemens shouted "with delight when I pile Hearts upon Mr. Ashcroft who makes such a good butt for our villainies."

There were some public functions still, though Clemens did his best to resist most of them. He went to Jamestown, Virginia, on the *Kanawha* for the Robert Fulton Day of the Jamestown "World's Fair," in late September. But ex-President Cleveland, the president of the Robert Fulton Memorial, a line of battleships, and almost a dozen other yachts all failed to show up for the ceremonies; instead, a squall and a driving rain came and Clemens called the entire affair "the completest and perfectest fiasco in history." He became interested in the Children's Theater of the Educational Alliance, exchanging many letters with Alice Minnie Herts and attending a benefit performance of *The Prince and the Pauper* on November 19, 1907. After attempting to excuse himself from the celebration of Carnegie's seventieth birthday dinner at the Engineers' Club, he finally relented and spoke at the gathering on December 9, getting revenge on Carnegie by dictating almost a week's assault on him in the autobiography.

But the autobiography was not autobiography at all as 1907 ended. Instead, the dictations were extemporaneous remarks on topics of almost as little interest to Clemens as to the present-day reader: a postal-check scheme (August 22), Marconigrams (October 18), the Knickerbocker Trust suspension of payments (November 1), the marriage of American girls to foreigners (October 11), all topics that must have taxed Miss Hobby's ability to remain awake. Two segments of dictation captured some of the glow of interest the 1906 material had generated. A four-day discussion of the art of platform-speaking (October 11 to 14) and the three-day satiric attack on Andrew Carnegie prompted by "St. Andrew's" birthday party (December 2, 10, 12) were lively, comic, and entertaining. But the concept with which the autobiography had begun was distinctly losing its place in the author's mind. More and more the dictations became compulsive and aimless monologue.

In spite of the artistic deterioration, the published segments appearing in the *North American Review* attracted wide attention. Letters came to Mark Twain with anecdotes and clippings which he incorporated into dictations. Harvey suggested that the

autobiography might be syndicated in newspapers, but honestly pointed out that thereby "the King will reach his 'submerged clientele.' It will not bring him in a penny though. If anyone gets anything it will be the Harpers."

Part of the difficulty with the autobiography lay in Mark Twain's growing sense of literary insecurity. One of his most important artistic traits had been his ability to gauge his audience. But the autobiography was now simply dull. Prohibitions against the publication of relatively innocuous material nevertheless became increasingly frequent. With similar insensitivity, when Duneka asked for a story for the Christmas 1907 issue of *Harper's Magazine,* Mark Twain sent him "Wapping Alice." The story was startlingly inappropriate for a Christmas issue of a magazine. It was the account of a maid in the Clemens household who claimed that a workman for the family had made her pregnant during an extended affair which was conducted in the Clemens family's basement. Clemens arranged an elaborate confrontation between the "seducer" and the "ruined maiden," coerced the young man to agree to marry Alice, and had Joe Twichell perform the ceremony. But "Alice" turned out to be a male transvestite, and Mark Twain concluded one version of his telling of the story with the observation that although the marriage was a long and happy one, it was predictably without issue.

Understandably, the Harper organization chose to select "Extracts from Captain Stormfield's Visit to Heaven" for the holiday issue. H. E. Rood of Harper & Brothers sent Clemens revised proof of the sardonic fantasy in September 1907. The confused author who had nominated "Wapping Alice" was squeamish about "Captain Stormfield." Miss Lyon recorded that he had "been so troubled over publishing" the story that he read it to Tuxedo friends for their reactions, surprised and pleased that they approved it. Since it was the payment from the periodical appearance of the "Extracts from Captain Stormfield's Visit to Heaven" which financed Clara's whim for a "suite" of rooms at Redding, the name Stormfield was, incidentally, the logical final choice for a name for the new house.

Mark Twain's loss of contact with his audience remains a sad enigma. The dictations from the autobiography for late 1907 and 1908, the choice of "Wapping Alice," and the fear of the reception of "Captain Stormfield" all suggest that the humorist was becoming tone deaf about his own work and its interest, perhaps an inevitable problem for an author approaching his mid-seventies. If ever in his life he now needed, and lacked, the strict and constructive critical standards which Olivia, and to some extent Clara, had provided him. They had vetoed inferior work with honest concern. Howells, too, had functioned as a keenly sensitive judge of Mark Twain's abilities in earlier days, but that relationship was no longer maintained by the aging authors. H. H. Rogers, now his closest companion, shrewdly controlled financial excesses but was not prepared to cope with literary extravagance. In Isabel Lyon, Clemens had a worshipper rather than a critic. Her raptures at everything he wrote can only have contributed to his inability to evaluate his success and his failure to consign the substandard literary output to his wastebasket.

<p style="text-align:center">iv</p>

Clemens' uncertainty and confusion extended to business matters. His relations with the members of the Harper dynasty were unsettling. John Larkin assured him, on December 18, 1907 (while the Knickerbocker Trust Company monies were still tied up), that the $25,000 minimum annual income clause in his contract would continue into 1908. Major Leigh reported an annual royalty of almost $23,000 due in March 1908, telling Miss Lyon when the payment came due that "while any demands will be met at once, still in these hard-time days, I hope you will see that the King doesn't spend money too rapidly." That same year, when the expiration of copyright on *The Innocents Abroad* was imminent, Clemens conceived the idea of extending the Mark Twain Company to protect and extend all his copyrights. Ashcroft

explained the history of the evolution of the organization to
Henry Rogers in early 1909:

> The incorporation was suggested by Mr. Ash-
> croft about three years ago, and Mr. Larkin, the
> counsel, for Harpers, also suggested it a year
> later. The principal reason for taking the step
> was that the copyright on "Innocents Abroad"
> had almost expired, and that other valuable
> copyrights would presently expire.

As the plans for transferring all Clemens' business matters to the
Mark Twain Company developed, the author's erratic business
investments in late 1907 and 1908 suggested that it was imperative
to relieve him of financial decisions.

Clemens gambled $10,000 in the stock of the Fleishman Bath
Company, a projected public bath at the corner of 42nd Street and
Sixth Avenue in New York. The original suggestion for the invest-
ment had come from John Stanchfield; but in 1908 Stanchfield
advised against sinking further capital into the establishment.
Clemens managed, with unusual good luck, to sell his original
purchase of stock without a loss.

He declined to invest in a platinum mine, but he did risk
money in silver-mine stock Julian Hawthorne was offering for sale,
"gambling on Julian Hawthorne's integrity and level headed-
ness." It was a final misplaced business confidence. In 1913, after
having sold $3,500,000 of stock in the Temagami Mine without
ever paying a dividend, Hawthorne and most of the other di-
rectors of the company were indicted for mail fraud. Hawthorne
served a one-year term in Atlanta Penitentiary, the last man on
whom Clemens blindly bestowed his commercial trust.

Clemens also invested almost $20,000 in the United Fruit Com-
pany. His capital in the Hope organ company seemed doomed
when Daniel Frohman wrote that the cost of the instrument—
$20,000—was too exorbitant for even Frohman to contemplate
installing one in his theater.

But it was Plasmon which continued to fascinate and to exasper-

ate Clemens as it always had. In December 1907, a few months after Clemens had met with the English Plasmon directors in London and the American Plasmon attorneys in New York City, he received an announcement from John R. Chamberlin that Chamberlin and J. D. Campbell had replaced Henry C. Davis and W. W. Baldwin as directors of the American branch of the company. Clemens wrote on the back of the notification, "I hereby tender my resignation vice. p. and director of the P.C. of America." A few days later, the new directors became peremptory: "We hereby demand that you deliver to our representative . . . all of the books of accounts, papers, vouchers, and all other property belonging to the Plasmon Company of America." It is uncertain whether the new directors were members of the old John Hays Hammond faction; regardless, Clemens was disinterested at the possibilities of dispute and litigation.

Social activity was another matter. In early January there was another farewell party for the Howellses, frequent "doe" luncheons at which Clemens was the only male (on January 14 and February 11, 1908) , and dinner parties with the Robert Colliers. Clemens attended a Lotos Club dinner in his honor on January 11, and went to a number of plays at the Children's Theater, of which he was now president.

He received a call from Elinor Glyn, the young author of *Three Weeks,* at the beginning of 1908 and unburdened himself of an opinion of her novel and the furor it was causing because of its depiction of adultery. To his later embarrassment, Miss Glyn printed a pamphlet transcribing Clemens' opinion that her characters had been "obeying a natural law in their instant coming together. God was to blame—if any blame is to be attached to a noble realization of His law—in bringing them together. They were obeying laws, unknown to themselves, and no strength of will, and no convention, could have kept those two apart."

From January 25 to February 6, Clemens and Ashcroft vacationed in Bermuda; and Clemens returned to Hamilton with Isabel and Henry Rogers for almost two months—February 27 to April 11. In spite of such perpetual motion, the two main attrac-

tions of the year were billiards and little girls. "It is dreadful that life has to be made up of extremes," Miss Lyon philosophized in her diary on January 10; "either the King's life is a blur with too much billiards, or it is black with none." The games, and card games, too, often lasted into the early-morning hours, and the "blur" was not always billiards-induced. On January 16, according to Miss Lyon,

> Ashcroft came to dine and for cards. We played Hearts until after 3 in the morning, and the King got drunk. He sailed around the room trying to reach the door and landing up in the corner by the Joan of Arc. He cast a gay little eye over at me in his unsteady gait, and said "I'm just practicing," as he sailed with light footsteps over to the door, and up to the bath room. Ashcroft began to spill his cards on the floor, and I picked up a discard of 27 cards and tried to arrange it as my hand—so much for the whole quart of scotch they—we—drank.

The following night Paine came for billiards, and at two-thirty in the morning Isabel

> wakened to hear the billiard-bang, and went down to find the King playing in a drunken haze. He was trying to drown out the chill, and couldn't move without reeling. It was a great thing to see. . . . It was wonderful to see the King pick up a ball and fondle it, and then try to hit it with his cue and be unable to touch it; but he swore splendidly. AB left the room and I gently took the King's cue away, and led him up to his room. He staggered and hit his head against one of the little angels on his bed post, and grabbed his dear head with a volley of oaths.

Although such entries in Miss Lyon's diary were rare, others signaled Clemens' increasing infirmity. On March 6, Miss Lyon came on him in the billiard room of their Hamilton, Bermuda, hotel,

"pale as death, leaning over the table, and the young German rubbing the back of his head. . . . It had been just a sudden 'crick in his neck,' and the pain is always so acute with him that it makes him weak." On April 23, while giving a curtain speech at the Children's Theater, Clemens suffered a memory lapse, "miscalled words, and seemed to have great difficulty in holding his thoughts together." Later in the year he suffered what he called a "sunstroke," which produced attacks of nausea and resulted in another memory loss.

Perhaps also somehow associated with his increasing age was his constant and almost compulsive interest in little girls. On his first trip to Bermuda in 1908 he made a close friend of Margaret Blackmer; on the second, he discovered Irene Gerken. As Miss Lyon described him, "his first interest when he goes to a new place is to find little girls" and "off he goes with a flash when he sees a new pair of slim little legs appear; and if the little girl wears butterfly bows of ribbon on the back of her head then his delirium is complete." He organized this "harem" into the Aquarium Club and gave each member an angel-fish pin. Clara was appointed the "Mother Superior" and Miss Lyon "The Chatelaine" of the group, and the list of the M.A.'s (Members of the Aquarium) swelled to a dozen. Clemens transcribed their names into his notebook—Dorothy Butes, Dorothy Quick, Dorothy Harvey, Dorothy Sturgis, Hellen Martin, Helen Allen, Irene Gerken, Margaret Blackmer, Louise Paine, Frances Nunnally, Jean Spurr, and Marjorie Breckenridge—careful to note the girls' ages, eleven and a half to seventeen years, averaging thirteen years. They visited him in a steady stream throughout 1908, but less frequently than his letters implored them to.

The best measure of his preoccupation was the energy and emotion which he poured into his letters to the angel fish. Of all the letters Clemens is now known to have written in 1908, ninety-four were to Members of the Aquarium—almost half the total correspondence. Almost always they were long, chatty, childlike letters, frequently composed over a number of days. All pleaded for visits. A large part of his eagerness for such company was

revealed by Mrs. H. K. Blackmer's letter arranging a visit by her daughter: "I'm sure you will think that she resembles more than ever your dear Susy." It seems inescapably true that Clemens was immersing himself in a milieu of small girls who were preferable to the adults who surrounded him. While he was diverting himself with contrived nostalgia, each of the adults around him was shattering under the strain of conflicting self-interests.

<div style="text-align:center">v</div>

Jean was adamant that she must be allowed to leave Katonah. On January 9, 1908, she and two sisters, Edith and Mildred Cowles, who were to serve as nurses, moved into a house at 57 Maple Avenue, Greenwich, Connecticut. They were accompanied by Jean's young friend Marguerite Schmidt, who may also have been a patient at Katonah. Miss Lyon and Clemens went to meet the quartet at the New York City station en route to the new cottage: "Poor Jean looks very very ill," Miss Lyon recorded. "She is so white and her once beautiful face is so drawn; her fingers have a curious movement. She is like a drooping lily." But the house at Greenwich shortly proved as unsatisfactory as Katonah, and an unidentifiable writer to Isabel blamed Clemens himself:

> We have been sore, though, at your king, for what has looked from outside like indifference about lonesome and afflicted and often misunderstood (??) brave pitiable beautiful Jean.

Miss Lyon replied:

> . . . That you should be sore with my King whose great wealth of love for Jean was never understood by *her*, could make me sad. . . .
> People have come to me and said, "Oh, do you know the cruel things that Jean is saying of her father and of her sister?" Jean has said to me

and to Clara many times that she doesn't want
her father to see her. . . . I have not told him
that Jean has had a serious return of her malady
since making the change [from Katonah to
Greenwich], for it depresses him for days. . . .
Two letters will come in the same mail—one to
me, one to the King—the one to me will be sweet
and affectionate, the one to the King will be full
of complaints of me and cruel accusations. But
we know.

On March 23, Clemens wrote compassionately to Jean:

I hope you will find a place that will be en-
tirely satisfactory to you and your friends—but be
sure it is close to New York, because I want you
to be near Dr. Peterson, and also near enough
for me to see you, and I can't stand long land-
journeys. However, you'll find the right place,
no doubt. When you think you have found it,
submit it to Dr. Peterson, and if it satisfies him
it will satisfy me.

On March 26, Dr. Peterson recommended to Miss Lyon that the
four girls might consider Gloucester, Massachusetts, as an alterna-
tive to Greenwich, and on April 18 Miss Lyon went there with
Edith Cowles and selected a cottage for the group.

Shortly after Clemens and Ashcroft visited Jean at Greenwich
on April 24, the girls moved to Gloucester, and her father again
hoped vainly for her happiness:

Jean dear, welcome to your new home, and
happiness therein! In earlier days I would not
have expected you to be otherwise than unhappy
in a new and strange home, but your spirit and
your philosophy have undergone great and be-
neficent improvement in these later days. . . . In
a word . . . the fine and fortunate disposition
you were born with is again in the ascendant—
and long may it keep its supremacy!

Unfortunately, the supremacy was short-lived.

When Jean apparently implied that the truth about her un-happiness was being kept from her father, Clemens was quite openly unimpressed:

> Evidently, there is something that has been kept from me—but that is right, and as it should be, unless it is something that I could remedy. Clara, Miss Lyon and Mr. Paine keep all sorts of distresses from me, and I am very thankful for it—distresses which they are aware I could not remedy, I mean. They know I desire this; for I am taking my holiday, now after 60 years of work and struggle and worry and vexation.

Indeed, when he planned a visit to Gloucester in June 1908, he declined Jean's insistent requests that he remain for several days: "I should like to tarry with you a considerable spell, but Dr. Peterson will not allow that. For your good he will restrict me to hours, not days." Then Jean tried to get a commitment to an overnight stay, but her father repeated his refusal:

> Certainly it *is* a pity that I can't stay all night in your house, but your health is *the* important thing, and I must *help* Dr. Peterson in his good work, and not mar it and hinder it by going counter to his judgment and commands.

Unable to enlist her father's sympathy or interest in any other way, Jean used Miss Lyon as an intermediary. Jean's long, charm-ing, frank, and confidential letters to Isabel, whom Jean called "Dear Lioness," catalogue some of the dilemmas Clemens himself was not interested in. The house in Gloucester was too small, Edith Cowles was terrifying both Jean and Marguerite Schmidt (whom Jean called Bébé), Mildred Cowles was threatening to jump off the rocks along the shore, and the accounting of money spent by the Cowles girls was haphazard and suspect. Clemens commented on the evaporated hopes for the new environment:

> I am disappointed, distressed, and low-spirited,
> for that dream of yours and mine has come to
> nothing. . . . I wish I could situate you exactly
> to your liking, dear child, how gladly I would
> do it. And I wish I could take your malady,
> and rid you of it for always.

It was an unusual expression of warmth and sympathy.

But when Clemens devised a new plan for Jean, she was "delighted and distressed, both. I had hoped to be with him [her father] this winter," but she and Bébé and Anna Sterritt were to be sent to Berlin instead. "Is it positively *settled* that I must go to Berlin?" she asked Miss Lyon. "I have a dread of it. I did *so* want to be in Redding." Dr. Peterson told Isabel that Jean was "expostulating against going to Germany, but I will write her that she must do so for the sake of her future." Jean was not reassured:

> I begged for an idea of how long I should have
> to stay over there (being as how I'm scared) and
> he [Peterson] said 6 or 8 months—that he felt
> sure I could return next summer. Now don't
> scare me, dear, into believing it may be longer!
> I can't stay away from father longer than that.

In spite of these repeated requests to be with her father, when Clemens told Mary Rogers of his younger daughter's departure for Berlin, he added, "and she is glad, for she likes Germany and the language."

Jean was solicitous about her drain on the family budget. She was frequently compelled to ask for additional money—always from Miss Lyon—and she once told the secretary:

> Of course with Father's money, I should be es-
> pecially careful. I feel very keenly all that he is
> doing for me and I have felt before that I have
> been too much of an expense, therefore I shall
> try above everything to keep our expenses down.

Clemens himself tried to persuade Jean not to "trouble about those financial matters; there will be no occasion for that."

Unlike Jean, Clara was not troubled in the least at her financial drain on her father's income. Clara and Clemens continued their professional rivalry in 1908. He had always teased her about her attempts to establish a career for herself without the benefit of being "Mark Twain's daughter," perfectly aware that his joking was "a vexation for her which was not wholly fictitious." But he continued to needle his older daughter about her inability "in the matter of dethroning me." And when Clara gave a recital at 21 Fifth Avenue on January 7, 1908, Isabel Lyon noted that

> The King didn't come down until the music was over, for he doesn't like a drawing room performance; but he listened over the ballusters, and I heard him gently clicking the billiard balls around in between times.

Clara continued to sing, on February 6 and at a large musicale on February 13, always accompanied by Will Wark and a violinist, Miss Marie Nicols. On May 16, 1908, the trio sailed on the *Caronia* for London. Clara made her English debut at Queen's Hall in June and gave another recital at Bechstein Hall on June 16. Both Clara and Wark wrote to Miss Lyon, whom they called "Nana Sing," explaining their expenses and asking for more money. (Ashcroft had told Isabel, during Clara's spring tour, "The good ship Clara Clemens ran ashore yesterday on the No Money shoals, while bound South. Cost of salvage, $300., which please remit.") Within a month of her arrival in England, Zocth Freeman the banker told Miss Lyon nervously, "We have to-day issued the *fourth* letter of credit for Miss Clara Clemens in answer to her cable asking for a renewal."

vi

Miss Lyon was involved in problems in early 1908 that were even more serious than Jean's or Clara's. She and Paine had become so antagonistic to each other that open warfare almost broke out.

The conflict originated over the possession and use of Clemens'
letters in Paine's biography. In January 1908 Samuel Moffett
called at 21 Fifth Avenue and told Miss Lyon,

> when I said the King was distressed to know
> that Paine had copied quantities of the King's
> early letters, that Paine gave him to understand
> that it was the King's particular wish that he
> should have them. The King said last night that
> the next thing Paine would be getting letters
> from Howells, and he proceeded to write Mr.
> Howells asking him not to comply.

But when Clemens asked Howells to withhold letters from Paine's
inspection, Howells replied that "your wish about your letters
comes, I am sorry to say, two months too late."

Miss Lyon wrote Paine her own views on the situation:

> The King has been talking about the volume of
> letters that Clara is going to compile, and asking
> for some old letters. I went up to the trunk tray
> that was in your room and found that some of
> the letters are gone. Have you taken them?

She felt, understandably, that since she and Clara were to edit
Clemens' letters, she was responsible for safeguarding the docu-
ments. On February 26, the distressed secretary telephoned

> Tino [a nickname for Paine] in Redding . . . to
> ask about letters that I am missing and that the
> King and Santa would hold me responsible for.
> He was cross and answered in a burst of ill tem-
> per that he had many letters and would take
> them when he wanted to. This is not quite right
> of Tino—and is a new and regrettable attitude.

Paine wrote Isabel a letter defending his urgent need to have full
access to all materials available in order to write the biography on
which he had invested two years and, he claimed, over $8,000, and
pointing out that brief excerpts from letters in his volume would

"do no more than whet the public appetite for her [Clara's] volume complete."

Clearly Paine and Miss Lyon were developing a serious conflict of interest regarding Clemens. The situation might have resolved itself, but later in 1908 another factor was added:

> Ashcroft came to my room with me and told me —after questioning me about Paine's friendship for me—that coming up in the train on Friday Paine sat with him and talked against me. Said that I am ruining my mentality, etc. with drugs, fenacetine—Why I can't even spell the word.

Phenacetine was an especially dramatic drug for Paine to accuse Miss Lyon of using. Clemens had blamed the destruction of his nephew Charles L. Webster on his addiction to it. In an autobiographical dictation that Paine could have overheard, Clemens remembered that Webster "took this drug with increasing frequency and in increasing quantity. It stupefied him and he went about as one in a dream. . . . In his condition, he was not responsible for his acts."

Miss Lyon was impressively responsible. Clara's and Jean's confidences to her and their expressions of affection for her suggest utter serenity. "You certainly have too much on your shoulders," one letter from Clara sympathized; "you poor dear good sweet kind courageous faithful Nana!" Another apologized when Clara "screamed to you for whiskey" and ended, "Most lovingly and affectionately and fondly and faithfully." But Isabel was apprehensive, nevertheless.

Her work and supervision of the construction at Redding were phenomenal. To accommodate Clara's expectation of a "suite" for herself, a loggia wing had to be added to the plans, beginning in February 1908, at an additional cost of $4,100. Miss Lyon selected tiles, gas fittings, a Cupid statue for the fountain, the Japanese burlap and grass cloth which was used instead of wallpaper in Clemens' rooms, and approved the payment of all the bills for a home which ultimately cost over $45,000. She received

the progress reports from Sunderland and Lounsbury and in-
spected the site personally on April 24 and 30. Clemens told
Dorothy Quick:

> Miss Lyon is working very hard, these days,
> getting the new house up-country ready. . . .
> She has been at it night and day, the past week,
> and has gotten all the furniture and the orches-
> trelle and a billiard table in, at last.

Miss Lyon earned her rare vacations, like the month-long stay in
Bermuda in the spring of 1908.

vii

That trip was recorded by Elizabeth Wallace, dean of women at
the University of Chicago, who was wintering in Hamilton. Miss
Wallace had been in Bermuda for Clemens' earlier brief trip with
Ashcroft, whom she nicknamed "The Pilot Fish" for his solicitous
attention to Clemens. But the longer trip—Clemens, Miss Lyon,
Henry Rogers, and Rogers' son-in-law W. E. Benjamin—allowed
Miss Wallace to meet an even more faithful retainer than Ash-
croft. "This time," she recorded,

> no Pilot Fish conducted him but instead a black
> eyed black haired Italian looking little woman
> who hovers about him with the tender care of a
> mother and daughter combined. This is the
> Little Secretary of the King and my heart's doors
> were open for her to come in and she came in
> and will remain forever as *Caranana*. With Mr.
> Clemens and Caranana came a tall distinguished
> looking man with a fine cut profile and clear
> young complexion. It was Mr. Rogers.

Miss Wallace described Clemens' fascination for little girls: "If a
child of ten or twelve happens to be anywhere within the radius of
his glance he is inevitably sure of seeing her":

Then begins the most delightful flirtation. The King nods—if that is not effective he beckons with his hand and sometimes he goes up to the child and makes a remark that seems to continue a conversation broken off at some remoter period. He is nearly always sure to win their hearts and the most familiar sight is to see him playing cards or billiards with a Margaret or an Irene or a Dorothy.

She reported, too, the warm and friendly rivalry that marked Clemens' friendship with Rogers:

One day as the Rajah came in to the dining room in his slow stately manner, the King who was already seated at the table said, "There he comes just like Gibbs' Lighthouse, stiff and tall turning his lights from side to side." The kindly simile was perfect in a way and I never afterwards saw the Rajah bearing down upon us without seeing the resemblance. The Rajah and the King love each other dearly and manifest their affection by abusing each other whenever the occasion offers and when it doesn't making the opportunity themselves. Our favorite amusement of an evening is to play hearts and the Secretary, who always keeps score, writes our names thus, The Author, The Rajah, The Dean, The Secretary. The Author usually prefaces the game by saying to the Rajah in a tone of kindly remonstrance "Now I hope you are not going to show your disagreeable disposition tonight. Do try to show us some pleasant sides of your character." The Rajah with a perfectly serious face replies in the same vein and this is kept up throughout the evening so skillfully that the Secretary and the Dean never grow weary, on the contrary they are convulsed with silent mirth. They—the King and the Rajah—both hold to the theory that the other would be a hopeless out-

cast were it not for his regenerating influence
and they assume a high moral tone when they
reason with one another.

Tranquility and indolence were soon to be replaced, and high
good humor would depart with Clemens' move to his Redding
home.

On June 3, Clemens changed the name of the nearly complete
dwelling from "Autobiography House" to "Innocents at Home"
and later in 1908 rechristened it, at Clara's insistence, "Storm-
field." He moved into the house on June 18 and was instantly
delighted with it. He gave total credit to Miss Lyon for its success.
When Archibald Henderson submitted a manuscript of an article
to Clemens, Ashcroft passed along an emendation: "The house—in
its design and decorations—is *totally* a product of Miss Lyon's
mind, and Mr. Clemens desires that credit be given her." To
Clara, Clemens' praise of Stormfield was either brutal or com-
pletely unthinking: "I do so delight in this home that the thought
of ever going back to that crude and tasteless New York barn,"
which Clara had herself decorated, "even to stay overnight, revolts
me."

Clara, still in Europe when her father moved into his new
home, may have had another cause for resentment of Isabel. Wark
explained that after the tour, "we are planning now to go to
France and settle down in some cheap country place (probably
Barbizon) in about two weeks." Clara confided to Miss Lyon that
"dear old W. is more wonderful all the time but I can't bear the
many many months still that separate us from freedom and frank
expression of the truth." Clara was cryptic, but just over two
months later, on September 7, 1908, the New York *World* was
not: "The engagement of his daughter, Clara, to Mr. Charles E.
Wark of this city, has been rumored," it claimed. "Miss Clemens
has been travelling in Europe for some months with a party of
friends. In the party is Mr. Wark" (p. 2) . Possibly Clara believed
that Isabel had "leaked" the rumor, with its connotation of dubi-
ous propriety, to the paper.

Perhaps a conflict was inevitable. As soon as Clara returned to the United States, they had a violent disagreement about the new home. Miss Lyon wrote in her diary:

> Santa misunderstood all my efforts in working over the house. My anxiety over the finishings, my interest in my search for the right thing for the King's house has all been misinterpreted, and the child says I am trying to ignore her. All my effort has been to please her, to keep her from the dreary search of hours and hours to find the right thing, or shape or color.

Two days later, Miss Lyon concluded that "somebody has put all these sickening ideas into Santa's head, and I feel that my interest in the house is dead forever."

The new house in which Miss Lyon's interest was dead was a substantial Italian villa, even to the reproductions of della Robbia figures imbedded in the walls. Clemens' own rooms, including a billiard room that was also the headquarters for the girls of the Aquarium, were on the ground floor, together with an enclosed loggia under Clara's suite and "Nightingale Cage" sleeping porch. A living room, dining room, kitchen, and an office for Miss Lyon were also on the ground floor. Upstairs were Clara's suite, her original rooms with bath, a bedroom with a connecting maid's room and bath ostensibly for Jean, four guest bedrooms, and three servants' bedrooms with bath. The terraced and landscaped grounds provided views for miles, and glass panes enclosed the loggia arches so that it could be used in winter. Clemens was so pleased and proud of his new home that in August he canceled his lease at 21 Fifth Avenue and settled into Stormfield permanently.

Nearby, in addition to the Paines, were Jeannette Gilder, Ida Tarbell, Dan Beard, and several other friends, a fledgling artists' colony. The Redding populace stood in awe of its new inhabitant—for whom even the New York trains would provide a special stop at the Redding station on the 4:15.

Miss Lyon moved into Stormfield herself—into the rooms Clara

had rejected. Her mother came from Farmington to the Lobster Pot cottage, and life should have been satisfactory. But Miss Lyon, who continued to "settle-in" and "shake-down" the Stormfield staff for weeks, was apprehensively nervous. In September she wrote, "The burden of this house is heavily on my shoulders. . . . I keep it there rather than in my heart *too* securely for if it were, or when it is taken from me, all the bleeding heart of me would be torn out with it."

Added to her already overwhelming duties, she now had the task of closing and dismantling the house at 21 Fifth Avenue. Her nervous and exhausted condition was reflected in her memories of the years there:

> In that house I saw the terrible sorrow and grief of the King, after Mrs. Clemens's death, and I saw the crying rage of servants dismissed by Jean and Clara. I saw Jean in her convulsions, and I saw Clara in her agony, and in her illnesses, and in her strugglings with her career, and in her hates and fierce lovings. And while my heart was full of loving for all of them, there was a long long lack of peace, and the stairs I climbed were often pitifully weary ones.

Among the few consolations for Miss Lyon was her increasing affection for Ashcroft, who willingly assisted her in the endless duties of her office.

In August 1908 the "sunstroke" that Clemens suffered at the funeral of Samuel Moffett produced in Miss Lyon a response that was distinctly proprietary in its sense of dedication. She wrote in her diary that on August 6, 1908

> Col. Harvey and I had a talk about a literary executor for the King and I told him how nearly Paine had called that for himself. Now Colonel Harvey is to do the editing of the Biog. Benares [her nickname for Ashcroft] and I have a moral obligation, now, in looking after the King. I shall

> not leave him for an hour unless Benares or an-
> other as good is here to look after him, and to-
> gether we must uphold him in our spiritual
> arms. The plan was for me to take Jean to Ger-
> many, but I must not go away from the King,
> ever.

She wrote Harriet Whitmore Enders, too:

> Colonel Harvey . . . and the 2 doctors . . . have
> vested me with the high moral obligation of
> never leaving the King alone again. And so some
> days I feel as if I were moving through this
> house with my spirit hands folded in prayer that
> I may be the right woman in the right place.
> Ashcroft will stand by me, and with me, for to
> *him* the obligation is the same.

Perhaps it is only coincidence that the same week Miss Lyon fired Miss Hobby, the stenographer brought into the household by Paine, "so that expense is closed up." She promptly replaced Paine's ally with a new stenographer, Miss Mary L. Howden, who answered an advertisement in September, became known as "Miss Mollie" in the household, and began almost immediately answering the deluge of letters that Clemens received.

A few days after Miss Lyon's pledge of allegiance, Clemens confirmed in a letter to Harvey the restrictions he wanted placed on Paine: The biographer would have to allow Harvey to exercise final approval and editorial veto of the biography, would have to limit his quotations from unpublished letters to 10,000 words and print the complete texts of no more than two or three letters in each volume of the biography, but would be allowed to "sprinkle" short quotations from letters with "considerable freedom" in his book.

Another incident with Paine and the unauthorized possession of letters came to light in October. On the fifteenth, Isabel Lyon

> discovered another of AB's indiscretions. He has
> had letters written from Mrs. Clemens to Mrs.

> Crane in his possession for over a year. The
> King's anger burned furiously, so he bade me go
> to the telephone and demand those letters. I did
> so—with Benar standing beside me to courage me
> up, and Paine said "certainly."

Paine appeared to be vanquished and Miss Lyon the victor in
their power struggle, with Ashcroft on her side. But Clara
Clemens had not yet chosen to exert her authority over her father.

viii

Part of Miss Lyon's self-imposed obligation was to keep Clemens
insulated from the intrigues and incriminations which surrounded
him, as much as possible; and the alliances and antagonisms of the
various factions escaped his notice almost entirely in mid-1908 as
he continued his eternal social pace. Paine lists the various func-
tions at which Clemens appeared: the Cartoonists' dinner, a Book-
sellers' banquet, a celebration of Queen Victoria's 104th birthday,
the dedication ceremonies of City College. In late June Lillian
Aldrich directed the dedication ceremonies of the Thomas Bailey
Aldrich Memorial Museum at Portsmouth, New Hampshire,
which Clemens felt compelled to attend. But he was so infuriated
at the mistress of the occasion, that "strange and vanity-devoured,
detestable woman," that he returned to Stormfield to dictate a
withering assault on Mrs. Aldrich for his autobiography. But in
1908 even the autobiography slowed down almost to a halt. In the
entire year there were only thirty-five autobiographical dictations,
and most of them only several hundred words in length. The
majority were annotations for a personal diary, in effect. The trips
to Bermuda and descriptions of various angel fish accounted for
five dictations (February 12 to 14, April 16 to 17) ; Mrs. Aldrich
earned five days of spectacular venom for her pretentious but
miserly behavior at her husband's memorial (July 3, 4, 7, 8, and
9) ; and two burglars at Stormfield provided copy for three days
(October 6, November 12, and December 8). Except for these

spurts of interest, nothing could capture Clemens' attention for longer than two consecutive days. If the dictations were still an accurate reflection of Mark Twain's mind, it was a mind characterized by aimless wandering and vacancy.

In August, when Moffett drowned, Clemens left Redding for the funeral, returning physically and emotionally shaken. After that excursion he rarely left the grounds of his new home. But guests poured in for week-long stays, and diversions with the angel fish and with plans for a Mark Twain Library in Redding were the sort of distractions his court arranged to keep him amused and pacified. Dorothy Quick and her mother, the Harper & Brothers staff, the Whitmores, and a dozen of the new neighbors visited. Clara came on September 8 with Will Wark, setting up a pattern of frequent visits. Ashcroft spent most weekends at Stormfield working on business plans. Clemens went to visit Colonel Harvey at Deal Beach, New Jersey, to discuss yet one more copyright scheme. And on the night of September 18, two burglars broke into the kitchen of the mansion, stealing silverware and creating lasting side effects. Isabel heard the intruders and surprised them as she descended the stairs to investigate. Claude Benchotte, a French butler, fired several shots; and Wark, Lounsbury, and the sheriff chased the two thieves, capturing them several hours later. The episode and ensuing trial were a severe strain to all the participants; but the ladies and servants suffered most. "Clara left for New York promptly & never wants to sleep in the house again. Miss Lyon & two of the maids will soon go away for a week" to recuperate, Clemens told Howells. Clara found an apartment at 17 Livingston Place in Stuyvesant Square and moved in on October 2.

After contemplating the purchase of a ten-dollar bulldog for protection, Clemens decided to secure the house with a burglar alarm, which was installed in early October. But the maids—indeed, all of the servants—were not reassured by the system. As a result of the burglary and the remoteness of Stormfield, the entire corps quit. It became Miss Lyon's job to find replacements. Teresa and Giuseppe Cherubini, the old Italian emigrees who had come with the Clemenses back to the United States in 1904, were re-

hired. A neighbor lad, Horace Hazen, offered himself as butler and was accepted. Miss Lyon was unable to depart from Stormfield for the rest she needed:

> There is such confusion over the servants, and the confusion lies not in the servant department, but in a part of the house that gives itself credit for a high line of conduct. . . . I dared not leave this house to a *certain* derangement, and a possible clearing out of the present working force. The servants do not want more than one head—hence the wearying wearying confusion.

A few days later she recorded that she was deep in "the mud of criticism—no, misunderstandings fired by C.C." Miss Lyon may well have voiced publicly as well as in the privacy of her diary her doubts about the propriety of Clara's behavior with Will Wark in spite of giving herself "credit for a high line of conduct." Clara was shortly to believe, at any rate, that Miss Lyon had circulated stories impugning her reputation.

Clemens, meanwhile, was entertained by the trial in Danbury of the two Stormfield burglars. He appeared, testified, posed with an automatic pistol, lectured, preened—he might well have pleaded guilty himself if it had assured him another day's headlines.

ix

Clemens was becoming so uninterested in routine financial affairs that Ashcroft as principal business adviser took a number of highly significant legal steps to relieve Clemens of the burden of such matters. An ornate organizational reshaping of Plasmon was put into effect. A United States auctioneer, Charles Shongood, liquidated the defunct Plasmon Company in 1908, and the Plasmon Milk Products Company was formed. Clemens was made president, Ashcroft was secretary and treasurer, and Mansfield Hobbs, an attorney friend of Ashcroft's, was vice-president. The London

Plasmon syndicate was to appoint a director to the American company's board and to supplement Clemens' $35,000 capital with an additional $20,000. By late 1908 the new company was about to attempt a resurrection, and Clemens was to ship Ashcroft to England at year's end to try to convince "Sir Thomas Lipton to come to a decision as to whether he would act as our selling agent" in the United States.

Ashcroft also had Hobbs draw up the documents incorporating the Mark Twain Company, with $5,000 capital stock, the organizational papers being filed on December 22, 1908. Clemens, Ashcroft, and Miss Lyon were the original officers of the company, but Ashcroft later mentioned that Jervis Langdon, Edward Loomis, and Zoeth Freeman were directors. Clemens executed a document on the incorporation of the company, assigning and transferring all his literary rights to it.

But he signed another legal form in the late fall of 1908 which he was himself to call

> the most amazing document that has seen the light since the Middle Ages. It bears date Nov. 14 last, and is a General Power of Attorney which hands me and all I own and all I ever *shall* own over to Ashcroft and Miss Lyon. Until June 1 [1909] I had never heard of that paper—yet I *signed* it.

However murky his recollection of signing the document (and he was to insist for some time that the signature was a forgery), his sober evaluation of its power was correct.

On November 14, 1908 (Miss Lyon was ill in bed on that date) Clemens appointed Ashcroft and Miss Lyon

> my true and lawful attorneys . . . to exercise a general supervision over all my affairs and to take charge of and manage all my property both real and personal . . . ; to lease, sell and convey any and all real property . . . ; to remand, receive and collect all dividends, interests and

moneys due and payable to . . . me; . . . to
sell, assign and transfer any and all stocks, bonds
and mortgages belonging or which may at any
time belong to me; to change any or all of my
investments and to make any investment of any
or all of the moneys belonging to me; to draw
checks or drafts upon any banks, banker or Trust
Company or any financial institution with which
or whom I have or may at any time hereafter
have moneys on deposit or to my credit.

It was comprehensive. And Clemens did indisputably sign it. Just
as indisputable is that Ashcroft had almost seven months' time
between the assigning and revoking of this power of attorney to
use it for personal gain. But whatever Clemens' hysterical suspi-
cions, Ashcroft did not exploit his total authority over Clemens'
property for illegal purposes.

 x

The guests continued to flood into Stormfield in such a stream
that Clemens was to say, "I am keeping hotel, and no train comes
or goes without bringing me a guest or robbing me of one."
Harvey brought Lord Northcliffe; Mr. and Mrs. Doubleday came
overnight. Elizabeth Wallace arrived from Chicago for Thanksgiv-
ing and was met at the station by Ashcroft with his hair tied up in
pink bows. "Caranana" had decorated him especially for her
arrival. Miss Wallace and Clemens danced a grand march to
Ashcroft's accompaniment on the orchestrelle, and the festivities
in general sounded like a pastoral farce.
 Jean provided a single inharmonious note. She, Anna, and
Marguerite Schmidt had boarded the *Pretoria* for Germany on
September 26, 1908. After getting settled, Jean explained to Miss
Lyon in detail the need for additional money to cover unantici-
pated expenses. Anna Sterritt angered Jean by saying "some
idiotic and impudent things about Bébé which were caused by

imagination, ignorance and perhaps a tinge of jealousy." But she was pleased with her progress under Professor Hofrath von Reuvers and was convinced he could cure her. She enrolled in a lecture course on Faust, made many friends among the American colony, and began a round of teas and luncheons. She even delivered her father's ghost story, "The Golden Arm," successfully to a charity benefit. She mailed Christmas presents for her father, Clara, and Miss Lyon on December 11. Then, without warning or explanation, she received a cablegram from Redding on December 17:

> You sail January ninth steamer Pennsylvania passage prepaid. Send Marguerite home. Dont cable.
>
> Father.

Why Jean was recalled from the only pleasant life she had known since the summer of 1905—to be sequestered at Unkeway Farm on Babylon, Long Island—why she was taken from the care of Professor von Reuvers, who appeared to be making successful efforts for her, and why she was suddenly separated from the teenage girl Marguerite Schmidt who was her closest friend remain mysteries. Nowhere in the extant documents or correspondence does Clemens mention a decision to bring Jean home after three months in Berlin rather than the six or eight that Dr. Peterson had recommended. The following year Clemens claimed that

> Jean was doubtful of the Berlin doctor, and sent home one of his prescriptions. Dr. Peterson said, "This will not do; order her home at once." Which we did, by cable. Jean responded with a cable saying she was well enough and asking leave to remain in Berlin at her own expense and support herself by teaching English. This grace was denied her. I would have denied it myself if I had known about it.

The statement is full of peculiar inconsistencies. If Jean was ordered home for medical reasons, why was it "graceless" to refuse

her permission to remain in Germany? And why would Clemens have agreed with the decision if he thought it was graceless? And why should he not have known about so important a decision, which could hardly have been kept from him once Jean returned to the United States? Nothing in the surviving record indicates that Miss Lyon was instrumental in keeping father and daughter apart, and if that were her intention, she would surely not have vetoed Jean's plea to stay in Berlin. Possibly the secretary used her influence with Dr. Peterson, affecting his decision to restrict the contact between Jean and her father; and indisputably Miss Lyon was terrified, with reason, of the unpredictable quirks in Jean's behavior. In addition, she was in close control of the household purse strings, and Jean was required in almost every communication to account for her expenses and to ask for additional funds. But her letters to "Dear Lioness" were always affectionate and cordial.

In 1909 Paine was to write Clemens, "Miss Lyon told Miss Gordon 'Jean Clemens and I can never live under the same roof, which means that she can never come home.' " On the bottom of this note Clemens commented, "To think—3 'friends' of mine knew of this and never reported it to me. Or to Clara?" No extant documents support Paine's claim.

For the present, however, the festivities continued through the end of 1908. Gabrilowitsch showed up in Redding on December 18 for a two-week stay, after Clemens assured Clara that she and "Gossip" would be welcome. Archibald Henderson arrived with the photographer Coburn; Gabrilowitsch played on the piano when no one was playing on the orchestrelle and sat with Clemens while Miss Lyon left to confer with Dr. Peterson about a new residence for Jean.

Ashcroft traveled back and forth almost daily. Clara was involved with a nominal "tour" under the direction of her new manager, George M. Robinson, who scheduled her concerts and recitals for a $300 monthly salary. But with Gabrilowitsch and Wark both paying her their attention, the singing schedule was erratic.

Even though Ashcroft was preparing to leave for England on Plasmon business—Miss Lyon's life had "lost something vital"—and even though Paine was about to embark on a trip to the Mediterranean to visit the *Quaker City* scenes from *Innocents Abroad,* it was a jolly Christmas. Robert Collier played an immense practical joke on the entire household by announcing in early December that he was sending Clemens a baby elephant for a holiday present. A "trainer" and a ton of hay followed—to be climaxed by a large wicker elephant which brought mixed joy and relief to the residents of Stormfield. Billie Burke came for a visit, and most of the household spent their time frolicking in the snow among the hills surrounding Stormfield. But it was the eye of the storm that was passing over Redding.

The peaceful interlude continued through January of 1909. Miss Lyon, speaking for Clemens, wrote Archibald Henderson that no assistance could be given his proposed biography of Mark Twain because Paine's exclusive rights must be honored. In contradiction, however, Ashcroft told Henderson that Miss Lyon was herself the literary executor of Clemens' estate. Clemens and Isabel traveled to New York to spend the latter part of January as the guests of the Robert Colliers. Originally, they planned to remain only from the twentieth through the twenty-third, but on the thirty-first Clemens told Dorothy Sturgis that he had remained ten days in order to celebrate Henry Rogers' birthday.

Clemens was diverted early in the year when he received a set of galleys of a book on Bacon by William S. Booth from John Macy and went "strenuously at work on an article taking sides in the Bacon–Shakespeare controversy." Even Miss Lyon attempted to dissuade him from the project: "His attack is not gentle, and not very clever," she said. But his interest kept up into early March 1909, when he told Jean:

> I am having a good time all by myself dictat-
> ing to the stenographer (Autobiography) a long
> day-after-day scoff at everybody who is ignorant
> enough and stupid enough to go on believing

Shakespeare ever wrote a play or a poem in his
life.

He subtitled the product of his enthusiasm as "From My Auto-
biography"; but *Is Shakespeare Dead?* exists both as a holograph
manuscript and in several typescript versions which Mark Twain
incorporated into the autobiographical sequence. On the first page
of the longhand first draft he wrote, *"Dictated Feb. 13, 1909."* It
was a simplistic book which took advantage of the sophisticated
arguments of George Greenwood's *The Shakespeare Problem Re-
stated* to make comic points about the dearth of biographical data
concerning Shakespeare. Greenwood was not amused, for in Mark
Twain's haste to publish his volume and in his growing absent-
mindedness, he had forgotten to give proper credit to Green-
wood's volume—from which he had quoted twenty-two pages. The
New York *Times* (June 9 and 10, 1909) and other papers at-
tempted to make sensational news of the literary theft, but Mark
Twain simply yawned and claimed that the scandal would benefit
the sale of Greenwood's book more than anything else would have.
He later claimed that he had obtained the permission of the New
York but not the London publisher and that the latter had caused
the embarrassment without checking into the matter.

Many years later Miss Lyon recalled the chagrin that everyone
but Mark Twain felt at the publication of the volume:

> He would wave the MS in grim triumph because
> he could get ahead of Greenwood, for Harpers
> would have to publish it. Harpers did not want
> to publish it, but they were under contract to
> print anything he wrote, and often Duneka and
> Major Leigh were distressed at the letters he
> sent them for immediate publication in Harpers
> Weekly. They were published but made no great
> stir. It was about this time that Colonel Harvey
> said to me: "Can't you get Uncle Mark *not* to
> have these ideas of his made public? His readers
> are not looking for such matter. . . . They want

only the beloved humorous side of him. And the
comment is that he is slipping intellectually."

Certainly the two uninspired brief articles in *Harper's Weekly* in
early 1909, "The New Planet" (January 30) and "A Capable
Humorist" (February 20), support Harvey's position.

<center>xi</center>

Isabel Lyon's health finally broke under the strain of her responsi-
bilities. On February 3, 1909, Clemens reported her "ill in bed
and under contract with the doctor to keep perfectly quiet for ten
days." On the ninth, he told Francesca Nunnally that the secretary
had been ill "these two or three weeks. It is a sort of nervous break-
down, attributable to too much work and care." On February 16
Miss Lyon wrote Hattie Whitmore Enders that Ashcroft (who had
returned from England on February 6) and she were to be
married. "The psychic moment hasn't come yet for telling the
King," she confided; "it won't make any difference in my life work
with the King. I'll stay right here, and Benares will come when he
can to be with us both." On the twenty-third of the month, Isabel,
still seriously unwell, went to Hartford for ten days, accompanied
by her mother. But her departure to the Heublein House to
recuperate proved to be a great strategic error.

Just as Isabel left for Hartford, Clara and her friend Mary
Lawton arrived in Stormfield for a visit. Clara had been persuaded
by Miss Lawton and Dr. Quintard that the financial restrictions
that Miss Lyon had placed on Clara were unwarranted, and she
apparently began insisting to her father that Miss Lyon was
embezzling his money. Clara's nagging had an effect on her father
that was noticeable even to outsiders. Mrs. Paine wrote to her
husband in the Holy Land that the

> poor old man is being driven almost crazy, and
> he said that until three weeks ago he thought he
> was happy and well off, but since then it has

been h—— and that if things did not get better
he would cut his G—— D—— throat—It would
not be surprising what he might do—

Mr. Ashcroft and Miss Lyon are to be mar-
ried!!! and it's a sworn secret just now, but I sup-
pose soon, what can *he* be thinking about but I
suppose they think that is the only way out and
the only thing to do since they have criticized
Clara.

Miss Lyon broke the news to "the King" while she was in Hart-
ford recuperating:

I can't go on alone carrying the dear weight of
wonderful Stormfield direction. Together we can
work for you. And you will have his love joined
with mine, and my love strengthened by his to
stand by you and yours as long as you need us.
. . . So I think, dear beautiful King, that before
I come back to you, we'll go quietly to New
York and be married.

Isabel Lyon apparently destroyed her diary for 1909. Her side of
the hysterical battle with Clara must be conjectured. To begin
with, all evidence indicates that her attempts to economize with
Clemens' money and to restrict Clara's prodigal expenses were
sincerely motivated. Harvey, Leigh, and Clemens himself had all
demanded austerity, and Miss Lyon followed their orders.

In addition, there is reason to believe that financial problems
were only superficial motivations in Clara's attack on Isabel.
Clemens' daughter certainly knew that the way to insure his
alienation against anyone was to charge embezzlement, and in
order to arouse his wrath against his secretary the older daughter
used the charge of misappropriation of his funds.

But underlying the financial charges were moral ones. Miss
Lyon had apparently been willing to point out that some of
Clara's activities with Will Wark were of dubious propriety—
indeed, of the identical sort that had prompted Clemens to with-

draw his support of Gorky and to regret having Elinor Glyn print his convictions about human instincts. Clara was curiously willing to spread the rumor that Miss Lyon "was going about everywhere taking my *reputation* away from me." Clara's reputation appears to have been a subject her father declined to argue over by 1909; and, to do him full justice, any charges Miss Lyon may have made were never a factor in the hostility that Clemens was to feel shortly toward the Ashcrofts. Almost thirty years after her father's death, when Clara hired a private detective to interview Miss Lyon, the former secretary explained that her marriage to Ashcroft was one of convenience:

> . . . She stated that she was the victim of a monstrous injustice; that she was innocent of all the charges made against her. She stated that the "family" and the biographer were jealous of her entirely friendly relation with Mr. C. and that, "to save the good name of Mr. C." and to avoid further trouble, she had taken a husband without loving him. She stated that her marriage was part of a deal whereby she would thus legitimize her standing in the household in consideration of the breaking off of all relations between C.C. and "Will." This deal, originated by Mr. C., who objected strongly to "Will," was honorably carried out by both women.

The logic of the agreement is obscure. But such sexual and moral conflicts were submerged in the more explicit financial accusations.

"Clara's suspicions were aroused by Dr. Quintard. He thought Miss Lyon and Ashcroft ought to be asked to furnish an account of their stewardship" in early March. By the eleventh of that month, Clara had hired an attorney named Jackson to protect her interests and Clemens wrote her protesting her aggressive behavior:

> Miss Lyon came to your mother as secretary, at $50 a month. She has never asked for more.

. . . She could not have been replaced at any
price. . . .

I have no suspicions of her. She was not
trained to business and doubtless has been loose
and unmethodical, but that is all. She has not
been dishonest, even to a penny's worth. All her
impulses are good and fine. . . .

I know Ashcroft and Miss Lyon better and
more intimately than I have ever known anyone
except your mother, and I am quite without sus-
picion of either their honesty or their honor-
ableness.

It was the last friendly appraisal Clemens was to make of Miss
Lyon's honesty.

When Ashcroft heard of Clara's intentions to examine the
household ledgers and account books, he called her and suggested
that the investigation would not be in Clara's own interest because
it would show the enormous sums which had been spent for her
costly and unsuccessful career as a singer. Ashcroft ominously took
four documents to Clemens within the next few days. Two defined
explicitly Ashcroft's duties as an officer of the Mark Twain Com-
pany, which Ashcroft established earlier to protect the writer's
various business interests; and two relieved Miss Lyon of all obli-
gations except those of "social secretary" and substantially raised
her salary to $100 a week. Another established her duties in
preparing Mark Twain's letters for publication, and a "Memo-
randum" recorded the fact that she had been authorized over the
past few years to purchase clothes and to make improvements in
the Lobster Pot cottage for which she was to repay Clemens. These
documents managed to allay Clemens' own doubts, if he had any.
On signing them, he wrote Clara:

Sunday, Mch 14.
Nothing is as it was. Everything is changed.
Sentiment has been wholly eliminated. All things
in this house are now upon a strictly business

basis. All duties are strictly defined, under sev-
eral written contracts, signed before a notary.

Since Isabel's functions were now to be totally social, Clemens
revoked her power of attorney to sign checks for him—a power she
had possessed and exercised since May 7, 1907.

On March 18, 1909, the Reverend Percy Grant married Ash-
croft and Miss Lyon in New York City with, as Clemens put it,
nine persons present if God was there. Clemens himself was there,
anyhow, and the couple, strangely morose and distant according to
Clemens' testimony, made the trip back to Redding in complete
silence. Clemens also noted that the newlyweds chose to occupy
separate bedrooms at Stormfield the night of the wedding.

However jaundiced his view was to become later, Clemens
showed no indication in late March that he was less than com-
pletely satisfied with the Ashcrofts' behavior. And Howells, who
visited Stormfield that spring, reported that the Ashcrofts "watch
over him with tender constancy." Clemens and Ashcroft traveled
to Norfolk, Virginia, on April 3, 1909, to attend the opening of
the railway Rogers had completed the year before. While there,
Ashcroft managed to act strangely over the firing of Horace
Hazen, the young butler hired the preceding autumn. Ashcroft
claimed that Hazen had been fired by Clara after a disagreement
about his wages and produced a letter of resignation from Horace;
later, both Horace and Clara claimed that they had reached a
satisfactory agreement regarding his salary but that Ashcroft had
forced Horace to resign and write a letter saying that Clara had
discharged him. In spite of such peculiar behavior on Ashcroft's
part (intended apparently to throw doubt on Clara's stability),
Clemens said:

> I was not willing to lose Ashcroft. I had sup-
> posed I could not do without either of them, and
> they were quite evidently of that opinion too;
> but Miss Lyon had grown so aggressive, and
> high-handed, and masterly, and fractious, and
> hysterical and insolent of late that if I didn't

> presently turn her out of the house she would
> turn me out.

Even the two Ashcrofts had some curious disagreements about their respective provinces. Isabel told Archibald Henderson on April 10, when the professor asked for biographical information about Clemens, "I have been associated with Mr. Clemens for nearly seven years—most intimately, whereas Mr. Ashcroft has seen him at close range for less than two years."

Clara continued her campaign. She made charges about Miss Lyon's wardrobe—purchased with Clemens' money. Isabel answered the accusations in a letter to Clemens on April 12, convinced that there was "some misunderstanding about the few garments I've bought . . . which . . . Miss Clemens in all sweetness and generosity" had authorized.

On April 15, Clara wrote her father, "You will give Miss Lyon her notice *right away* I hope," and the same day Clemens provided Mrs. Ashcroft with the thirty-day notice that was a part of the March 13 contract. He sent his written notification to the room of his secretary of six years by a maid, who returned to his quarters with a more courteous acknowledgement than he had any right to expect: "Thank you so much for doing in so kind a way, the thing that I have been expecting," Isabel said. "And I now accept my dismissal from your service, to take place any time you shall choose within the month." After a few days of arranging affairs and moving her own belongings, Isabel left Stormfield. Ashcroft came for business matters on April 17, left, and Clemens apparently never saw him again.

xii

The treachery which Clemens finally convinced himself was true depressed him to the point that he recollected an earlier attempt at suicide. Two days after Ashcroft left for the last time, the shaken master of Stormfield

> called to my mind *my* experience of 1866 and I
> told it at dinner. I put the pistol to my head but
> wasn't man enough to pull the trigger.
>
> Many times I have been sorry I did not suc-
> ceed but I was never ashamed of having tried.
> Suicide is the only really sane thing the young or
> the old ever do in this life.

Funereal brooding was perhaps not mere coincidence. When Clara
wrote later about the revelations, she used a strange simile to de-
scribe her feelings: "The shock was so great to me to learn that
such things *could* happen in the world that for a while it seemed as
if nothing much worse had *ever* happened to me and it was no
more surprising than if I had discovered that Jean or Susy was
plotting my death." And in 1940, ninety-year-old Dan Beard
remembered that once the Ashcrofts got Clemens' signature on the
comprehensive power of attorney, "The stage was all set to get rid
of the old man—." There is no substantiation for such a "plot," but
it may well have seemed possible to Clemens and his daughter.

Clara wanted more than the banishment of the Ashcrofts, what-
ever real or imagined plots she believed them capable of, and she
set out to get revenge. In late April, Henry Rogers "had a call
from Clara this morning," in which the daughter unburdened
herself of her suspicions. Rogers told Clemens, "In the last two or
three years I had my suspicions of things, which you in your good
natured way have overlooked." Rogers agreed to supervise an
audit of all the Clemens household books for the preceding two
years, and placed the chore in the hands of Miss A. Watson,
Katharine Harrison's assistant. On the twenty-ninth, Rogers sum-
moned Ashcroft to his office; and by May 4, Ashcroft was prepar-
ing to turn over vouchers and checkbooks to the financial adviser.
But Ashcroft could not resist the temptation to write Clemens a
letter after his first visit with Rogers:

> Mr. Rogers seems to be of the same opinion
> that many of your other friends are, viz: that the
> ghastly treatment accorded to Miss Lyon during
> the past few weeks by a member of your family

> is a mightily poor return for the way in which
> she has, since Mrs. Clemens' death, looked after
> you, your daughters and your affairs. . . . As
> you have already stated, the charges emanated
> from a brain diseased with envy, malice and
> jealousy, and it is only when one forgets this
> fact that one views them seriously.

By the time Ashcroft wrote his indictment, new factors were at
work in the conflict, and the possibility of an amicable settlement
was lost.

xiii

Jean Clemens had disliked her place in Babylon, Long Island, at
first sight. "I hadn't been there ten minutes," she told her father,
"when I telephoned Clara and told her I could not stay there."
She continued:

> I really couldn't write you from Babylon, be-
> cause, as I have already said, I didn't want to
> start complaining as soon as I had gotten back
> and I was so anxious to get away and leading
> such an utterly empty life that I couldn't find
> a thing to write about.

She moved in March to "Wahnfried," a cottage she liked in Mont-
clair, New Jersey, supervised by Miss Edith Clapp, a nurse. She
had still never seen Stormfield by mid-April 1909. Clara had an
interview with Dr. Peterson on the eleventh of that month, and on
the thirteenth Peterson traveled to Stormfield. On the fourteenth,
Clemens and Paine called on the doctor to try to convince him
that Jean's presence at Stormfield would not upset either Jean or
her father—"he was reluctant to believe me. In fact didn't believe
either of us." Peterson finally agreed, full of apprehension, to
allow Jean to make a one-week trial visit to Redding, and Clemens
assured her, "Dear child you will be as welcome as if it were your

mother herself calling you home from exile!" Jean finally wrote her name in the Stormfield Guest Book on April 26, 1909, triumphantly giving her address as "Stormfield." She was never to leave again; indeed, an adjoining 125 acres of land with barns and livestock, called "The Italian Farm," became hers. Ironically, Ashcroft had arranged the purchase of the property for Clemens in February for $4,200 as one of his final transactions in his capacity as business manager; and Jean was to manage it until her death.

With Paine back from his trip to the Holy Land, with Jean at Stormfield, and with Clara directing affairs from 17 Livingston Place, the Ashcrofts were fighting a losing battle in exile. As soon as Isabel was given her notice and had moved into the Lobster Pot—now called "Summerfield"—Clara fired Teresa and Giuseppe because they were representative of the "Lyon faction" and reestablished Claude Benchotte in charge of the household staff.

In early May, Lounsbury provided the further ammunition needed for a final assault on Isabel. Clemens had given her the land and the cottage in 1907 and in late 1908 had offered to lend her the money necessary to renovate the Lobster Pot. According to his later testimony, Miss Lyon had told him the total costs of the work had been $1,500. Clemens wrote off $500 of that amount as a Christmas present to Isabel in 1908, and among the various documents of the March 13, 1909, legal transactions, Ashcroft gave Clemens four notes of $250 each to secure the balance of the debt. But Lounsbury insisted that the work on Summerfield had cost over $3,500, not $1,500. With the same glee that marked his investigations of the Blisses, Dan Slote, Webster, Paige, and the officers of Plasmon in his earlier financial history, Clemens pursued the Ashcrofts with a bookkeeper's zeal. Miss Watson—who saw Clemens' behavior as less than rational—was replaced by an accountant of John Stanchfield's named W. J. Weiss. What was discovered was that on a number of occasions a workman who labored at both Stormfield and Summerfield was paid by a single check, with no separate accounting for Miss Lyon's share of the charges. By late May, Clemens decided that he wanted the cottage

and land redeeded to him so that Mrs. Ashcroft would be required to leave the vicinity altogether.

While Isabel's nerves were shredding under the assault, Ashcroft retained his calm self-assurance. He wrote Archibald Henderson in late May:

> There is a rather distressful situation at Storm-field. Mr. Clemens has practically abandoned the place, the present occupants being his two semi-insane daughters. He says: "This house has gone to hell, and I'm going to get out of it." One of his daughters has brought charges of dishonesty, etc., against Miss Lyon (Mrs. Ashcroft), and Mr. Rogers, at the time of his death, was kindly acting as arbiter between the two parties.

Rogers' death on May 19—as Clemens was en route for a visit with him—was a crushing blow: "This is terrible, terrible, and I cannot talk about it," Clemens told the reporters who met his train at Grand Central Station. "I am inexpressibly shocked and grieved. I do not know just where I will go." It also removed from Clemens' life an arbiter who might have struck a judicious balance between the excesses of Clara on the one hand and the Ashcrofts on the other.

But on about May 28, Clemens wrote, Ashcroft made one of his "blunders." He bragged to young Harry Lounsbury about Clemens, "I can sell his house, over his head, for a thousand dollars, whenever I want to!" Clara and Paine, puzzled at the arrogance of Ashcroft's boast, searched and discovered the comprehensive power of attorney that Clemens had signed in November 1908 and now immediately revoked.

Ashcroft acknowledged the revocation in a registered letter on June 3, 1909; he also told Clemens:

> Mrs. Ashcroft's health has been seriously undermined owing to the unjust and unfounded accusations made against her, and she is on the verge of a breakdown. Her doctor orders imme-

> diately a complete change. As I have important
> business to attend to in England, some of which
> you are acquainted with, we shall probably sail
> in a few days to be gone about four weeks.

Apparently Stanchfield, who was handling the investigation of the
Ashcrofts after Rogers' death, suggested that it would be prefer-
able to the Clemens faction if the couple remained in the United
States until the results of the audit were available. The Ashcrofts
chose to sail on June 8, in spite of Stanchfield's request; neverthe-
less, Clemens' claim that they fled surreptitiously to avoid prosecu-
tion was clearly false. Not only did Clemens have Ashcroft's
registered letter stating their plans; but when Stanchfield attached
both Summerfield and Mrs. Ashcroft's house in Farmington, Isa-
bel immediately booked passage back to the United States to
answer the charges.

xiv

The *contretemps* with the Ashcrofts grew serious enough to stir
Mark Twain to literary activity, and he produced one of the most
remarkable manuscripts of his entire career. In 1911, Charles T.
Lark, then attorney for Clara, wrote of the manuscript of *Is
Shakespeare Dead?* that it was

> about the last work which he wrote out in long-
> hand. I understand that the only complete manu-
> script which he wrote personally after this one
> was his account, in a very lengthy letter ad-
> dressed to W. D. Howells, of his experiences in
> connection with the Lyon-Ashcroft controversy.

Clara was to claim later that, in the aftermath of the Ashcrofts'
departure, the document Lark referred to was written for legal use
by her father:

> Father left me *one* weapon to use in case they
> troubled me any more and I used it.—He wrote

out a full description of their entire story of dis-
honesty which I was to publish if there was no
other way to keep them quiet.

In fact, the document to which Clara and Lark referred became
publicly known for the first time in 1970.

It was simply an installment of the autobiography in a new form
which Mark Twain devised for his memoirs in April of 1909. He
told Howells on April 17 about his dissatisfaction with the dic-
tated autobiography. Miss Hobby had been unsatisfactory, and so
apparently had Miss Howden, because she was replaced by a male
stenographer, W. E. Grumman, on February 3, 1909. But it was
dictation itself that Mark Twain had come to dislike:

> My mind's present scheme is a good one; I
> could not like it better if I had invented it my-
> self. It is this: to write letters to friends & *not
> send them.*
>
> I will now try it on you as a beginning, & see
> how it works. Dictating Autobiography has cer-
> tain irremovable drawbacks.
>
> 1. A stenographer is a lecture-audience; you are
> always conscious of him; he is a restraint. . . .
>
> 2. You are not talking to yourself; you are not
> thinking aloud—processes which insure a free
> & unembarrassed delivery—for that petrified
> audience-person is always there, to block that
> game. . . .
>
> But that scheme—that new-born scheme—that
> splendid scheme—that all-comforting, all-satisfy-
> ing, all-competent scheme—blows all these ob-
> structing and irritating difficulties to the winds!

The idea was of course one that Clemens was thoroughly familiar
with. For years he had been writing choleric letters without mail-
ing them.

The first attempt was a failure. Two days after announcing the
idea, Mark Twain attempted a "Twichell Letter": "Joe dear," he
began, "I think I will write you a letter—but you'll never see it."

The subject was, predictably, American Christian missionaries, but after only a few pages, and those mostly newspaper clippings, the inspiration played out.

Beginning on May 2, however, and continuing intermittently until October 21, 1909, Mark Twain composed the "Ashcroft-Lyon Manuscript," 429 pages of diatribe against Miss Lyon and Ashcroft, supplemented by pages of newspaper clippings, miscellaneous letters, statements of account, and similar "exhibits." The document is a literary curiosity. Conceived as a "Howells Letter," it began as a chronological account of the couple's treachery. But as new revelations came to light during the composition of the manuscript, and as Mark Twain suddenly remembered grievances he had forgotten to include in their proper chronological order, sequential arrangement dissolved into random and often contradictory accusations. Among the charges was the criticism that Isabel had wasted time making pincushions in Dublin. Mark Twain claimed that she had also kept requests of Jean's from him—when Jean could obviously have made all her requests face to face on his occasional visits to her.

He insisted that the secretary herself or Ashcroft had initiated the rumors of their impending marriage in 1907, rather than Charlotte Teller. Although he admitted that when Isabel came to the Clemens' employ in 1902, "she was slender, petite, comely, 38 years old by the almanac, and 17 in ways and carriage and dress," nevertheless

> there is nothing about her that invites to intimate personal contact; her caressing touch—and she was always finding excuses to apply it—arch girly-girly pats on the back of my hand and playful little spats on my cheek with her fan—and these affectionate attentions always made me shrivel uncomfortably—much as happens when a frog jumps down my bosom. Howells, I could not go to bed with Miss Lyon, I would rather have a waxwork.

She was, he said, "an old, old virgin, and juiceless, whereas my passion was for the other kind." Incongruously, even though Isabel was supposedly seeking to marry her employer, "why, Howells, every week-end was spent by her and Ashcroft in her bedroom, part of every day and at night, too sometimes till past midnight, and with the door shut!" Lecherous behavior on the part of a juiceless old virgin, according to Mark Twain's account, was enhanced by her attire:

> She would get herself up in sensuous oriental silken flimseys of dainty dyes, and stretch herself out on her bepillowed lounge in her bedroom, in studied enticing attitudes, with an arm under her head and a cigarette between her lips, and imagine herself the Star of the Harem waiting for the eunuchs to fetch the Sultan; and there she would lie by the hour enjoying the imaginary probabilities.

Isabel was also guilty of having drunk all but three of the forty-eight bottles of Scotch consumed at Stormfield in July and August of 1908, according to Mark Twain, and, most absurd of all, he insisted that she had been "much the laziest white person I have ever seen, except myself."

Ashcroft was "guilty" of selling Clemens Spiral Pin stock, of having fired Horace Hazen, of having presented a number of legal documents for Clemens' signature which the forgetful old man could not remember signing, and of having an excessively florid prose style.

But the Clemens family comes off more poorly than the Ashcrofts do in the "Ashcroft-Lyon Manuscript"; all three Clemenses were illogical and lacking in compassion; and Clara's and Jean's harassment of the defenseless and high-strung secretary and her mother was needlessly vicious. The manuscript is a geyser of bias, vindictiveness, and innuendo. It proceeds in no systematic order, and it ends with the quite irrelevant and almost irrational comment about Peary and Cook both discovering the North Pole. It is

obvious that Mark Twain was unable to maintain comic distance from the material or intelligent involvement with it. The "affronts" were too personal, too recent, and by his own thinking too important for Mark Twain to achieve humor. A vain old man's sense of indignity at having two "servants" gain notoriety and publicity at his expense pervades the "letter." Perhaps Mark Twain finally realized that his new scheme for autobiography had a flaw: It was more self-incriminating than self-revealing. It removed perspectives which art requires. It condemned a gullible and foolish man for misplacing his trust for so long in such obviously corrupt antagonists as the Ashcrofts whom he created in his own mind. He never attempted again, at any rate, to utilize his letter-autobiography structure.

xv

Clemens developed an unbecoming sanctimoniousness when he described the situation to Elizabeth Wallace:

> The Ashcrofts have wrecked their life—and *so* foolishly! . . . They are in disgrace—an irremediable disgrace—and nothing to blame for it but their own greed and treachery. She was borne from her house sick, yesterday. Will she ever be brave enough to return?

Isabel did return, to face dockside interviews and headlines in papers on both sides of the Atlantic. "Twain Charges False," headlined the New York *American* when Mrs. Ashcroft sailed from England.

Clara became revealingly nervous while Isabel was in mid-ocean:

> I hear that Miss Lyon is on her way home and she will probably have long conversations with the newspapers—drat her!—I *do wish* if she does that you personally would make a simple state-

> ment for all the papers saying that you were
> grateful to me and my friends for discovering
> Miss Lyon's dishonesty etc.—because just now be-
> fore a winter of concerts it may create a harmful
> atmosphere for me if you remain perfectly silent
> and allow all this to seem a mere difference be-
> tween women.

If she knew her charges were sound, why should Clara expect the internationally published conflict to be diminished to "a mere difference between women"? The New York *Telegram* (July 13, 1909), the *American* (July 14) and a third unidentified clipping proclaimed "She Will Make Twain Explain His $4,000 Suit" and "Mark Twain Must Explain." Also, just as Clara feared, Isabel told the reporters that she "blames the whole trouble on the 'artistic temperament' of Miss Clara Clemens."

When Ashcroft followed Isabel to the United States in late July, he provided the New York *Times* with even more provocative copy explaining the behavior of the elder Clemens daughter. He said that his wife, whom he oddly referred to by her maiden name,

> probably would have been supplanted two or
> three years ago, but the elder daughter had musi-
> cal and other ambitions, and thought more of
> them than of taking care of her old father and
> filling her mother's place.
>
> One's vocal ambitions, however, sometimes ex-
> ceed one's capabilities in that direction, and the
> bitter realization of this has, in this instance,
> caused the baiting of a woman who has earned
> and kept the admiration and respect of all of
> Mark Twain's friends. . . .
>
> Fortunately Miss Lyon is in a position to prove
> that the bulk of the money was paid to Clara
> Clemens herself for the expenses of concert tours
> and the delightful experience of paying for the
> hire of concert halls destined to be mainly filled
> with "snow" or "paper," for the maintenance of
> her accompanist, Charles E. Wark, and to defray

other cash expenditures that an embryonic Te-
trezzini is naturally called upon to make.

Clemens continued to maintain total silence at these accounts, but
Clara and Jean found a method for gaining satisfaction and
vengeance.

Isabel traveled with her mother to the Redding cottage, where
the Clemens brigade awaited her. When the former secretary did
not present herself at Stormfield, Clemens' attorney Charles Lark
took Jean as a witness and went to Summerfield on July 17. Lark
met Isabel and her mother, declined to allow Isabel to consult her
own attorney, told her that Clemens was prepared to present a
complaint to the grand jury unless Isabel signed a deed and
vacated the cottage. At first, Lark generously allowed the two
women two months to move, but at Jean's suggestion he changed
the departure date to September 1, 1909. After leaving to have the
deed drawn up over the weekend, Lark discovered that he could
have the necessary papers prepared the same day. He and Jean
returned and Mrs. Ashcroft signed the deed and also wrote
Clemens a check for $1,500, the amount she had borrowed on the
cottage. (Clemens had apparently rescinded his $500 Christmas
gift against the loan.) The two interviews between Lark and
Isabel, which Jean recorded in a twenty-four-page account her
father incorporated into the "Ashcroft-Lyon Manuscript," left
both Isabel and her mother in hysterical collapse.

Lark then decided that he would require Mrs. Ashcroft's signa-
ture on a lease agreement, which would reinforce the legal guaran-
tees of their departure by September 1. The prospect of
confronting the two terrified women in the cottage was so compel-
ling that on the twentieth, Clara went along as witness and
recorder of the event—both Clemens and Paine declined that
office. When Lark and Clara arrived with the lease, they met a
hysterical Mrs. Lyon. Clara wrote:

> Her face was flushed and she gesticulated ner-
> vously as she addressed him [Lark] in a loud tone
> of voice:

"You took an unfair advantage of us last Sat-
urday and did not keep your word for you prom-
ised us to go away and bring back the deed in
two or three days but instead of that you came
back with it the same day and therefore it is not
legal. My daughter does not even *know* what she
signed and we are both of us *crazy;* you intimi-
dated her into giving her signature by threaten-
ing to arrest her if she didn't."

As soon as Ashcroft returned to the United States, he echoed the
charges against Lark for intimidation of his wife:

Three days after her arrival, without being per-
mitted the benefit of counsel, when alone with
her mother in the cottage, and, as she says, by
threats and intimidations, she was induced to
sign a paper, the purport of which she knew not,
and give a check for $1,500., the amount of a
mortgage she had raised on the property. All of
which transpired at a time when, as her doctor
says, she was a physical and nervous wreck.

Legally, there seemed to be the strong likelihood of a draw.

But during that summer of 1909 Ashcroft and Stanchfield's
accountant Weiss audited—independently—the Clemens family
bank accounts. Weiss compiled voluminous "schedules" of ex-
penses: Clemens' accounts, Jean's expenses, charges for remodel-
ing the cottage, household expenses, concluding with "Notes and
Comments." The two points of contention were distilled into very
simple figures: (1) Miss Lyon used $3,500 of her employer's
money to refurbish her home, while claiming to have used only
$1,500, and (2) Miss Lyon had drawn checks on Clemens' bank
account for "cash" or "household expenses" for $6,789 between
March 1907 and February 1909.

Ashcroft explained in a letter to Stanchfield exactly the cause
for confusion:

No accounts were ever kept of the household
expenditures, nor was Miss Lyon ever requested

or instructed to do so. The items Mr. Lark seems to question are cash items. According to Mr. Rogers' audit, during this time $6789. was drawn in cash, an average of $282. per month—a mere bagatelle when you consider the receipts and disbursements passing through her hands, which were: receipts, $342,751.; disbursements, $279,-536. Out of this $6789., part of the servants' wages was paid—the pay-roll for servants amounting to about $5,000.; also, out of this $6789., the sum of approximately $3,000. was paid in cash to Miss Clara Clemens for her accompanist, Mr. Wark, her manager, Mr. Charlton, part of the expense of her concert trips, a trip to Nova Scotia, and many other items. Every cent of the balance was used for the expenses of the house, traveling expenses, and other payments in Mr. Clemens' or his daughters' interests.

As a practical man, you are aware that it is extremely difficult, if not impossible, to go back two years, and take a stub entry showing an amount of say $100. drawn in cash, and technically account for each cent of it. The only records ever kept were the brief stub entries, which was the manner in vogue when Miss Lyon assumed her duties. It can only be said that not $1. was spent dishonestly, and it was all disbursed for the best interests of Mr. Clemens. Never during her administration was she asked to make an accounting or to keep any record of cash expenditures. She was practically a member of the family and treated as such.

Nevertheless, Ashcroft did attempt to account for the cash disbursements in two meticulous, if unverifiable, statements he prepared for Stanchfield. Clemens had spent $550 of the cash; servants had been paid $2,625 in cash; traveling expenses accounted for $918. Clara had spent $1,950—in addition to the $13,220 in check stubs which had gone for her tours. The balance,

$1,006 of "miscellaneous items," included $320 of "receipted bills for which no checks had been drawn," $75 of Miss Lyon's own salary, and $55 in tips for the Robert Colliers' servants during the January 1909 visit. That left, as Ashcroft pointed out, about $5 a week unaccounted for as household items.

By this point, rational explanations were of course useless. Clara claimed that she rarely received cash payments. Clemens said that it was against the "rule of the house" to pay servants' wages with cash. The whole family believed that Miss Lyon had used Clemens' money to satisfy her expensive tastes in dressing and in furnishing her cottage. The Clemenses—perhaps aware that their charges against Isabel exposed gullibility and stupidity on their own parts—decided with professed seriousness that Miss Lyon had hypnotized Clemens, thereby ensnaring him in her spell. Such utter nonsense was first suggested by Mary Lawton to Clara: "Mary Lawton, the psychic, said she had hypnotized you," Clara told her father, "and it certainly looked like it." The idea surprised Clemens:

> I had never thought of that. The suggestion looked reasonable—particularly since no *other* plausible way had been discovered of accounting for the enslaved condition I had been in for the past two or three years.

But such a notion alleviated Clemens' own sense of guilt, and he readily accepted it as an explanation for his actions in the "Ashcroft-Lyon Manuscript."

xvi

Although the Ashcrofts would have seemed enough to occupy Clemens full time in mid-1909, a steady procession of guests filed into Stormfield, unaware of the battle being waged around them. And Clemens made a number of short trips: to a Lotos Club dinner for Andrew Carnegie, to a testimonial dinner for William

T. Jerome on May 7. In early June he traveled to Baltimore to
deliver a commencement address at the Misses Tewkesbury's
school for Frances Nunnally's graduation; but the trip brought on
another attack of illness similar to the one he suffered at Samuel
Moffett's funeral. Now, however, the doctors diagnosed it as indis-
putably angina pectoris. Rogers' death had broken Clemens'
health more conclusively than any other event: His best friend, his
most trusted adviser had died so unexpectedly and in the midst of
such violent suspicions about allegiances that it could not help but
leave Clemens in deep isolation. After Rogers' death and the
Ashcrofts' departure, Paine recorded that "Mark Twain lived
curiously apart from the actualities of life."

He received and read proof for the dollar book edition of *Ex-
tracts from Captain Stormfield's Visit to Heaven* in mid-year.
Clemens' diffidence at its publication is difficult to understand.
The slangy, vernacular speech of the Captain, salted with nautical
terms, is felicitous. Good-natured spoofing of some of the tradi-
tional images of Heaven were basically innocuous. Discovering
that Earth was known in Heaven as The Wart or the tediousness
of wearing wings and eternal psalm-singing, for example, were
harmless jabs at the fundamental concept of Paradise. Serious
issues cropped up in the rigidly edited text only rarely. A mother
seeks a baby who is a grown woman when she arrives in Heaven,
and the mother is bitterly disappointed. DeWitt Talmage is
mocked because of his intention to "fling his arms around Abra-
ham, Isaac and Jacob, and kiss them and weep on them." The
analogy of Heaven to an absolute monarchy is discussed by Storm-
field with his friend Sandy. And Sandy explains to the Captain
that he enjoys the company of even a French angel, "if I ever have
the luck to catch him engaged in anything that ain't indelicate."

And there were lawsuits and countersuits, claims and counter-
claims, meetings between John Stanchfield's assistant Charles Lark
and the Ashcrofts' attorney Mansfield Hobbs to divert Clemens
once he convinced himself that Ashcroft and Isabel had plotted a
scheme to embezzle everything he owned. By September 7, 1909,

in spite of the previous charges and threats, Clemens, Jean, Clara, and Paine signed a "discharge of all indebtedness and obligations to Ralph W. Ashcroft and Isabel Lyon Ashcroft from the Mark Twain Company." In the New York *Times* for September 12, 1909, an article headlined "Mark Twain Suits All Off" commented on the complicated legal positions:

> On their parts the Ashcrofts ratify and confirm the conveyance to Mark Twain by Mrs. Ashcroft of the house known as the Lobster Pot. . . .
>
> In addition Mr. and Mrs. Ashcroft have agreed to withdraw the suits which they brought against Mark Twain and Miss Clemens for defamation of character.
>
> On the other hand Mark Twain has agreed to drop his suit against Mrs. Ashcroft for an alleged loan of $3,050 and has removed the attachment which he had caused to be placed on the property of his former secretary at Farmington. Reparation has also been made for the hard things which the Ashcrofts alleged had been said of them by the author and Miss Clemens. Mark Twain has signed a document acquitting Mrs. Ashcroft of all blame for her conduct of his affairs while she was in his employ as his secretary. Miss Clara Clemens has also to the satisfaction of Mr. and Mrs. Ashcroft retracted the criticisms she is alleged to have made on Mrs. Ashcroft.

Clemens claimed the story was totally untrue and wrote a letter to Adolph Ochs, owner of the *Times*, claiming that "the interviewer had a personal grudge against me, and the sub-editor who accepted the interviews without verification of their alleged facts had also a personal grudge against me." But the article at least suggests the extent and the complexity of the lawsuits it was necessary to file and retract in order to untangle the affair. And Clemens finally

broke his silence and composed a public statement about the Ashcrofts for Melville Stone—"Clara wants it in the Associated Press, but if I alone were concerned I wouldn't take any notice of the rotten Ashcrofts."

Ashcroft resigned from the Mark Twain Company's board of directors; the attachment on the Farmington house was lifted. Ashcroft retained his position with the Plasmon Milk Products Company, the role in which Clemens had first encountered him, as an ally, five years earlier.

The Ashcrofts moved to Brooklyn and then, in 1910, to Racine, Wisconsin. Clara told Mrs. Whitmore after her father's death that he had reached the point "where he couldn't mention her name without having a heart attack." He did mention her name constantly, of course, most extensively in the "Ashcroft-Lyon Manuscript" on which he wrote as late as October 21, 1909.

What can be seen through the haze of accountants' figures, bitter personal conflicts, and the malicious accusations between the principals is this: Miss Lyon did, indeed, consider herself, with reason, a member of the family and was the person in the household most effectively devoted to its head. Her capacity for figures and accounts was no more trustworthy than Clemens' own, but her methods were never criticized until Clara unleashed her attack in early 1909. Isabel probably did expend about $2,000 more on the renovations of her own cottage than the $1,500 she officially borrowed. That she did so as premeditated embezzlement could only be persuasive to a mind so confused that logical counterargument was unacceptable. She assumed a relationship that did not exist. She presumed that her employer would be as unconcerned over the money spent to improve her corner of his property (which she originally intended to will back to his estate at her death, according to Clemens) as she was over the inequitability of a monthly salary of $50 for seven years for duties that expanded without limit. She could well have claimed that a fee for the interior decorating of a $45,000 house would have more than covered the costs of her own cottage. The very fact that Isabel

never made a defense of her Lobster Pot expenses suggests just as easily her shocked silence at the injustice of the accusations as guilt. Undoubtedly she had become overly protective toward Clemens and possibly as jealous of his daughters as his daughters were of her. Her mistake was in not questioning whether Clemens' loyalty to her was as compelling and powerful as her loyalty to him.

Ashcroft was more of a problem. Against him Clemens could find only the most elusive suspicions. The general power of attorney that gave Ashcroft and Miss Lyon complete control over Clemens' property was intended by one or both of them to give the couple complete authority over his estate after his death, or even during his lifetime if senility should warrant it. Edward Loomis' evaluation of the situation years later was basically accurate: "If he hadn't acted when he did, Clara would have inherited zero." But if Clemens did not wish Ashcroft and Isabel to control the Mark Twain Company and all his assets, he could have declined to sign the several documents which vested absolute control in them. Possibly, as he claimed, the signatures were obtained and notarized by fraud; more likely, they were placed on documents when he was so befuddled and indifferent that he could confuse his own ennui with "hypnosis." Many years later, when she was in her seventies, Isabel would claim "that she soon discovered that she had taken a viper unto her bosom; that her new husband . . . proved to be a forger and all-around crook for whose actions she was equally blamed. Thus, for offering herself as a martyr to the cause of peace and harmony in the C. household, her character had become eternally damned." But, except for firing young butler Horace Hazen and selling a stock certificate (putting all the proceeds into Clemens' bank account) —both legal acts under his power of attorney—Ashcroft took no recorded advantage of his powerful legal position.

The "eternal damnation" of which Miss Lyon spoke in her customary hyperbole even in her old age was pronounced by Clara and Paine and endorsed at least playfully by Clemens himself. In

one of the last literary enterprises of his life, "Advice to Paine," on how to behave when entering Heaven, Clemens told the biographer, "Be always kind, always forgiving—let bygones be bygones. Send the Lyon-Ashcrofts a fan." Of course, Clemens continued to hate the pair, her more than him because she had gained—and earned—his affection and confidence. In 1910, Clemens told Clara (who was still seeking, and got, approval for her overthrow of the secretary) that Miss Lyon was "a liar, a forger, a thief, a hypocrite, a drunkard, a sneak, a humbug, a traitor, a conspirator, a filthy-minded and salacious slut pining for seduction and always getting disappointed, poor child."

Clara, with undiminished malice and with Paine's help, removed every trace of Isabel and Ashcroft from her father's biography and records. Every time Miss Lyon's name appeared in the autobiographical dictations it was struck out and replaced with "my secretary." When Elizabeth Wallace was preparing her little memoir *Mark Twain and the Happy Island,* Paine warned her, "I hope there is nothing . . . in the book, concerning Miss Lyon, as Mrs. Gabrilowitsch feels very strongly on this point." He even cautioned against using the nickname "the King":

> Events made it ugly and distasteful and a sickening memory to all of us . . . when ever we recalled its former constant use (and the manner of it,) by one who had poisoned the very air of that beautiful spot.

Paine was, in fact, almost as vindictive toward the Ashcrofts as Clara. On the day after Jean and Lark obtained Isabel's signature on the deed to Summerfield, Clemens wrote Clara, "God will punish Paine. I know it. Because he is so intemperately glad over yesterday's tragedy." Paine was made the manager of Clemens' business affairs on July 17, 1909; he had the restrictions removed from his use of unpublished material in his biography. He signed an agreement with Clemens on July 24 to take over the editing of the volumes of letters. And, noting the coincidence that it was the first anniversary of the burglars' break-in at Stormfield, Clemens

announced on September 18, 1909, in his Stormfield Guest Book
that the Ashcroft affair was completely settled.

xvii

Still the guests poured into Stormfield. After a lengthy summer
illness in New York, Ossip returned to Stormfield in September.
He and Clara gave a recital for 525 guests as a benefit for the Mark
Twain Library, in which Clemens found diversion:

> Detachments and squads and groups and
> singles came from everywhere—Danbury, New
> Haven, Norwalk, Redding, Redding Ridge,
> Ridgefield, and even from New York: some in
> 60-h.p. motor-cars, some in buggies and carriages,
> and a swarm of farmer-young-folk on foot from
> miles around—525 altogether. . . .
> The artists were received with great welcome,
> and it woke them up, and I tell you they per-
> formed to the Queen's taste! The program was
> an hour and three-quarters long and the encores
> added a half-hour to it. The enthusiasm of the
> house was hair-lifting.

Even more hair-lifting, Clara and Ossip decided that evening to
marry. Although they had first met in 1897 and expressed varying
levels of emotion for almost ten years, the actual decision was
abrupt and came as a surprise to the household. Jean wrote to
Marguerite Schmidt, who had come to the United States to live in
New York City with Edith and Mildred Cowles, "On 21 Sept. my
sister decided to get married. She will wed Ossip Gabrilowitsch
next Wednesday and leaves to reside at Potsdam or at Berlin the
12th of October!"

Clemens was pleased at the October 6 wedding: Twichell offici-
ated, Jean was the bridesmaid, and Jervis Langdon was the
groomsman. The Gilders came (the last time that Clemens was to
see Richard Watson Gilder, who died the following month) . The

Hapgoods, Clara Gordon, the bride's nurse, and Dr. Angenette Parry, her doctor, were also there. The father of the bride showed his obstinate insensitivity about Clara's wedding day by wearing his scarlet Oxford robes in what was his habitual but perhaps unconscious impulse to center attention on himself. And he was pleased that Gabrilowitsch had, as he put it in a letter, "squelched Clara's 'career.' "

There is no other evidence that Clemens was distressed with Clara. But she had disrupted his household, evicted his business manager and his social secretary, and was now deserting him herself. Clara's new tour manager, R. E. Johnston, wrote Clemens that the thirty-one engagements booked for Clara had to be canceled because of her precipitate marriage, and Johnston expected Clemens himself to write a public letter of explanation. Even more strange, Clemens declined invitations to go to New York, when an attack of appendicitis delayed Ossip's departure, because he did not wish to tell Clara goodbye again: "I do not wish to do that," he explained, "as the chances are against my ever seeing her again." There must have been something more strained than either Jean or Clemens would admit about the departure.

At last, Clemens admitted Jean to the intimacy she had so long craved. He wrote Clara a description of the younger daughter whom he was at last getting to know:

> Jean is a surprise and a wonder. She has plenty of wisdom, judgement, penetration, practical good sense—like her mother—and character, courage, definiteness, decision; also goodness, a humane spirit, charity, kindliness, pity; industry, perseverance, intelligence, a clean mind, a clean soul, dignity, honesty, truthfulness, high ideals, loyalty, faithfulness to duty.

Jean was nearing thirty when her father apparently for the first time recognized her substantial worth. And her health was so sound that she even represented her father at a Fulton-Hudson

celebration in late September, when Clemens himself decided not to attend.

Her duties at Stormfield were, as she catalogued them for Marguerite Schmidt, quite incredible for a woman so recently considered a helpless invalid:

> Here is what I did yesterday. Got up at ten minutes of seven, breakfast at 7:20; changed clothes and leave for the post office at 8:00. Return, 9:05. Exchange a few words with my father while giving him his newspaper, quick look at the letters of which I read two; change clothes and leave for Georgetown where I went to buy several kinds of "feed" for my new chickens. Return to the farm around 11:30. Unpacked bags, fed the chickens, water my "hepatica" plants and return here around 12:15. Work without stopping until 1:00 on my father's accounts, then the bank book which had just arrived. Lunch from one o'clock to 1:20, leave for the farm at 1:30 after having given four letters to Katie to deliver to my father if by chance he had finished his work before my return. Arrived at the farm, I worked till 4:15. . . . Returned on foot about 4:30, I prepared myself a little (very little) for tea and since I was a little late, I did not go up to my room until 5:20. From then until quarter of seven I worked without stopping to write checks, address envelopes, go over the accounts and write a business note for my father. At 7:00 we had dinner and after dinner I played billiards with my father until 9:00! Arrived in my room, I was finally allowed to look at the newspaper, the first in four or five days and to read a little in a book. I went to sleep (I was already in bed) at 10:00.

And, she told Marguerite, the schedule was not unusual; Jean was that busy almost every day.

Her father marveled at her energy and at her work at her farm. He prepared a good-humored description of her chores for use by a newspaper:

> Jean's farm adjoins mine. She cultivates a good many acres, and raises hay, and poultry, and eggs, and taxes, and various other desirable things which she sells to me at a margin of profit: the kind of margin you sometimes see around a picture—where there's more margin than picture.

In spite of her father's affection and playfulness, Jean felt the old tensions occasionally. She told Bébé that she was compelled to do things she did not want to "in order that my father shall not grow too angry and tell me to go to the devil. For, although he is very good and generous, when he has an idea in his head, it's like melting marble with a piece of ice to make him change his mind!!"

Paine was an almost daily visitor at Stormfield, and he recorded in his notebook the flurries of guests, conversations, billiard games, and increasing chest pains that Clemens relieved with a hot-water bottle and huge draughts of hot water. It was an indolent, aimless, pleasant existence, except for the angina, and Paine's social function was to provide diversion and to deflect occasional rages.

Some of the incipient ideas which Mark Twain had barely mentioned in *Extracts from Captain Stormfield's Visit to Heaven* became his central concern in "Letters from the Earth"—in many ways a serious and straightforward continuation of the Captain Stormfield story. Possibly it was exactly that vernacular voice, patterned on Captain Ned Wakeman, whom Clemens had known and admired in California in 1866 and had appropriated in earlier literary works, that distressed the humorist when it spoke of theological matters in comic terms. But the materials themselves were to become the topics for the fallen angel Satan in Mark Twain's most sustained literary effort of the autumn of 1909.

On November 13, he was working, as he told Elizabeth Wallace,

on "Letters from the Earth," and "if you will come here and see us I will—what? Put the MS in your hands, with the places to skip marked? No. I won't trust you quite that far. I'll read messages to you." The letters took the form of a secret correspondence from Satan (visiting Earth during a spell of banishment) to St. Michael and St. Gabriel in Heaven. Satan's eleven numbered communications catalogue the absurdity of human behavior, in an extended satire on the tenets of orthodox theology.

The tension of the "Letters" was an old familiar one: God had created the universe and man as an experiment in *"Automatic law,"* but man—"a marvelous curiosity," Satan calls him—has attempted to impose on the universe his own absurd and perverted morality. Man, Satan reports, has imagined that he will go to Heaven—but a Heaven devoid of "the supremest of his delights, the one ecstasy that stands first and foremost in the heart of every individual of his race—and of ours—sexual intercourse." Instead, man has invented a hymn-singing, harp-strumming "deafening hurricane of sound—millions and millions of voices screaming at once and millions and millions of harps gritting their teeth at the same time!"

Satan also describes the Christian theology for his friends—its contradictions of belief in a just God against the record of the Old Testament. The senseless expulsion of Adam and Eve from Eden, the destruction of all humanity except Noah's family in the Flood, the creation of disease, and the invention of the house fly are among the beneficences for which man praises "an All-Just and All-Forgiving and All-Pitying Being who never answered a prayer."

"Letter VIII" returns to the question of sexuality, commenting on the inequity of the seventh commandment and the man-made laws of monogamy when polyandry would better suit female sexual appetite. With ribald humor Satan comments on man's incompetency at lovemaking in comparison with woman's ability and interest. (It is perhaps no coincidence that Notebook 38, of the same period, is filled with the punch lines of a number of classic dirty jokes.)

The final three letters return to a recounting of the deluvian

portion of the Old Testament and to an indictment of both man and the heartless God man has invented. Even the New Testament receives its share of ridicule—for it removes the one relief which man's God had overlooked in his original creation, the blessing of Death:

> Life was a fever-dream made up of joys embittered by sorrows, pleasure poisoned by pain; a dream that was a nightmare-confusion of spasmodic and fleeting delights, ecstasies, exultations, happinesses, interspersed with long-drawn miseries, griefs, perils, horrors, disappointments, defeats, humiliations, and despairs—the heaviest curse devisable by divine ingenuity; but death was sweet, death was gentle, death was kind; death healed the bruised spirit and the broken heart, and gave them rest and forgetfulness; death was man's best friend; when man could endure life no longer, death came and set him free.

So God invented Christ, and Christ invented Hell, to insure eternal rather than merely mortal suffering.

By late 1909 the sentiments voiced by Satan in "Letters from the Earth" were commonplace thoughts for Mark Twain. The ending of *The Mysterious Stranger* and *What Is Man?*, for example, had derided the vanity of human behavior and the absurdity of historical theology. What marks the earlier of Satan's letters as different and important is the tone embodied in them. Satan is detached from the events and attributes which he describes, more detached than any of the other divine commentators in Mark Twain's writing career. The pose does not last—the final three letters are strident in their scoffing and indignant at the stupidity of humankind. But in the first two-thirds of the document, language and voice and attitude combine to produce a literary text in which rancor and vituperation are noticeably absent. The earlier letters are humorous rather than polemical—for once during the last literary efforts, the sardonic author was able to channel his

energies with precision and control to achieve the artistic balance
he had so long sought.

xviii

On November 18, 1909, Clemens and Paine sailed to Bermuda,
planning to remain until after Clara's departure for Europe. Jean
stayed behind at Stormfield, making occasional trips to New York
for treatments from Dr. Peterson. She preferred Dr. Quintard,
whom she described as "having a woman's complexion; he is small,
round, with laughing blue eyes and light auburn hair." And rela-
tions between Jean and Peterson were somewhat strained. Jean
told Marguerite Schmidt:

> Do you remember the difficulties that Dr. P.
> made before he would let me come here? Well,
> Thursday after I had seen him, he was glad to
> have succeeded in making me come back from
> Berlin and return home! Really I found him a
> little overwhelming and I told him that I, too,
> was glad to have come back from Germany and
> then I laughed, saying but *you* haven't made me
> go home. He wanted to insist until I told him
> that it was with much difficulty that my sister
> had obtained permission for only a week's visit
> and since I didn't want to argue with him, I
> didn't continue the discussion although I would
> have liked to for his manner irritated me. But he
> has not dared to speak of Miss Lyon, he knew
> enough to keep quiet on that subject.

But Peterson continued to treat Jean; and when a sympathizer
afflicted with epilepsy wrote Clemens a letter of condolence at
Jean's death, Clemens replied to his query concerning treatment,
"Apply to Peterson."

Clemens and Paine spent the days in Bermuda in habitual
fashion. Most of Clemens' time was occupied by Helen Allen, the

fifteen-year-old daughter of the United States consul in Bermuda, who had visited Clemens in November. Her parents insisted that he stay at their home, Bay House, rather than at the hotel. And he told Francesca Nunnally that he drove "two or three hours every afternoon with my hosts, after school hours, over these fine roads, in this fine air, with the brilliant blues of the sea always in sight, and have thus driven the dyspeptic pain in my breast almost entirely away. Also the furious thoughts about Miss Lyon and Ashcroft, that pair of professional traitors and forgers." Jean became distressed over some of the instructions about paying bills during Clemens' absence and had to be reassured that "Bless you, I *didn't* distrust your intentions, and as for your honesty, I *couldn't* impeach it. No one can do that. You misquote me, dear, and you misunderstood me." Carriage rides, incessant talk, and some slight literary work occupied the old man's days and kept his temper even.

In late 1909 Mark Twain had been commissioned by *Harper's Bazaar* to write an essay on "The Turning Point of My Life" (published in that magazine's issue of February 1910). He began with the "Parable of the Two Apples," a long and belabored fable on Circumstance, which neither Paine nor Jean liked. Their displeasure, according to Paine, brought on an attack of Clemens' angina. A second version, the one published in 1910, was written in Bermuda in November or December and proved more acceptable. Its basic thesis was that the turning point of his life was a case of the measles which, through an inexorable chain of succeeding events, led to his choice of a literary career. External events—which Mark Twain recorded with close fidelity to his biography—had coincided to move him in an unalterable direction, with choice and free will totally absent from the process. The cause-and-effect sequence was more often than not farfetched, but the article gained pristine approval from Howells as the best thing Mark Twain had ever written.

In the same time span he wrote—or, more accurately, edited—"Marjorie Fleming, the Wonder-Child," which he published in the December 1909 issue of *Harper's Bazaar*. The article was little

more than a collection of letters, poems, and quotations from the journals of the precocious little girl who had died before she was nine and who had fascinated Mark Twain for over thirty years.

Financial and business matters were not allowed to bother Clemens; Ashcroft's brainchild, the Mark Twain Company, conducted an active business under his successors, Loomis, Lark, and Paine. It negotiated a deal with the Edison Company for a motion picture of *The Prince and the Pauper* for a $150 permissions fee; it copyrighted *Is Shakespeare Dead?* in the name of the Mark Twain Company. It took over Clemens' interests in the old Fentress Land Company involvement with the Tennessee lands, an affair which continued to occupy attention even after Clemens' death.

The Mark Twain Company also threatened its first litigation, against the Player's Navy Cut tobacco company for an advertisement in the *Illustrated London News* containing Mark Twain's endorsement of its brand of tobacco. Clemens explained to Elizabeth Wallace:

> In England Ashcroft committed a forgery in the second degree upon me, and sold for £25 my name (and words which I would not have uttered for a hundred times the money.) Sh—! say nothing about it—we hope to catch him and shut him up in a British jail.

If Ashcroft sold the endorsement while he was in England in the summer of 1909, he had the authority still of being the secretary of the Mark Twain Company, even though his power of attorney from Clemens had since been officially revoked.

Although it died slowly, Plasmon finally died. Ashcroft reported back from London on July 17, 1909, that he had finally made a splendid contract with Lipton to market the product in the United States. But Lipton apparently had second thoughts about the project and withdrew his support after consulting with "his Chicago people." A young man named Haithwaite, apparently a friend of Ashcroft, tried to negotiate with the Mark Twain Com-

pany to purchase Clemens' shares in the Milk Products Company, but Haithwaite declined to pay the $35,000 par value which Clemens set as his asking price. Ashcroft, who retained his position in the company, told Lark that the foundering organization would sink unless Clemens provided additional funds, a suggestion that was sensibly declined. Finally, by December 11, 1909, while Clemens was in Bermuda,

> The office has been discontinued and all the bills of the Company have been paid through a pro rata contribution of the shareholders, our friend Ashcroft to this end actually producing the sum of $90 in cash. Mr. Clemens's pro rata portion was $350, which sum was advanced by Mr. Loomis.

The grand, decade-long scheme was over, having cost Clemens at least $50,000 in losses and an unpardonable expense of time and energy.

xix

Clemens and Paine decided to return to Stormfield for Christmas, docking in New York on December 20, 1909. Jean met the boat and tried to arouse her father's enthusiasm for the holidays. She asked Marguerite Schmidt to spend the holiday with her: "my father is absolutely disinterested in Christmas and it is primarily on that account that I am begging you."

Clemens returned to Stormfield a few days before Christmas, where he watched Jean decorate the house, buy and wrap presents, and manage household affairs with her usual energy. On December 23, after a quiet evening, they said good night to one another. The morning of Christmas Eve, as Bébé was on her way to Stormfield, Jean died. Up early to make final preparations for Christmas, she entered the bathroom at seven o'clock for her bath. An hour later, Katy Leary became anxious about her. Breaking

into the bathroom, Katy found Jean in the tub. "In the opinion of E. H. Smith, the examining physician of the county, death was due to drowning," evidently during an epileptic seizure. Paine was summoned immediately, and Jervis Langdon arrived the following day from Elmira, New York.

The condolences flooded into Stormfield. But those who knew Clemens best knew that there was no consolation possible to a man whose share of grief and tragedy had long since exceeded all justice. Clara, ill in Germany, could not be told the news immediately, but her father wrote her with the weariness, joy, and envy which were his response to death:

> O, Clara, Clara dear, I am so glad she is out of it and safe—safe! I am not melancholy; I shall never be melancholy again, I think. You see, I was in such distress when I came to realize that you were gone far away and no one stood between her and danger but me—and I could die at any moment, and *then*—oh then what would become of her! For she was wilful, you know, and would not have been governable.
>
> You can't imagine what a darling she was, that last two or three days; and how *fine*, and good, and sweet, and noble—and *joyful*, thank Heaven! —and how intellectually brilliant. I had never been acquainted with Jean before. I recognized that.

That, indeed, was the tragedy—not that Jean was dead but that he had "never been acquainted with Jean before" her death.

In his Guest Book he wrote:

> Christmas Day—she lies in her coffin at the other end of this room, beautiful in death.
> *Night.* At 6 P.M. The hearse and carriages moved toward the station. Jervis and Katy will take Jean to Elmira, where her mother, and Susy and Langdon lie buried. A snow-storm was raging. Clara is in Germany.

Unable because of the almost constant pains of angina to make the strenuous trip to Elmira, Clemens stayed at Stormfield writing his final segment of autobiography, "The Death of Jean." Paine hovered solicitously, played the orchestrelle, and attempted to alleviate the loneliness and gloom that hung over the home.

Jean's death was to destroy forever Mark Twain's creative voice. Clemens told Paine that "The Death of Jean" "can end my autobiography. It is the final chapter." The manuscript began strangely, with a two-page account of the purpose of the autobiography to extend copyright on his earlier books, a purpose by this time unnecessary because of a new law providing a forty-two-year copyright term. The elegy also contained a diatribe against Miss Lyon, contrasting her secretarial capacities with Jean's, and a description of the daughter's willfulness when under the influence of epileptic attacks which Paine decided to omit from the printed version. The document that resulted, after the editorial decisions were made, was still unusual for several reasons.

In it, understandably, Mark Twain equated Jean's death with the most recent preceding one in his family, Olivia's. The passage Paine deleted blamed Olivia's death on the strain of ministering to Jean's attacks; the characters of the two women were compared. Jean's body, like Olivia's, reassumed its youthfulness miraculously as it lay in the coffin.

More important, the grief Mark Twain expressed at Jean's death had some of the rhetorically ceremonial quality of his writings on the death of Olivia. Jean's dog, like the two horses Olivia had purchased in 1904, would "not be neglected." Some books that Jean had arranged for Mark Twain's autograph became sacred: "Her hand has touched them—it is an accolade—they are noble now." In the midst of such comments, there was nevertheless sincere grief, intensified by the briefness of their life together at Stormfield and the total isolation the father now felt: "We were together; *we were a family!* the dream had come true—oh, preciously true, contentedly true, satisfyingly true! and remained true two whole days."

The pathos, heartbreak, and guilt were expressed even more

revealingly in a letter Clemens wrote Clara shortly after he composed "The Death of Jean":

> I don't know why you should love me, I have not
> deserved it; and the love Jean manifested for me
> astonished me daily. I recognized its sincerity,
> but could not divine the source of it, nor what
> had bred it and kept it alive, any more than I
> divine why you love me nor how you keep it up.
> But I was deeply grateful to Jean for that un-
> earned love, and I am deeply grateful to you for
> yours.

It would have been a moment logically for Mark Twain to continue some of the topics in "Letters from the Earth," with the ideas of those letters overlapping into the eulogy or the communication with Clara. But, except for the comments on the blessings of death, there are few echoes. The despicable nature of human existence, the burden of unearned disease, the malice of a divinity who could strike down the unoffending daughter—none of these possibilities was exploited.

Even in his desolation, however, Clemens remembered the Ashcrofts, who had, as he was to rationalize it, kept Jean from him. He told Mrs. Whitmore:

> Doubtless all Hartford has listened to the other
> side—and *believed* it. I judge so because in to-
> day's and yesterday's avalanche of sympathizing
> letters and telegrams Hartford is substantially
> unrepresented.

Mrs. Whitmore advised, "Do not try to revive the past issues about Isabel Ashcroft. . . . Here, she is on her own ground and reaps that advantage."

What remained was the desolation of Mark Twain, now totally alone, and the almost automatic impulse to write. To have survived the blow of Jean's death was his tragedy, and to have transformed the tragedy into literature was, if not redemption, at least the response that mitigated grief. With all its mistaken directions,

"The Death of Jean" was Mark Twain's last attempt to convert his life to literature and to expiate the guilt which had stalked him throughout his career. He was the Derelict at last.

<center>XX</center>

On New Year's Day, 1910, Clemens wrote Elizabeth Wallace, "The pain in my breast has come back—so I am leaving for Bermuda next Wednesday, for an indefinite stay." He made a brief trip to visit the Edward Loomises' house and meet Howells (Loomis, who was the husband of Clemens' niece Julia, was by this time a director of the Mark Twain Company), and then he left for Bermuda with Claude Benchotte: "I have Claude, best of butlers, valets and everything else, with me," he told Miss Wallace. "He lives at Hamilton House, but is in close touch with me by telephone and bicycle."

Paine and his wife moved into Stormfield, keeping a skeletal staff of servants on hand. Clemens apparently had little thought of returning to Redding permanently, as his suggestions and directions to Paine on February 5, 1910, suggest:

> As I shall probably see Stormfield but seldom, hereafter, & then only flittingly, we can go on reducing expenses there & get them well down. . . .
>
> And suppose you discharge all servants not absolutely necessary to your little family's needs— thus diminishing food-expenses & wage-bill. . . .
>
> I want Katy to remain, & be always there when Clara or I come. I shall keep Claude myself.

Paine followed Clemens' instructions and sold Jean's farmhouse and forty acres of her land and was instructed to administer the proceeds of the sale for a Jean L. Clemens Memorial Building at the Mark Twain Library in Redding.

There was some dissension between Katy Leary and Mrs. Paine

over the management of Stormfield. Clemens wrote the house-
keeper a letter vesting all authority in her:

> I enclose page 1 of a letter just received from
> Mrs. Ossip. It troubles me because she seems to
> have gotten the impression (the superstition),
> that your authority as housekeeper is not *su-
> preme*. But it *is* supreme. There is no house-
> keeper but you. . . .
> Mrs. Paine is my *guest*—that is all. She under-
> stands this, and will not endeavor to help you
> keep house. . . .

It sounded like the beginning of another act in a decade-old play.

Whatever "Mrs. Ossip's" suspicions and their source, she de-
cided to return to the United States quite unexpectedly. Clemens'
letters to her on March 12 and 24 welcomed and rejoiced in her
plans to arrive at Stormfield. Paine later claimed that Clara was
summoned home by cable when it became apparent her father was
dying, but her plans had been made a month earlier than that.
Possibly another power struggle was looming. Clara, who still
drew impressively on her father's bank account with her letter of
credit after her marriage, may have planned another assault on
imagined competitors for the family wealth. Her father may have
sensed Clara's fears, for he wrote her that Paine's management of
the finances had reduced Stormfield expenses by over a third so
that Clemens no longer felt financially "cramped."

Most of the financial matters were handled by the officers of the
Mark Twain Company, not by Clemens himself. While in Ber-
muda, the retrenching speculator made one last fling at invest-
ment. He wrote back to Paine that he would like to sell for
$70,000 the Utah Consolidated stock that he had purchased for
$90,000 four years earlier. "I am very tired of Utah," he ex-
plained.

He was tired, for that matter, of business and speculation in
general. He had struggled throughout the ten years of the twenti-
eth century against the specter of poverty which had never really
existed. In a letter he had written back in May of 1889 in honor of

Walt Whitman's seventieth birthday, Mark Twain catalogued breathlessly if callously the "great births" of mechanical, techno-logical, and political progress of the preceding seventy years. After his list of marvels, he adjured the poet to "wait thirty years, and *then* look out over the earth. You shall see marvels upon marvels added to those whose nativity you have witnessed; and conspicu-ous above them you shall see their formidable Result—Man at almost his full stature at last!" Although Clemens would not live to observe the perfected world he forecast, twenty years after his projection he found himself ironically betrayed and in large measure destroyed by the very "marvels" he so grandly exalted and Man—at least those with whom he had been associated—far from the realization of that "full stature" he had so blithely predicted.

In February 1910 Clemens had asked Paine for one of the "Mysterious Stranger" fragments, which the secretary mailed to Bermuda; but Mark Twain apparently did no work on the manu-script. He wrote the brief "Advice to Paine," published in part in *Mark Twain, A Biography*. The "advice" was slight both in length and conception. It was in a sense a burlesque etiquette for the proper manners Paine should practice when entering Heaven. But even in its slightness it was an unusual document. At Jean's death, Mark Twain had written, "Shall I ever be cheerful again, happy again? Yes. And soon. For I know my temperament. . . . My temperament has never allowed my spirits to remain depressed long at a time."

True to his temperament and to the creative instincts which not even personal tragedy could suppress, he took up his pen for a final comic effort in "Advice to Paine," which, however slight, was at least an attempt. The irrepressible spirit, battered and eroded by a decade of torment, struggled to the very last.

Clemens wrote some instructions about Clara's and Ossip's wills which seemed important to him in Bermuda, and he praised Loomis and the other directors of the Mark Twain Company, telling Loomis "how thankful I am to have a Mark Twain Com-pany such as *I* have got—sterling men, every one, and to the last

degree capable." He attacked the novels of Will N. Harben for their illogic in his final notebook. But these fitful activities were only flickers in the twilight existence that marked Clemens' final months.

The young Helen Allen fascinated and exasperated him. She took his dictation, but without the adulation and interest he expected from an angel fish. She preferred the company of young men, which affected Clemens with unseemly jealousy. Her parents, Mr. and Mrs. William H. Allen, watched over Clemens. In fact, Paine had written the Allens a long and almost condescending letter before Clemens' arrival in Hamilton, describing the close attention that would have to be given to their guest:

> Now, as to the other matters; you have already realized, of course, that Mr. Clemens has to be protected from the great number of people who wish to use him as the means of their own social advancement, or as an ornament for their drawing-rooms and dinner tables. Of course he likes to go sometimes and he likes to see certain people, but it is pretty difficult to know just where are the right places to go, and who are the right people to see. . . .
>
> He is also to be guarded from business propositions of every sort—schemes, plans, investments, and the like. These things have been his undoing through a long period of years. He has never made an investment that brought him a return, however promising it may have seemed in the beginning. He does not wish ever to make an investment again. But, as I have said, he is impulsive, enthusiastic, and likely to fall in with the suggestion of a plan which would only mean discomfort, worry and nightmare for him later on, and he has had enough of such things.

In effect, the Allens were expected to be Clemens' guardians as well as hosts.

They did their job well. Clemens played golf with Woodrow Wilson, visited with the ubiquitous Dorothy Quick briefly—she found him "years older and very worn. The once erect figure was a little stooped. He no longer threw back his chest, but the old flame was in his eyes." Mr. and Mrs. Robert Collier arrived in early March—they had "adopted" Clemens the preceding year—and stayed for several weeks. But a siege of bronchitis settled in and was complicated by an especially severe recurrence of the angina. After booking passage to return to the mainland on April 23—"I don't want to die here for this is an unkind place for a person in that condition"—he suffered a serious and major relapse, perhaps even a stroke, in late March. Allen wrote Paine a letter advising that "matters had become very serious indeed. Mr. Clemens had had some dangerous attacks, and the physicians considered his condition critical."

On the other hand, there is some slight, provocative evidence that suggests the Allens' anxiety may have been motivated by their concern for Clemens' attachment to their daughter as well as for his physical deterioration. Letters Clemens was writing in late March betray neither a lack of lucidity nor a faltering penmanship. The dying man's jealousy of Helen's interest in another man, named Arthur—whom Clemens described as "a man qualifying as neither a groom nor gentleman but blending both capacities" but whom Paine discreetly called "a small playmate of Helen's"— interlaced the pages of his final notebook, on the cover of which Paine circumspectly wrote that it must not be offered for sale or inspection until fifty years after Mark Twain's death. There was also a manuscript, which Paine sequestered for decorum's sake, of notes to and about Helen. Portions of it may well have been written after Paine arrived in Bermuda, for one of the notes told Helen, "I would God I had some Paine-killer." Others, occasionally written in his simplified-spelling code, contained endearments somewhat inappropriate from a seventy-five-year-old man to a girl not yet sixteen:

> I think you are very pretty and sweet and dear
> and cute, Helen—in fact I *know* it.

> I wish I could trade places with Teddy [her toy
> bear?].

> Who is saccharine? It will be best to tell you in
> private, Helen.

And, finally, Albert Lee, an employee of Robert Collier who was
in Bermuda in March, claimed that he knew

> some story . . . which . . . is something very
> terrible that happened in Bermuda shortly be-
> fore M. T.'s death. . . . It is something un-
> printable. . . .

It is difficult to interpret what such scanty evidence implies. But it
is at least possible that Clemens' jealousy erupted into an overt
expression that frightened or offended the Allens. Perhaps Helen,
the last of the fifteen-year-old surrogates for lifelong sweetheart
Laura Wright, was the object of improper comments or even
actions.

Whatever the motivation, Paine, equipped with morphine,
hypodermic needles, and instructions from Dr. Quintard, sailed
for Bermuda on April 2. For ten days, Paine administered the mor-
phine, took Clemens on brief rides, and watched over him as he
slept fitfully and read in *Jude the Obscure*. The nights of April 8
and 9 Clemens suffered attacks which Paine thought would prove
fatal. On April 12, 1910, Clemens, Paine, and Claude boarded the
Oceana and made the trip back to the United States. Clemens was
under heavy sedation most of the trip, from both the injections of
morphine and what Paine called "milder remedies which we had
brought." The New York *Times* reported later that on the few
occasions when he was not under sedation Clemens "tried to
smoke on the steamer while returning from Bermuda, and only
gave it up because he was too feeble to draw on his pipe."

The Colliers had originally planned to meet Clemens at the
dock with their automobile, and he proposed to "lodge with my
small mamma," as he called Sallie Collier, for a week or two. Such
plans were obviously impossible now, and Clemens was carried off

the ship and taken directly to Stormfield. Lounsbury met the train and drove the small party to the house itself. Clemens insisted on alighting from the carriage without help but had to be carried to an upstairs bedroom, where the death watch began.

Epilogue: THE LAST VOYAGE

Dimly I heard some one murmur "Blessed are the dead that the rain falls on," and then the owl-eyed man said "Amen to that," in a brave voice. . . .

"The poor son-of-a-bitch," he said.

—F. Scott Fitzgerald, *The Great Gatsby*

On April 14, as the *Oceana* docked, Clemens had his final attack of angina pains. "The physicians denied him the morphine, now, as he no longer suffered acutely." Clemens' speech became slurred, and he believed that Gabrilowitsch, who arrived at Stormfield with Clara on the seventeenth, could understand him better than the other attendants. It is at least possible that, as the last entry in his notebook was in German, he was lapsing into that tongue occasionally during his final days.

As those days, and life, dragged on, Clemens' mind wandered and his speech became even more inarticulate. "He had," Paine said to the Allens, "slipped out of life's realities, except during an occasional moment." According to one newspaper obituary, "even on his death bed, when he had passed the point of speech, and it was no longer certain that his ideas were lucid, he would make the motion of waving a cigar, and smiling, expel empty air." On the twenty-first, he tried to write several notes, but the words were almost illegible. One asked for spectacles and a glass pitcher. Another, written to Clara on the last day of her father's life, may have had a special pathos. "Dear," it read, "You didn't tell me, but I have found out that you. Well, I . . . " and the scrawl became indecipherable. The words "became persuaded" or "become personal" appear likely as additional ones in the note. Although the

evidence is slim, the dying father had perhaps realized in a lucid interval or had been told by Ossip that Clara was five months pregnant and was attempting to communicate his awareness of the expectation of a grandchild.

Paine recalled for the Allens that on April 21, 1910, Mark Twain's

> voice got a little better later in the day, and he said several intelligible words to Gabrilowitsch. In the afternoon he lapsed into unconsciousness. His breath grew gradually weaker, and so his life went out. I was not in the room at the moment, as even the physicians did not expect it quite so soon. They hardly thought he would live through the night, but believed he would keep on breathing for some hours. All at once, however, the breathing suddenly stopped, but that was all; there was no struggle of any kind.

Dr. Quintard and Clara both recorded what they believed to be Mark Twain's final words. Taking Clara's hand, he said, "Good-bye dear, if we meet—" Curiously, not one of the obituary or news stories of Mark Twain's death mentioned the phrase, but quoted his request for spectacles as his last words. And a month earlier, he had written Elizabeth Wallace a coda more felicitous to his beliefs: "Isn't this life enough for you? Do you wish to continue the foolishness somewhere else? Damnation, you depress me!"

Mark Twain's body was dressed in one of the white cashmere suits and carried downstairs to the living room at Stormfield. A wreath of laurel leaves, made by Dan Beard, rested on the coffin. Clara spent a half hour alone in the room the following morning, and then, while all Redding businesses and stores closed, the coffin was carried to New York to the Presbyterian Brick Church. Four hundred people were invited to the brief ceremonies conducted by Twichell and the Reverend Henry Van Dyke:

> The service was very brief and simple, such as he would have approved. Afterward, all who wished to do so, had a chance to take a farewell

> look. All the quiet and dignity and beauty had
> come back to him. He was like a fine piece of
> marble, and it was a most impressive scene to
> see those thousands file by, look at him for a
> moment, gravely, thoughtfully, and pass on. All
> sorts were there, rich and poor; some crossed
> themselves, some saluted, some paused a little
> longer to take a closer look, but no one offered
> to pick a flower, or to make any display, of any
> sort. It was one of the most impressive spectacles
> I have ever witnessed.

More than three thousand mourners passed by, and at five o'clock
the doors of the church were locked in order that the funeral party
could take the special train to Elmira.

The car carrying the body to the Langdon home contained the
Gabrilowitsches, the Loomises, the Langdons, the Colliers, Mrs.
Gilder, Paine, Duneka, Major Leigh, Katy Leary, and Claude
Benchotte. At three-thirty on April 24 the Reverend Samuel
Eastman conducted another brief service in the parlor in which
Clemens and Olivia had been married. The coffin was opened
once more and then sealed and carried to the Langdon family plot.
And there, in a driving rain, beside Olivia, the infant Langdon,
Susy, and Jean, Mark Twain was buried. As his old friend Joe
Goodman, a Western comrade from forty-eight years earlier, told
Paine, "I am grieved—and yet glad that Mark made so good an
ending. God knows how mortally afraid I was that somebody
would land him in a dime museum before the finish."

But he was, like Jean, "safe" at last.

After her father's death Clara continued to live at Stormfield
until the birth of her daughter Nina in August 1910. She con-
tinued to badger the Ashcrofts, sending Lark to Racine, Wiscon-
sin, with the "Ashcroft-Lyon Manuscript" to coerce Ashcroft into
returning the manuscript of *Is Shakespeare Dead?* to her. She kept
close vigil on all literary documents, removing all references to the
Ashcrofts, and to Will Wark, from them. Through Paine, she even
controlled the photographs which Elizabeth Wallace could repro-

duce in her *Mark Twain and the Happy Island.* "I should avoid any *'affectionate'* photographs with young girls," Paine cautioned "Betsy" Wallace. "Clara feels pretty strongly about that."

Paine, as the literary editor of the Mark Twain Estate, was a willing participant in the suppression of the unpleasant facts. On February 6, 1910, he had sent Clemens a bit of doggerel which suggested his own attitude toward Isabel:

> Who feeds on bromide and on Scotch
> To keep her nerves at highest notch?
> Who makes of business-books a botch?
> *The Bitch*

And as late as 1926 he wrote to Harper & Brothers his revealing opinion of independent studies of Mark Twain:

> I think on general principles it is a mistake to let any one else write about Mark Twain, as long as we can prevent it. . . . As soon as this is begun (writing about him at all, I mean) the Mark Twain that we have "preserved"—the Mark Twain that we knew, the traditional Mark Twain —will begin to fade and change, and with that process the Harper Mark Twain property will depreciate.

And the "preserved" Mark Twain was kept fairly intact through Paine's term as literary editor (until 1937) and indeed until shortly before the death of Clara in a San Diego motel in 1962.

The Ashcrofts moved to Montreal in 1913, separated in the early 1920s, and were later divorced. Ashcroft remarried in 1927 and died in Canada in 1947. Isabel returned to New York, worked for many years at the Home Title Company in Brooklyn, and lived at 7 Charles Street in Manhattan. She died in 1958 at the age of ninety-five. In the interval between her banishment from the Clemens family and her death she never uttered a recorded word of reproach or bitterness against "the King." She was even humane enough to stipulate that the diaries on which much of this biog-

raphy is based were not to be made available for research until after Clara's death.

In her diary entry for January 15, 1905, Isabel had written, "Some day the penalty for having such perfect living will come." Much later, she added a postscript: "After 28 yrs. Jan 3/33. No penalty attaches itself to perfect living. No penalties ever attach themselves to joys." Her devotion never wavered, nor did her willingness to assist those scholars and researchers who sought her out. Her diaries and notebooks, after passing through the guardianship of Samuel C. and Doris Webster, were deposited in the Mark Twain Papers at Berkeley. And finally, over sixty years after the death of Mark Twain, an accurate record of the final ten years of his life could be written without injury to any of the principals.

The task is left to interpret what this record means. That it is true, and that for over half a century the complete facts of Mark Twain's last decade were unavailable, is not enough. The record is true—and frequently unpleasant. It is true—and even harsh. It is true—and ultimately tragic. But even that would not justify its being true—and public.

Something more seems to illuminate the dry facts of Mark Twain's last decade than mere deterioration suppressed in the interests of his public image. He was a man of contradictory impulses all his life. His business instincts, his literary activities, and his domestic relationships had always thrived in spite of tensions and anxieties which kept him guiltily introspective for decades and decades. An indisputable and almost overwhelming sense of inferiority competed inside him with a vanity and an aggressiveness that compelled him to seek the public spotlight whenever he could.

Fear had been the controlling emotion of his life: fear of poverty, fear of offending and alienating his family and friends, fear of being mistaken by his audience. He moved insecurely in all the worlds he inhabited, much like the mysterious stranger in a dream world who obsessed him in his fiction. He created in his own imagination a "Langdon caste" which he convinced himself he could enter only by amassing a spectacular fortune; but even

after he had achieved that goal in the mid-1880s he continued to pursue wealth with a zeal and a recklessness that a Langdon would only have condemned. He feared poverty although there had never been any poverty facing him—even during the period of his bankruptcy.

To compensate for his fear of poverty he spent lavishly—foolishly. He invested, almost always unwisely, but compulsively; it would take a diligent scholar days to identify and catalogue all the slips and sheets of numbers: dollars, shares, profits, losses, and similar mathematical scribblings in the Mark Twain Papers. He lived ostentatiously, with a retinue of servants, cooks, maids, and nurses that must have exceeded his family's needs. Even his residences—Hartford, Dollis Hill House, Riverdale-on-the-Hudson, the Villa di Quarto, Stormfield—were increasingly spectacular, palatial, and needlessly vast. He ordered special railway cars for his travel; he wandered on Grand Tours of Europe to "economize"; and he tended to boast publicly of his income from book royalties and investments to even casual acquaintances.

When she was delirious, dying of spinal meningitis in her twenty-fifth year, Susy Clemens said, "Up go the trolley cars for Mark Twain's daughter. Down go the trolley cars for Mark Twain's daughter." And, palpably sensing no ambiguity in the ominous chant, her father recorded it in his notebook only as evidence of Susy's affection for him. But the same insensitivity that marked his relationship to his family from 1900 to 1910 had also been an undercurrent in his domestic life during the halcyon years of his marriage. He sought, understandably, the support and the praise of his wife and daughters. He craved their adulation, but his domination often produced the opposite result. As they grew older but no less dependent, his daughters became more aware of his vanity, his unpredictable rages, and his expectations for "Mark Twain's daughters." Even as early as December 1886 Clemens confessed to Howells his discovery that

> all their lives my children have been afraid of
> me! have stood all their days in uneasy dread of

my sharp tongue & uncertain temper. The accus-
ing instances stretch back to their babyhood, &
are burnt into their memories: & I never sus-
pected, & the fact was never guessed by *anybody*
until yesterday. Well, all the concentrated griefs
of fifty years seemed colorless by the side of that
pathetic revelation.

However hyperbolic the statement sounds, there were obvious
antagonisms that Mark Twain created in his family during the
"good years" but felt compelled to conceal. And it was her father
who regretted that Susy almost made a successful adjustment to
Bryn Mawr—away from him—during her freshman year.

The list of his gaucheries could be extended. But essentially he
was confused and tormented by the role of an often tyrannical
paterfamilias and the urge to be petted and admired by his family.

The same ambiguity marked his friendships and enmities out-
side the agoraphobic family circle. Howells, Twichell, his brother
Orion, almost anyone who came to know him well and to gain his
confidence also gained at least his occasional distrust and suspi-
cion. His volatile temperament could explode without warning
and inflict exactly the injuries he attempted so strenuously to
avoid.

Finally, his fears about his literature had plagued him from the
beginning of his writing career: Was he a journalist or a writer of
books? Was he a comedian or a moralist, or were the two roles
identical? Was his proper vein the raucous Western tall tale or the
genteel historical romance? These were questions he debated from
the 1860s until the end of his life, and the volumes in his collected
works are the transcript of that debate. He could "demean" him-
self and reach what he called his submerged clientele, or he could
write books like *The Prince and the Pauper* or *Joan of Arc* and
receive the approval of the literary establishment instead of pro-
digious royalties.

The dilemma was not that Mark Twain had to discover some
theoretically perfect literary voice by reconciling the antagonisms
within him. Quite the contrary, the tensions and uncertainties and

complexities involved in the process of literary decision-making were in themselves the richness of his writing. Throughout the nineteenth century he was able to channel his energies into creative impulses, to sublimate many of his resentments and his affections into literary use. His opinion of a betrayed trust might express itself with classic understatement in Jim's speech to Huck defining "trash" after the two outcasts are separated in the fog: "Dat truck dah is *trash;* en trash is what people is dat puts dirt on de head er dey fren's en makes 'em ashamed." His growing convictions about conscience as the all-controlling force in man's destiny could appear in fictional guise as Huck's famous debate in Chapter 31 of *Huckleberry Finn.* His political and economic ideas found an ideal method of expression in the tension between a nineteenth-century Yankee from Connecticut and the practices of the country ruled by Arthur. His own conflicting temperamental impulses were objectified in the twinning themes of *The Prince and the Pauper, Pudd'nhead Wilson,* and "Those Extraordinary Twins."

And even when the transmutations of his belief and his biases into art were less than successful, Mark Twain managed to capture in his literature the essential humanity of his own doubts and indecisions. Much of his literature was based on the honest, unsophisticated, and imperfect pose of a man who lived by his memory and whose craft was always basically autobiographical. He *was* the people's author and spokesman, as his publishers advertised him. He could dismiss plot (as in *Huckleberry Finn*), violate traditional forms (as in the autobiography), and fail to sustain his original intention (as in almost everything he wrote). The ability to recognize his own failures was often his strength with a demotic audience. Mark Twain simply "told himself" in his writings, and what he lost in structure and cohesiveness he gained in identification through honesty. Paine phrased the quality as aptly as anyone ever has: Mark Twain "reached the heart of the world . . . because he was so limitlessly human that every other human heart . . . responded to his touch."

Until 1900 Mark Twain managed to retain control over his universe, over his despair, pessimism, frustration, and insensitiv-

ity, by his artistic capacities. But when deaths, disloyalties, and his
own old age dulled his creative instincts, when he outdistanced in
tragedy his own ability to transmute fact into literature, he was
crippled. When his vanity, fed by his court of worshippers, de-
flected his energies, he was adrift like the derelict ship he de-
scribed in his poem. Something occurred which made the adversity
and the conflicts no longer convertible into finished art. Age was
itself a contributing factor. The death of his most sensitive critic
was another. His ostentation, symbolized by his white suits and
crimson Oxford robes, multiplied unchecked by constructive re-
strictions. His fear of isolation, his insomnia, his interminable
games of billiards and only desultory literary activity were all the
geriatric manifestations of a personality that had never been quite
able to endure itself. And the junkyard of unfinished manuscripts
and ill-conceived literary ideas was the most enduring testimony
of the failure of Mark Twain to retain creative control over his
world.

According to one critic, Mark Twain's "despair represents the
increasing inadequacy of his adjustment as demands upon it mul-
tiplied in severity through his personal disasters." While that is
true, it is true too that nothing he had learned in the nineteenth
century could ever have provided a satisfactory basis for adjust-
ments to life in the twentieth. His resiliency turned brittle under
the constant torments; his ability even to maintain sensitive con-
tact with his world suffered as he was protected and insulated from
it by his palace guard. Paine admitted Mark Twain's idiosyn-
crasies:

> With his strength he had inherited the weak-
> nesses of our kind. With him, as with another,
> a myriad of dreams and schemes and purposes
> daily flitted by. With him, as with another, the
> spirit of desire led him often to a high moun-
> tain-top, and was not rudely put aside, but lin-
> geringly—and often invited to return. With him,
> as with another, a crowd of jealousies and re-
> sentments, and wishes for the ill of others, daily

went seething and scorching along the highways
of the soul. With him, as with another, regret, re-
morse, and shame stood at the bedside during
long watches of the night; and in the end, with
him, the better thing triumphed—forgiveness and
generosity and justice—in a word, Humanity.

But Paine muted the weaknesses—the very weaknesses that made
the abortive and fragmented literature of Mark Twain's last years
all the more impressive because of the conditions under which it
had been attempted.

The bitterness which permeated *What Is Man?*, "Letters from
the Earth," the "Mysterious Stranger" fragments, much of the
autobiography, and most of the shorter political writings was a
rage at the obscenity of life. Like Huck, Mark Twain had "been
there" himself.

SOURCE NOTES

Notes have been keyed to page and line numbers of the text in order not to intrude them on uninterested readers. Since an overwhelming majority of them refer to previously unpublished documents, however, the scholar may locate the originals without difficulty. The following abbreviations have been used:

MS	Manuscript
PH	Photocopy
TS or TSS	Typescript or typescripts
RWA	Ralph W. Ashcroft
CC	Clara Clemens
OLC	Olivia Clemens
SLC	Samuel L. Clemens
IVL	Isabel Lyon
HHR	Henry H. Rogers
CWB	Clifton Waller Barrett Collection, Alderman Library, The University of Virginia, Charlottesville, Virginia
Berg	The Henry W. and Albert A. Berg Collection, The New York Public Library
Harvard	Harvard College Library, Cambridge, Massachusetts
HEH	Henry E. Huntington Library and Art Gallery, San Marino, California
MTM	Mark Twain Memorial, Hartford, Connecticut
MTP	The Mark Twain Papers, Bancroft Library, The University of California, Berkeley
Princeton	Princeton University Library, Princeton, New Jersey
Yale	American Literature Collections, Beinecke Library, Yale University, New Haven, Connecticut

275

AMT	*The Autobiography of Mark Twain,* ed. Charles Neider, New York, 1959
Enchantment	Dorothy Quick, *Enchantment, A Little Girl's Friendship with Mark Twain,* Norman, Oklahoma, 1961
FoM	*Mark Twain's Fables of Man,* ed. John S. Tuckey, Berkeley, 1972
Happy Island	Elizabeth Wallace, *Mark Twain and the Happy Island,* Chicago, 1913
HHR	*Mark Twain's Correspondence with Henry Huttleston Rogers,* ed. Lewis Leary, Berkeley, 1969
HHT	*Mark Twain's Hannibal, Huck and Tom,* ed. Walter Blair, Berkeley, 1969
LE	Mark Twain, *Letters from the Earth,* ed. Bernard DeVoto, New York, 1962
Life as I Find It	Mark Twain, *Life as I Find It,* ed. Charles Neider, New York, 1961
LLMT	*The Love Letters of Mark Twain,* ed. Dixon Wecter, New York, 1949
LMT	Mary Lawton, *A Lifetime with Mark Twain,* New York, 1925
Mary	*Mark Twain's Letters to Mary,* ed. Lewis Leary, New York, 1961
MFMT	Clara Clemens, *My Father, Mark Twain,* New York, 1931
MMT	William Dean Howells, *My Mark Twain,* New York, 1910
Mr. Clemens and Mark Twain	Justin Kaplan, *Mr. Clemens and Mark Twain,* New York, 1966
MSM	*Mark Twain's Mysterious Stranger Manuscripts,* ed. William M. Gibson, Berkeley, 1969
MTA	*Mark Twain's Autobiography,* ed. Albert Bigelow Paine, New York, 1924
MTB	Albert Bigelow Paine, *Mark Twain, A Biography,* New York, 1912
MTFM	Caroline Thomas Harnsberger, *Mark Twain, Family Man,* New York, 1960
MTHL	*Mark Twain–Howells Letters,* eds. Henry Nash Smith and William M. Gibson, Cambridge, Massachusetts, 1960
MTL	*Mark Twain's Letters,* ed. Albert Bigelow Paine, New York, 1917
MTLW	*Mark Twain the Letter Writer,* ed. Cyril Clemens, Boston, 1932
MTN	*Mark Twain's Notebook,* ed. Albert Bigelow Paine, New York, 1935
MTSatan	John S. Tuckey, *Mark Twain and Little Satan,* West Lafayette, Indiana, 1963
My Husband	Clara Clemens, *My Husband, Gabrilowitsch,* New York, 1938
A Pen Warmed-up in Hell	*A Pen Warmed-up in Hell,* ed. Frederick Anderson, New York, 1972
SMT	Edith Colgate Salsbury, *Susy and Mark Twain,* New York, 1965
Will Bowen	*Mark Twain's Letters to Will Bowen,* ed. Theodore Hornberger, Austin, 1941

INTRODUCTION

Page: line
xvi:15 *LMT,* p. xi.
xxiv:20 *LLMT,* pp. 349–50.
xxv:5 *LE,* p. 40.

xxv:29 *SMT*, p. 313.
xxvi:7 *MTB*, p. 1339.
xxvi:24 *MTFM*, p. 207.
xxvii:24 Notebook 5, TS p. 8, MTP.
xxviii:13 "The Death of Jean," MS pp. 40–41, MTP.

PART I: INDIAN SUMMER (1900 TO SUMMER 1904)

Page: line
3:15 SLC to Laurence Hutton, January 1, 1900, Princeton.
6:25 Notebook 32b, TS p. 64, MTP.
6:31 *HHR*, p. 425.
7:6 February 12 and June 7, 1900, MTP.
8:6 *HHR*, p. 430.
8:11 February 12, 1900, MTP; see also *MTL*, pp. 689–92, 695.
8:17 *MTLW*, pp. 105–06.
8:21 SLC to Samuel E. Moffett, May 17, 1900, MTP.
8:27 *MTHL*, p. 717.
8:32 *HHR*, p. 444.
9:2 SLC to Samuel E. Moffet, May 17, 1900, MTP.
9:6 James M. Baldwin, *Between Two Wars—1861–1921*, pp. 111–12.
9:14 SLC to Pamela Moffett, April 25, 1900, MTP.
9:18 *Will Bowen*, p. 27.
10:22 SLC to A. S. Hogue, n.d. [1898?], MTP.
10:25 January 12, 1900, *MTLW*, p. 93.
10:28 *HHR*, p. 439.
10:33 SLC to MacAlister, March 10, 1900, CWB.
11:7 CWB, PH in MTP.
11:10 SLC to MacAlister, March 9, 1900, CWB.
11:32 SLC to MacAlister, December 5, 1900, CWB.
12:29 McClure to SLC, January 11, 1900, MTP.
13:2 *Ibid.*, January 16, 1900, MTP.
13:8 *Ibid.*, January 28, 1900, MTP.
13:12 *MTB*, pp. 1100–01.
13:16 *HHR*, pp. 428–29.
13:30 SLC to Frank Bliss, March 30, 1900; to MacAlister, March 17, 1900; to
 Harvey, April 12, 1900, MTP.
14:16 *MTB*, p. 1109.
14:20 *Ibid.*
15:7 DV #239, MTP.
15:13 *MTHL*, pp. 715–16; *MTL*, pp. 694–95; *HHR*, p. 434.
15:19 Twichell to SLC, July 15, 1900, MTP.
15:22 *Ibid.*, August 24, 1900, MTP.
15:27 DV #393, MTP.
15:32 *MSM*, p. 24.
16:11 *Ibid.*, pp. 136–37, 156.
17:5 *MTB*, pp. 1100–01.
17:7 *Life as I Find It*, p. 334.
17:23 *Ibid.*, p. 331.
17:27 *A Pen Warmed-up in Hell*, p. xvii.

17:34 *MTB,* pp. 1125–26.
19:27 *AMT,* p. 326.
20:8 *MTB,* p. 1121.
21:5 February 24, 1901, Louisiana State University Library, PH in MTP.
22:18 *MTHL,* p. 726.
22:26 Goodell to SLC, MTP; SLC to Goodell, December 31, 1900, in the pos-
 session of William M. Gibson, PH in MTP.
23:4 Andrew Langdon to SLC, December 31, 1900, MTP.
23:22 SLC to Matthews, Columbia, PH in MTP.
23:33 SLC to Robert N. Stanley, January 21, 1901, MTM; SLC to Edmund
 Kirby, January 22, 1901, CWB.
24:20 Edmund Norton to SLC, February 23, 1901, with marginal notation,
 MTP.
24:25 See *MTB,* pp. 1133–34, for additional commentary.
24:34 *MTL,* pp. 704–05.
25:4 September 5, 1901, MTP.
25:12 *MTB,* p. 1143.
25:16 December 9, 1901, MTP.
25:29 *MTL,* p. 705.
26:2 OLC to Grace King, Louisiana State University Library, PH in MTP.
26:21 New York *Tribune,* February 15, 1901.
26:29 March 10, 1901, MTP.
29:11 April 14, 1901, CWB.
29:15 To Mrs. Trask, December 30, 1901, Berg.
30:2 SLC to Frank Bliss, August 26, 1901, University of Texas Library.
30:10 *Ibid.,* August 29, 1901, University of Texas Library.
30:24 *MTB,* p. 1139.
32:17 September 8, 1901, University of Texas Library; *MTL,* pp. 713–16.
32:20 To A. H. Thayer, July 17, 1901, Harvard University Library.
33:2 SLC to Whitmore, August 27, 1901, MTP.
33:6 September 8, 1901, Yale University Library, TS in MTP.
33:14 October 15, 1901, TS in MTP.
33:19 December 7, 1901, MTP.
34:8 Documents File, 1900, MTP.
34:11 *MTL,* p. 706; Notebook 34, TS p. 8.
34:25 August 14, 1901, MTP.
34:28 OLC to Samuel Moffett, September 17, 1901, TS in MTP.
35:6 Mrs. Erna Eskuche, Documents File, 1901, MTP.
35:30 *HHR,* p. 466.
35:35 OLC to Samuel Moffett, September 17, 1901, TS in MTP.
36:5 *MTB,* p. 1152.
36:34 Notebook 34, TS p. 21b, quoted in Howard Baetzhold, "Found: Mark
 Twain's 'Lost Sweetheart,'" *American Literature,* 44:425 (November,
 1972) .
37:9 SLC to MacAlister, April 24, 1901, CWB.
37:22 October 27, 1900, CWB.
37:27 August 27, 1900, MTP.
38:1 Wright to SLC, February 4, 1903, MTP.
38:9 SLC to Frank Bliss, March 18, 27, July 13, MTP; to George Harvey,
 May 4, Yale.

38:12 See *HHR*, pp. 465, 472–73, 477–78.

38:26 SLC to Frank Bliss, October 27, 1901, UCLA.

38:34 TSS in MTP.

39:6 Frank Bliss to SLC, March 7, 1902, MTP; SLC to Harvey, February 26, 1902, MTP.

39:9 October 27, 1902, MTP.

39:11 Notebook 35, TS pp. 24–25.

39:21 Anderson Auction Catalog, 1931.

39:27 Notebook 34, TS pp. 13–17.

39:30 October 14, 1901, Harvard University Library.

40:4 December 26, 1901, University of Texas Library.

40:14 December 8, 1901, *MTHL*, p. 735.

40:28 *MMT*, p. 83; *MTHL*, pp. 732, 733.

40:31 SLC to James Ross Clemens, June 13, 1902, PH in MTP.

42:7 MTP, printed with silent corrections in *LLMT*, p. 333.

42:17 *HHR*, p. 509.

42:33 *LLMT*, p. 338.

43:16 *HHT*, pp. 15–20.

43:29 A. C. Bedford to H. H. Rogers, February 4, 1902, MTP.

43:33 See her letters of March 21 and April 8 to William E. Benjamin, *Mark Twain's Letters to the Rogers Family*, ed. Earl J. Dias, pp. 39–41; and *HHR*, p. 484.

44:6 May 23, 1902, MTP.

44:11 *HHR*, pp. 493–95.

44:16 To Whitmore, November 12 and 24, MTM and MTP respectively.

44:26 *My Husband*, p. 17.

44:31 *HHR*, p. 485.

44:34 *My Husband*, p. 25.

45:11 OLC to Mrs. Whitmore, May 27, 1902, MTM.

45:27 *HHR*, p. 487.

45:30 Notebook 35, TS p. 10.

45:31 *LMT*, p. 182.

46:4 *HHR*, p. 490.

46:14 *Ibid.*, p. 496.

46:17 *HHR*, p. 497.

46:26 SLC to Dr. W. L. Hawkes, April 23, 1903; Hawkes to SLC April 30, 1903, MTP.

46:34 *HHR*, p. 511.

47:4 *MTN*, p. 377.

47:6 November 3, 1902, MTP.

47:8 SLC to Whitmore, September 26, 1902, MTP.

47:10 *MMT*, p. 90.

47:21 SLC to Muriel Pears, October 13, 1902, MTP.

48:4 SLC to Whitmore, November 5, 1902, MTP; see also Notebook 35, TS p. 28.

48:33 *MTL*, pp. 719–21; *MTB*, pp. 1158–61.

49:30 SLC to Duneka, "Thursday" [1902?], Berg.

49:35 *MMT*, p. 90.

49:36 *MTL*, pp. 722–26.

50:6 October 18 and 23, 1902, MTP.

50:9 Arthur L. Scott, ed., *On the Poetry of Mark Twain,* pp. 116–22.
51:12 *HHR,* p. 511; Notebook 35, TS pp. 30, 31.
51:28 SLC to Laurence Hutton, November 6, 1902, Princeton.
52:2 *LLMT,* pp. 339–40.
52:5 September 15, 1902, Berg.
52:25 *MTL,* p. 734.
53:10 SLC to W. D. McCrakan, December 5, 1902, MTP.
53:11 See W. D. McCrakan to SLC, December 4, 11, and 16, 1902, January
 7, February 7, and March 2, 1903, all in MTP.
53:13 December 15, 1902, CWB.
53:21 "Notes re: 'Christian Science,' " Berg.
54:7 Edward H. Anderson to SLC, April 20, 1903, MTP.
54:10 Bliss to SLC, April 25, 1903, MTP.
55:22 SLC to Whitmore, October 18, 1902, MTP.
55:27 *Ibid.,* November 9, 1902, MTP.
56:10 *AMT,* p. 339.
56:19 January 5, 1903, MTP.
57:7 *MTB,* pp. 1191–92.
58:10 IVL Diary, January 3, 1903, MTP.
58:28 *MTB,* p. 1190.
58:31 SLC to Thomas Bailey Aldrich, January 23, 1903, Harvard University
 Library.
59:4 April 20, 1903, *HHR,* p. 524.
59:7 SLC to Hutton, March 18, 1903, Princeton.
59:10 IVL to Whitmore, April 24, 1903, MTP.
59:24 *HHR,* p. 527.
59:29 *MTHL,* pp. 765–66; May 7, 1903, MTP.
60:1 IVL to Whitmore, January 13, 1903, MTP.
60:11 SLC to Whitmore, April 5, 1903, MTM.
60:24 SLC to Mrs. Whitmore, June 16, 1903, MTM.
60:33 *MTN,* p. 383.
60:36 On June 23, she wrote a Dr. Frau Bree, "In September we are going
 to California or Europe, we are not sure yet which is better" (TS in
 MTP) .
61:20 *MMT,* p. 87.
61:32 *MTN,* p. 386.
63:17 SLC to Bergheim [February 6, 1903], MTP.
63:19 Wright to SLC, May 14, 1903, MTP.
63:23 Notebook 36, TS pp. 4–5.
63:33 "Plasmon's Career in America, as recounted by R. W. Ashcroft," Sep-
 tember 22, 1904, MTP.
64:3 *HHR,* p. 516.
64:5 *Ibid.,* pp. 520–21.
64:27 SLC to Duneka, April 27, 1903, IVL copy in MTP.
64:31 TS in MTP.
64:36 Collier to SLC, May 4, 1903, MTP; *ibid.,* May 28, 1903, CWB.
65:4 Quoted in *HHR,* pp. 525–26.
65:15 TS in MTP.
65:18 *HHR,* p. 526.
65:29 IVL to Whitmore, May 29, 1903, MTP.

66:5 SLC to Jacobs, June 11, 1903, MTP.

66:8 *HHR*, pp. 531–32.

66:17 "To the Stockholders of the American Publishing Co.," CWB.

66:22 Bliss to SLC, June 27, 1903, CWB.

66:26 Both "As Regards the Company's Benevolences" and the notebook entries are published in *HHR*, pp. 533–34.

67:7 July 2, 1903, Princeton.

67:11 *MTL*, p. 741.

67:13 July 18, 1903, CWB.

67:27 OLC to CC, July 5, 1903, TS in MTP.

67:30 SLC to CC, July 5, 1903, TS in MTP.

67:34 SLC to CC, July 17, 1903, TS in MTP.

68:24 Gilder to SLC, August 4, 1903, Berg, PH in MTP.

68:34 *HHR*, p. 634.

69:29 Frank Bliss, "Clemens Negotiations 5 Aug. 1903 to" in CWB.

69:33 Bliss to Rogers, September 16, 1903, MTP.

70:3 *MTN*, p. 381.

70:21 Arthur W. Higgs to George Gregory Smith, September 18, 1903, and Smith to SLC, September 20, 1903 and October 7, 1903, MTP.

70:29 SLC to Dr. Parker, October 14, 1903, CWB.

70:33 *HHR*, p. 526; George W. Reeves to SLC, October 19, 1903, CWB; SLC to Reeves, October 20, 1903, CWB.

71:7 Smith to OLC, November 2, 1903, MTP.

71:24 *MTHL*, p. 775.

71:26 *MTA*, I, 195–218.

72:8 Autobiographical Dictation, 1904, MTP.

72:15 IVL Diary, 1903, p. 38, MTP. The *Italian Gazette* reported, however, on January 12, 1904, that the Countess had been visiting in Rome since the preceding December 19.

72:19 Countess Massiglia to Mrs. Janet Ross, November 6, 1903, MTP.

72:23 Autobiographical Dictation, 1904, TS p. 122, MTP.

72:30 Plaisant to SLC, November 27, 1903; George Gregory Smith to Plaisant, November 28, 1903, MTP.

72:33 Smith to SLC, December 12, 1903—two letters, both in MTP.

73:7 "The Countesss Massiglia," DV #351a, MTP.

73:20 IVL Diary, February 28, 1904, MTP.

73:25 SLC to Duneka, February 8, 1904, PH in MTP.

73:30 *HHR*, pp. 557–58.

74:4 Sebastiano Cecchi to SLC, January 30, 1904; Paolo de Plaisant to SLC, February 4, 1904; George Gregory Smith to SLC, February 6, 1904, all in MTP.

74:7 Notebook 37, TS p. 6.

74:9 *Ibid.*, TS p. 9.

74:22 On September 25, 1903, Harold Wheeler, John Hays Hammond's general manager of the company, offered Clemens $3,500 worth of stock (MTP), and in early 1904, when the Clemens family was already immersed in the frustrations concerning the countess, Butters wrote him a letter offering to restore the 250 bonus shares if Clemens would purchase additional stock from Butters.

75:3 SLC to Stanchfield, MTP.

75:13 Paine #122, MS p. 1, MTP.
75:23 DV #356, MTP.
75:30 SLC to MacAlister, September 6, 1902, CWB.
75:33 December 1, 1903, CWB; *HHR*, pp. 544–45.
76:4 March 21, 1904, Berg; April 7, 1904, CWB.
76:14 *HHR*, pp. 544–45.
76:29 December 30, 1903, Washington University, quoted in part in *FoM*,
 p. 249.
77:2 MTP.
77:8 SLC to Duneka, January 8, 1904, Berg.
77:14 January 5, 1904, TS in MTP.
77:18 MS p. 2; see *HHR*, pp. 542–43, for details about Reeves.
77:30 April 2, 1904, MTP.
78:6 *MTHL*, p. 778.
78:18 IVL Diary, February 28, 1904, MTP.
78:21 Notebook 37, TS p. 7, MTP.
79:34 SLC to C. J. Langdon, February 14, 1904, MTM.
80:9 *Ibid.*, June 19, 1904, MTM.
80:19 *HHR*, p. 542.
81:3 SLC to Mary Mapes Dodge, December 18, 1903, PH in MTP.
81:8 SLC to Grocco, n.d., MTP; Dr. Nesti to SLC, February 10, 1904, MTP.
81:22 Notebook 37, TS p. 10; SLC to Sue Crane, May 20, 1904, MTP.
82:8 Notebook 37, TS p. 9.
82:10 *MTN*, p. 386.
83:6 SLC to Sue Crane, March 8, 1904, MTP.
83:16 May 13, 1904, PH in MTP.
83:36 May 9, 1904, Yale.
84:6 *MTL*, p. 761; SLC to Twichell, June 8, 1904, Yale.
84:8 *AMT*, p. 344.
84:22 *LMT*, pp. 228–29.
84:29 IVL Diary, June 5, 1905, MTP.
84:34 *MTHL*, p. 785.
85:9 SLC to C. J. Langdon, June 8, 1904, MTM.
85:10 Notebook 37, TS p. 12.
85:13 *HHR*, p. 570.
85:15–16 *MTHL*, p. 785; *HHR*, p. 569; *MTL*, p. 758.
85:21 *MSM*, pp. 30–31; SLC to C. J. Langdon, June 19, 1904, MTM.
85:25 June 8, 1904, telegram to C. J. Langdon, MTM, also recorded in Note-
 book 37, TS p. 12.
85:27 *MTL*, p. 760.
85:28 SLC to Twichell, June 8, 1904, Yale.
86:27 SLC to Mrs. Frank Cheney, July 21, 1904, MTM, published in part in
 SMT, p. 398, as is the letter from Mrs. Cheney to which SLC refers
 (pp. 271–72).
86:36 *MTHL*, p. 787.
87:2 *MTB*, pp. 1221–22.
87:3 SLC to C. J. Langdon, June 13, 1904, MTM.
87:7 *Ibid.*, June 19, 1904, MTM.
87:18 *Ibid.*, June 26, 1904, MTM.
87:27 Baldwin to Kirch, June 25, 1904, MTP.

88:2 Arcangeli, Gatti & Co. to Dr. Kirch, July 22, 1905, MTP.
88:12 In the margin of a letter from Sebastiano Cecchi to SLC, June 28, 1904,
 MTP.
88:16 SLC to Mason, July 23, 1904, MTP.
88:21 IVL Diary, July 5, 1904, MTP.
89:1 *MTFM,* p. 211.
89:29 IVL Daybook, February 2, 1906–1907, MTP.

PART II: GÖTTERDÄMMERUNG (SUMMER 1904 TO SUMMER 1907)

Page: line
93:5 June 30, 1902, MTM.
93:17 [December 10, 1902], MTM.
94:12 September 3, 1905, TS in MTP.
94:22 IVL Diary, December 14, 1904, January 15, May 21, and June 3, 1905,
 MTP.
94:27 IVL Diary, April 23, 1905, MTP.
95:14 Quoted in Ralph W. Ashcroft to John B. Stanchfield, July 30, 1909,
 MTP.
95:21 SLC to CC, "Sunday Afternoon," TS in MTP; *Mr. Clemens and Mark
 Twain,* p. 373.
95:26 December 28, 1904, MTP.
96:12 To Mrs. Franklin Whitmore, June 25, 1910, MTM.
96:31 IVL Diary, July 16, 1904, MTP.
97:1 *Ibid.,* July 22, 1904, MTP.
97:16 *MFMT,* p. 256.
97:19 IVL Diary, August 3, 1904, MTP.
97:21 *Ibid.,* August 5, 1904, MTP.
97:23 *HHR,* pp. 579–80.
98:4 SLC to MacAlister, November 9, 1904, CWB.
98:5 Twichell to SLC, October 27, 1904, MTP.
99:25 March 22, 1905, MTP.
99:31 *Harper's Weekly,* March 18, 1905; April 8, 1905; July 15, 1905; August
 12, 1905; October 21, 1905; and November 4, 1905.
100:7 IVL Diary, February 22, 1905, MTP.
100:11 "IVL Notes re: What Is Man?," Berg.
101:9 *FoM,* p. 218.
101:14 IVL Diary, March 21, 1905, MTP.
101:17 Duneka to SLC, April 7, 1905, MTP.
102:8 RWA to SLC, September 19, 1904, MTP; October 14, 1904, MTP;
 and Stanchfield to SLC, January 23, 1905, MTP.
102:14 Harold Wheeler to S. Melville Bergheim, August 26, 1904, MTP.
102:18 RWA to SLC, September 4, 1904, MTP.
102:25 "Plasmon's Career in America, as recounted by R. W. Ashcroft," Sep-
 tember 22, 1904, MTP.
102:27 Hammond, Wheeler, and Butters were being sued for libel and slander
 by RWA, with SLC agreeing to pay half the court costs and lawyers'
 fees to appeal the suit (RWA to SLC, July 19, 1905, MTP).
103:3 Hammond to RWA, August 29, 1905, in MTP, as are copies of
 RWA's various "publications."

103:6 *New York Law Journal,* August 23, 1905, p. 1.

103:27 SLC to RWA, September 2, 1905 (IVL copy) , MTP.

103:32 RWA to SLC, November 2, 1905, MTP.

104:3 See *HHR,* p. 492, n. 2.

104:19 Lewis to RWA, April 27, 1905; RWA to Stanchfield, May 1, 1905, MTP.

105:15 April 23, 1905, Brown University Library.

105:20 IVL Diary, March 25, 1905, MTP.

105:23 IVL to Dear Sir, April 5, 1905; Stoeckel to IVL, April 8, May 23, and
 June 9 and 19, 1905, MTP.

105:34 IVL Diary, May 5, 1905, MTP.

106:5 SLC to Aldrich, May 17, 1905, Harvard.

106:8 *HHR,* p. 589.

106:11 *HHR,* p. 587; Twichell to SLC, July 3, 1905, MTP.

106:14 IVL Diary, June 7, 1905, MTP.

106:16 IVL Daybook, June 14, 1905, Antenne-Dorrance Collection, PH in
 MTP.

106:20 IVL Diary, July 16, 1905, MTP.

106:22 July 16, 1905, CWB.

106:25 SLC to Muriel Pears, July 26, 1905, Yale.

106:32 SLC to W. E. Benjamin, June 1, 1905, PH in MTP.

107:5 IVL to John Larkin, June 17, 1905, MTP; Larkin to SLC, May 29, June
 20, 1905, MTP.

107:16 Cecchi to SLC, November 4, 1904, MTP; Stiattisi to SLC, February 6,
 1905, MTP; SLC to Stiattisi, February 19, 1905 (IVL copy) , MTP.
 On August 25, 1906, Miss Lyon recorded in her diary that "the lawyers
 aren't going to say that the suit is given up—for you can't ever say
 what such as the Massiglia might do. They might suddenly become the
 assailers, instead of the assailed" (MTP) .

107:32 IVL Diary, November 29, 1905, MTP.

108:7 February 3, 1905, MTP.

108:12 SLC to Starr, February 26, 1905, MTP.

108:25 Kirch to Mr. Barbour, July 19, 1905, MTP.

108:32 IVL Diary, September 3, 1905, MTP.

109:1 Starr to SLC, March 21, 1906, MTP; marginal reply in unknown hand.

109:14 IVL Diary, May 21, 1905, MTP.

110:28 TS in MTP.

110:31 Duneka to SLC, June 15, 1905, MTP.

110:31 IVL Daybook, June 6, 1905, Antenne-Dorrance Collection, PH in MTP.

111:5 *MTSatan,* p. 68.

111:13 IVL Diary, July 4, 1905, MTP.

111:21 *HHR,* p. 589.

111:27 IVL Diary, July 7, 1905, MTP.

111:30 *Ibid.,* July 12, 1905, MTP.

112:4 "IVL Notes on the Duneka Letters," April 2, 1938, Berg.

112:8 June 7, 1905, MTP.

112:13 IVL Diary, July 13, 1905, MTP.

112:16 *MTL,* p. 775.

112:17 SLC to Duneka, Berg.

112:18 Duneka to SLC, September 18, 1905, MTP.

112:29 Willis F. Johnson, *George Harvey,* pp. 181–82.

112:33 September 19, 1905, MTP.

113:5 IVL Diary, September 26, 1905, MTP.
113:7 TS in MTP.
113:10 *MTL*, p. 779.
113:11 *HHR*, p. 601.
113:17 IVL Diary, October 6, 1905, MTP.
114:19 *HHR*, p. 595.
114:21 *Ibid.*, p. 597.
114:24 SLC to Katherine Clemens, August 31, 1905, *MTLW*, p. 96.
114:26 August 3, 1905, TS in MTP.
114:27 SLC to CC, September 3, 1905, TS in MTP.
115:3 October 16, 1905, MTP.
115:8 June 29, 1905, TS in MTP.
115:14 September 3, 1905, TS in MTP.
115:17 December 6, 1905, CWB, PH in MTP.
115:22 SLC to CC, "Mid-June" 1905, PH in MTP.
115:31 August 3, 1905, TS in MTP.
116:28 SLC to Mrs. T. B. Aldrich, September 16, 1905, Harvard.
116:29 IVL Diary, October 7, 1905, MTP.
117:1 *MTFM*, p. 220.
117:10 October 20, 1905, TS in MTP.
117:20 IVL Diary, September 21 and October 18, 1905, MTP.
117:26 *HHR*, p. 602.
117:28 May 20, 1905, MTP.
118:1 From an unpublished memoir by Gene Gowning—Clemens' buggy
 driver that summer—quoted in an unpublished paper, "Mark Twain
 in Dublin, New Hampshire," by Zachary Goodyear, PH in MTP.
118:14 Doris Webster note in IVL Diary, TS p. 110½, MTP.
118:16 IVL Diary, November 30, December 15 and 23, 1905, MTP.
118:25 *Ibid.*, December 17, 1905, MTP.
118:27 *MTL*, p. 786.
119:6 IVL Diary, January 18, 1906, MTP.
119:9 *Ibid.*, December 7, 1905, MTP.
119:19 *Ibid.*, December 27, 1905, MTP.
119:35 *Mary*, p. 59.
121:7 IVL Diary, January 27, 1906, MTP.
121:20 *Ibid.*, February 2, 1906, MTP.
122:1 February 18, 1906, TS in MTP.
122:3 IVL Diary, February 28, 1906, MTP.
122:18 *Ibid.*, March 15, 1906, MTP.
122:21 *Ibid.*, March 16, 1906, MTP.
122:23 October 9, 1906, TS in MTP.
122:31 IVL Diary, May 6, 1906, MTP.
123:4 *Ibid.*, February 6, 1906, MTP.
123:7 *Mary*, p. 63.
123:12 TS in MTP.
123:22 IVL Diary, March 24, 1906, MTP.
123:25 SLC to Gertrude Natkin, March 24, 1906, TS in MTP.
123:27 IVL Diary, March 25, 1906, MTP.
123:29 April 26, 1906, Harvard.
126:3 IVL Diary, January 19, 1906, MTP.
126:9 *Ibid.*, February 4, 1906, MTP.

126:16 *Ibid.,* February 16, 1906, MTP.
126:19 *Ibid.,* March 12, 13, 1906, MTP.
127:9 SLC to Gertrude Natkin, February 3, 1906, TS in MTP.
127:12 February 5, 8, 1906, TSS in MTP.
127:15 March 18, 1906, TS in MTP.
127:27 April 9, 1906, TS in MTP.
127:31 April 28, 1906, TS in MTP.
128:11 See Howard Baetzhold, "Found: Mark Twain's 'Lost Sweetheart,'"
 American Literature, 44:414–29 (November, 1972).
128:28 January 8, 1906, MTP.
129:1 International Spiral Pin Company to SLC, November 24, 1906, MTP.
129:3 Larkin to SLC, January 12, 1906, MTP.
129:6 Larkin to SLC, September 5, October 4, 1906, MTP.
129:12 Ames to Mary Lawton, October 26, 1905, MTP, with a note by SLC
 on the envelope to preserve it for his autobiography; SLC to Skinner,
 May 7, 1906, PH in MTP.
129:19 Mann to SLC, December 30, 1905, MTP; SLC to Mann, January 3,
 1906, MTP.
129:21 IVL Diary, February 22, 1906, MTP.
129:34 SLC to "Gentlemen," January 10, 1906, MTP.
130:9 SLC to MacAlister, January 16, 1906, CWB.
130:13 C. Breneron Sharpe to SLC, March 3, 1906, MTP; RWA to SLC,
 January 16, 1906, MTP.
130:21 RWA to IVL, March 28, 1906, MTP.
130:27 SLC to Mrs. Ditson, March 5, 1906, IVL Daybook 1, MTP.
130:35 Herbert Welsh to SLC, December 15, 1906, IVL marginal notes for
 reply, MTP.
131:12 March 14, 1906, Lilly Collection, Indiana University, PH in MTP.
131:21 Duneka to SLC, February 17, 1906, MTP, IVL marginal notes for
 reply.
131:26 Harvey to SLC, September 11, 1906, SLC marginal note for reply, MTP.
132:3 IVL Diary, May 25, 1906, MTP.
132:10 *Ibid.,* June 8, 1906, MTP.
132:14 Doubleday to SLC, May 16, 1906, MTP.
132:18 IVL Diary, May 24, 1906, MTP.
132:23 See *MTHL,* pp. 818–19.
132:32 IVL copy in the possession of Bigelow Cushman, PH in MTP.
133:3 IVL Diary, August 25, 1906, MTP; F. N. Doubleday to SLC, August 24,
 1906, with marginal notes for reply, MTP.
133:6 Doubleday to SLC, August 29, 1906, MTP.
135:22 Carnegie to Doubleday, December 17, 1906, MTP.
135:25 "IVL Notes on What Is Man?," Berg.
135:35 See *MTHL,* pp. 813–14.
136:2 IVL Diary, June 11, 1906, MTP.
136:4 See *MTHL,* p. 812.
136:19 IVL Diary, January 14, 1906, MTP.
136:23 Knickerbocker Publishing Company to SLC, December 13, 1906, IVL
 marginal notes for reply, MTP.
136:27 *MTB,* p. 1268.
138:2 Autobiographical Dictation, April 4, 1906, *MTA,* I, 312.

138:23 M. A. DeWolfe Howe, *Memories of a Hostess,* p. 251.

139:18 IVL to Muriel Pears, April 9, 1906, IVL Daybook 1, MTP.

139:19 IVL Diary, April 8 and 9, 1906, MTP.

140:25 *HHR,* p. 607; IVL Diary, June 23, 1906, MTP.

140:30 S. G. Niles to SLC, June 19, 1906, IVL marginal notes for reply, MTP.

140:31 *HHR,* pp. 607, 610.

141:3 June 24, 1906, IVL Daybook 1, MTP; the announcement had appeared on exactly the date Clemens remembered: "Neither Harper & Brothers nor the *North American Review* will publish in book form Mark Twain's papers on 'Christian Science.' All orders now on file will be cancelled."

141:9 Frederick Leigh to SLC, December 28, 1906, IVL marginal note for reply, MTP.

141:14 October 19, Documents File—1905, MTP.

141:34 SLC to Duneka, June 4, 1906 (IVL copy), PH in MTP.

142:2 SLC to Dorothy Quick, February 9, 1908, inside the front cover of *Mark Twain's Library of Humor,* Vol. I, MTP.

142:6 June 4, 1906 (IVL copy), PH in MTP.

143:9 SLC to IVL, July 10, 1906, MTP.

142:19 SLC to Duneka, June 13, 1906, IVL Daybook 1, MTP; IVL Daybook 1, inside back cover.

142:28 *HHR,* pp. 611–12.

142:36 SLC to IVL, July 10, 1906, MTP.

143:13 SLC to CC, August 3, 1906, TS in MTP.

143:15 *Mary,* pp. 38–39.

143:27 "Extracts from Jean's Diary," June 9, 1906, p. 3, MTP.

143:29 *Ibid.,* June 10, 1906, p. 3, MTP.

144:2 Peterson to IVL, June 23, 1906, MTP.

144:19 "Extracts from Jean's Diary," June 28, 1906, p. 4, MTP.

144:24 IVL Diary, June 12, 1906, MTP.

144:36 *Ibid.,* June 20, 1906, MTP.

145:16 n.d., Berg.

145:23 IVL Diary, June 15, 1906, MTP.

145:30 *Ibid.,* June 25, 1906, MTP.

146:6 *Ibid.,* June 29, July 8, August 8, 1906, MTP.

146:16 SLC to IVL [July 10, 1906], PH in MTP.

146:30 *Mary,* pp. 62–63.

146:33 Isabel Lyon Notes, Berg.

146:36 *Mary,* p. 42.

147:5 IVL Diary, August 17, 1906, MTP.

147:16 SLC to CC, August 28, 1906, TS in MTP.

147:22 *Mary,* pp. 54, 62, 66.

147:35 November 13, 1906, TS in MTP.

148:4 *Mary,* p. 93.

148:16 IVL Diary, September 28, 1906, MTP.

149:13 "Extracts from Jean's Diary," July 4, 1906, p. 5, MTP.

149:32 *Ibid.,* August 13, 1906, p. 7, MTP.

150:7 IVL Diary, September 29, 1906, MTP.

150:9 September 27, 1906, PH in MTP.

150:11 IVL Diary, October 3, 1906, MTP.

150:14 October 9, 1906, Berg.
150:28 October 2, 1906, TS in MTP.
150:31 SLC to Aldrich, October 2, 1906, Harvard.
151:4 SLC to CC [October 9, 1906], TS in MTP.
152:7 "Extracts from Jean's Diary," October 4, 1906, pp. 11–12, MTP.
152:15 IVL Diary, October 10, 1906, MTP.
153:3 Autobiographical Dictation, April 6, 1906, MTP.
153:10 SLC to CC, August 3, 1906, TS in MTP.
153:17 John Howells to SLC, September 19, 1906, MTP.
153:21 October 12, 1906, MTP.
154:16 IVL unnumbered Daybook, January 1907, MTP.
154:30 *Mary*, p. 69.
155:1 *HHR*, p. 618.
155:6 *Mary*, pp. 79, 81.
155:10 *HHR*, p. 620.
155:21 IVL Diary, October 27, 1906, MTP.
155:26 *Mary*, p. 84.
155:34 *Ibid.*, p. 93.
156:26 "S.L.C. to C.T.," privately printed, New York, 1925, "Foreword," p. 6.
156:30 IVL Diary, October 24, 1906, MTP.
157:2 SLC to MacAlister, November 29, 1906, CWB.
157:4 SLC to Jean [December 7, 1906], TS in MTP.
157:14 *MTB*, p. 1344.
157:16 IVL Diary, December 10, 1906, MTP.
157:36 "Copyright Hearings, December 7 to 11, 1906," Washington: Government Printing Office, 1906, p. 116.
158:27 *Ibid.*, pp. 120–21.
159:5 IVL Diary, December 21, 1906, MTP.
159:18 IVL Daybook 3, December 17, 1906, MTP.
160:14 "Extracts from Jean's Diary," October 21, 1906, pp. 14–15, MTP.
161:14 IVL Diary, January 3, 1907, MTP.
161:18 *Ibid.*, January 4, 1907, MTP.
161:34 *Ibid.*, February 3, 1907, MTP.
162:3 *Ibid.*, January 12, 1907, MTP.
162:4 *HHR*, p. 624.
162:8 IVL Diary, January 16, 1907, MTP.
162:12 *Ibid.*, January 19, 1907, MTP.
162:20 *Ibid.*, January 20, 1907, MTP.
162:23 *HHR*, p. 625.
162:30 IVL Diary, July 30, 1907, MTP.
163:23 November 14, 1906, MTP.
163:27 November 19, 1906, MTP.
164:20 Autobiographical Dictation, March 26, 1907, MTP.
164:31 IVL Diary, February 14, 1907, MTP.
165:7 *Ibid.*, March 11, 1907, MTP.
165:28 *Ibid.*, February 26, 1907, MTP.
166:2 SLC to Jean, April 22, 1907, TS in MTP.
166:5 See SLC to Edith Ellis Baker, May 2, 1907, PH in MTP, and *MTLW*, pp. 154–56.

166:8 IVL Diary, May 10, 1907, MTP.
166:10 SLC to CC, July 27, 1907, TS in MTP.
166:13 IVL Diary, May 29, 1907, MTP.
166:28 IVL Daybook 3, MTP.
166:35 *MTL,* p. 806.
167:6 IVL Diary, June 8, 1907, MTP.
167:8 *Ibid.,* June 21, 1907, MTP.
167:15 *Ibid.,* January 10, 1907, MTP.
167:16 George O'Connor to SLC, January 15, "1906" (i.e., 1907), MTP.
167:30 "Extracts from Jean's Diary," December 19, 1906, p. 19, MTP.
168:10 *Ibid.,* February 4, 1907, p. 23, MTP.
168:16 January 11, 1907, *MTFM,* p. 228.
169:8 "Extracts from Jean's Diary," January 14, 1907, p. 22, MTP.
169:13 January 17, 1907, *MTFM,* pp. 231–32.
169:15 SLC to Jean, January 26, 1907, TS in MTP.
169:20 January 1, 1907, CWB.
169:26 IVL Diary, March 25, 1907, MTP.
169:31 May 14, 1907, TS in MTP.
169:35 [May 26, 1907], TS in MTP.
170:2 IVL Diary, June 11, 1907, MTP.
170:5 *HHR,* p. 625.
170:19 On January 20, according to Miss Lyon's record, Clara "went back to
 Katonah" after coming to New York to see Ossip Gabrilowitsch on
 the nineteenth; on February 13, she passed through New York, again
 seeing Ossip, en route to Atlantic City with a sore throat (SLC to
 Jean, February 14, 1907, TS in MTP; IVL Diary, March 28, 1907,
 MTP).
171:2 TS in MTP.
171:5 IVL Diary, March 29, April 3, 1907, MTP.
171:10 IVL Diary, June 17, 1907, MTP.
171:13 *Ibid.,* July 8, 1907, MTP.
171:20 *HHR,* p. 625.
171:31 IVL Diary, April 12, 1907, MTP.
171:32 *Ibid.,* April 9, 1907, MTP.
172:5 *Ibid.*
172:12 June 8, 1907, Item 281, Charles Hamilton Catalog 15, 1966.
172:16 IVL Diary, June 13, 1907, MTP.
172:27 *Ibid.,* June 19, 1907, MTP.
173:1 *Ibid.,* May 22, 1907, MTP.
173:6 Clippings in Scrapbook 30, MTP.
173:9 IVL Diary, July 25 and 26, 1907, MTP.
173:14 *MTB,* p. 1405.
174:1 Carlotta Welles Briggs to Dixon Wecter, November 4, 1947, MTP.
174:17 *MTB,* p. 1384.
174:30 IVL Diary, June 3, 1907, MTP.
175:23 *MTB,* p. 1394.
175:28 IVL Diary, January 14, 1907, MTP.
175:32 *MTB,* p. 1396.
177:10 *Ibid.,* p. 1402.

PART III: THE DERELICT (SUMMER 1907 to 1910)

Page: line

181:19 Karl Kelsey to SLC, April 1, 1907, MTP, IVL marginal notes for reply.
182:2 Matthews to SLC, March 1, 1907, MTP, IVL marginal notes for reply.
182:4 McClure to SLC, February 28, 1907, MTP, IVL marginal notes for reply.
182:11 Henderson to SLC, August 26, 1907, MTP.
182:17 *MTHL*, p. 838.
182:24 John Howells to SLC, August 3, 1907, MTP, and May 29, 1907, MTP.
182:26 Howells to SLC, August 3, 1907, MTP.
182:34 IVL Diary, August 5, 1907, MTP.
183:5 Howells to SLC, August 8, 1907, MTP.
183:8 See IVL Diary and *MTB*, p. 1445.
183:18 IVL Diary, October 23, 1907, MTP.
183:27 RWA to SLC, May 14, 1907, MTP, IVL marginal notes for reply.
183:29 See John Winthrop Loveland to SLC, November 19, 1907, MTP.
184:2 "What Happened," Paine #124, MTP.
184:8 *HHR*, p. 635.
184:30 IVL Diary, October 29, 1907, MTP.
185:2 *Ibid.*, September 1, 1907, MTP.
185:12 *Ibid.*, September 8, 1907, MTP.
185:15 SLC to Frances Nunnally, TS in MTP.
185:24 Anna Sterritt to IVL, August 24, 1907, MTP.
185:30 October 2, 1907, TS in MTP.
186:6 IVL Daybook 4, October 5, 1907, MTP.
186:11 October 8, 1907, TS in MTP.
186:15 SLC to Jean, December 1 and 21, 1907, TSS in MTP.
186:24 SLC to Jean, December 21, 1907, TS in MTP.
186:28 January 14 [1907], MTP.
186:32 IVL Diary, September 12, 1907, MTP.
187:9 A. Radclyffe Dugmore, "Stormfield . . ." *Country Life in America*, 15:608–09, April 1909.
187:17 IVL Diary, September 28 and September 1, 1907, MTP.
187:20 *Ibid.*, October 15, 1907, MTP.
188:3 IVL to Mrs. Gertrude Quick, August 1, 1907, MTP.
188:10 IVL Diary, August 23, 1907, MTP.
188:13 SLC to Dorothy Quick, August 11, 1907, MTP.
188:29 Autobiographical Dictation, July 24, 1907, MTP.
188:36 IVL Diary, October 13, 1907, MTP.
189:9 *HHR*, p. 639.
190:1 IVL Diary, August 1, 1907, MTP.
190:4 *Ibid.*, September 9, 1907, MTP.
190:12 Duneka to SLC, August 2, 1907, with IVL marginal note for reply, MTP.
190:27 Rood to SLC, September 30, 1907, MTP.
190:32 IVL Diary, September 15, 1907, MTP.
191:25 Leigh to SLC, December 12, 1907, MTP.
191:28 Leigh to IVL, March 6, 1908, MTP.
191:31 See IVL Diary, October 27, 1908, MTP.

192:9 "Memorandum for Mr. Rogers re: Clemens' Matter," Ashcroft-Lyon
 Folder 2, MTP.
192:17 Stanchfield to SLC, September 27, 1907, MTP.
192:21 Bismark Moore to SLC, December 29, 1908, MTP.
192:24 Julian Hawthorne to SLC, August 8, 1908, with IVL marginal note
 for reply, MTP.
192:29 See Maurice Bassan, "A Critical Biography of Julian Hawthorne," un-
 published Ph.D. dissertation, University of California at Berkeley,
 1961, pp. 266–71.
192:31 "Securities Bought. 1908 & 1909," Ashcroft-Lyon Folder 2, MTP.
192:34 Frohman to SLC, April 4, 1908, MTP.
193:3 IVL Diary, October 10, 1907, MTP.
193:9 Chamberlin to SLC, December 11, 1907, IVL marginal note for reply,
 MTP.
193:12 Chamberlin to SLC, December 14, 1907, MTP.
194:33 IVL Diary, January 17, 1908, MTP.
195:4 *Ibid.*, March 6, 1908, MTP.
195:7 *Ibid.*, April 23, 1908, MTP.
195:8 *HHR*, p. 657.
195:8 IVL Diary, August 6 and 13, 1908, MTP.
195:9 *MTB*, pp. 1458–59.
195:15 IVL Diary, February 28, 1908, MTP.
195:18 *Ibid.*, April 1, 1908, MTP.
195:21 Stormfield Guest Book, entry of September 27–29 [1908], MTP.
195:27 Notebook 38, TS p. 3, MTP.
196:3 September 21, 1908, MTP.
196:17 IVL Diary, January 9, 1908, MTP.
197:10 "Eva" to IVL and IVL reply, Daybook 4, February 16, 1908, MTP.
197:20 March 23, 1908, TS in MTP.
197:23 Peterson to IVL, March 26, 1908, MTP.
197:36 May 20, 1908, TS in MTP.
198:13 May 21, 1908, TS in MTP.
198:18 June 14, 1908, TS in MTP.
198:24 June 19, 1908, TS in MTP.
198:33 Jean to IVL, August 1, 4, and 5, 1908, MTP.
199:6 [July 2, 1908], TS in MTP.
199:10 Jean to IVL, August 1, 1908, MTP.
199:13 *Ibid.*, August 4, 1908, MTP.
199:21 Peterson to IVL, August 15, 1908, and Jean to IVL, August 5, 1908,
 MTP.
199:25 *Mary*, p. 123.
199:33 Jean to IVL, August 1, 1908, MTP.
199:35 August 9, 1908, TS in MTP.
200:6 Autobiographical Dictation, October 4, 1908, MTP.
200:8 *MFMT*, p. 277.
200:20 New York *Times*, June 14, 1908, Section C, p. 3.
200:25 RWA to IVL, March 5, 1908, MTP.
200:28 Freeman to IVL, July 7, 1908, MTP.
201:11 IVL Diary, January 22, 1908, MTP.
201:14 *MTHL*, pp. 828, 829.
201:20 IVL Diary, January 23, 1908, MTP.
201:30 *Ibid.*, February 26, 1908, MTP.

202:2 Paine to IVL, January 28, 1908, in "Ashcroft-Lyon Manuscript," MTP.
202:11 IVL Diary, July 26, 1908, MTP.
202:19 *AMT,* p. 256.
202:24 CC to IVL, June 24, 1908, MTP.
202:26 *Ibid.,* February 27, 1908, MTP.
203:1 IVL Diary, January 7 and 27, 1908, MTP.
203:8 SLC to Dorothy Quick, June 14, 1908, MTP.
205:3 "Diary of Elizabeth Wallace," pp. 49, 70, 73–74, PH in MTP.
205:10 SLC to Jean, October 2, 1908, in *MFMT,* pp. 276–77.
205:15 RWA to Henderson, February 16, 1908, in my possession.
205:20 SLC to CC, July 18, 1908, PH in MTP.
205:25 Wark to IVL, June 24, 1908, MTP.
205:28 CC to IVL, June 24, 1908, MTP.
206:11 IVL Diary, May 2, 1908, MTP.
206:29 *Mary,* p. 123.
207:8 IVL Diary, September 3, 1908, MTP.
207:22 *Ibid.*
208:6 IVL Diary, August 8, 1908, MTP.
208:15 IVL to Hattie Whitmore Enders, August 17, 1908, MTM.
208:18 IVL Diary, August 4, 1908, MTP.
208:22 Mary L. Howden to IVL, September 23, 1908, MTP.
208:31 SLC to Harvey, August 10, 1908, Harvard, PH in MTP.
209:5 IVL Diary, October 15, 1908, MTP.
210:27 *MTHL,* p. 835.
210:28 SLC to Jean, October 2, 1908, TS in MTP.
210:30 Cyrus Miller to RWA, September 28, 1908, MTP.
210:31 William Wainwright to SLC, October 9, 1908, MTP.
211:1 SLC to CC, October 6, 1908, PH in MTP.
211:2 IVL Diary, October 9, 1908, MTP.
211:11 *Ibid.,* October 20, 1908, MTP.
211:13 *Ibid.,* October 26, 1908, MTP.
212:3 See Frank Presbrey to SLC, December 1, 1908, MTP, and "Memo-
 randum for Mr. Rogers re: Clemens' Matter," Ashcroft-Lyon Folder
 2, MTP.
212:7 RWA to Charles T. Lark, November 2, 1909, MTP.
212:13 "Memorandum for Mr. Rogers," Ashcroft-Lyon Folder 2, MTP.
212:15 Item 281, Charles Hamilton Catalog 15, 1966.
212:24 SLC to William R. Coe, June 16, 1909, PH in MTP.
213:10 "Exhibit A," Revocation of Power of Attorney, June 1, 1909, Ashcroft-
 Lyon Folder 2, MTP.
213:19 *HHR,* p. 659.
213:25 Elizabeth Wallace to her mother, November 28, 1908, MTP.
213:31 Jean to IVL, October 8, 19 and 20, 1908, MTP.
214:1 Jean to IVL, October 8, 1908, MTP.
214:14 SLC to Jean, December 17, 1908, MTP.
214:33 "Ashcroft-Lyon Manuscript," MS p. 49, MTP.
215:21 Undated note, Ashcroft-Lyon Folder 2, MTP.
215:26 IVL Diary, December 18, 1908, MTP; SLC to CC [December 12,
 1908], Hannibal Mark Twain Museum, PH in MTP.
215:30 IVL Diary, December 30, 1908, MTP.

215:34 George L. and George M. Robinson to SLC and IVL, various dates in 1908. MTP.

216:2 IVL Diary, December 30, 1908, MTP.

216:17 IVL to Henderson, January 14, 1909, in my possession.

216:19 RWA to Henderson, February 13, 1909, in my possession.

216:22 SLC to Margaret Blackmer, January 3, 1909, Yale.

216:24 January 31, 1909, Columbia, PH in MTP.

216:28 SLC to Frances Nunnally, February 17, 1909, TS in MTP.

216:30 IVL Diary, January 10, 1909, transcribed into IVL notes on *Is Shakespeare Dead?*, Berg.

217:2 SLC to Jean, March 3, 1909, TS in MTP.

217:7 Folger Shakespeare Library, PH in MTP.

217:19 "Marjorie Fleming, the Wonder-Child," Paine #15, MS p. 3, MTP.

218:2 IVL Diary, February 17, 1909, as transcribed in IVL notes, Berg.

218:9 SLC to William R. Coe, PH in MTP.

218:11 SLC to Frances Nunnally, February 9, 1909, TS in MTP.

218:17 IVL to Hattie Whitmore Enders, February 16, 1909, MTP.

219:9 Mrs. Paine to Paine, March 8, 1909, HEH, PH in MTP.

219:19 n.d., "Ashcroft-Lyon Manuscript," MTP.

220:4 CC to Mrs. Franklin Whitmore, June 25, 1910, MTM.

220:25 "Report of Miss X," DeVoto Papers, Stanford University, PH in MTP.

220:31 "Ashcroft-Lyon Manuscript," MS pp. 2–3, MTP.

221:12 SLC to CC, March 11, 1909, "Ashcroft-Lyon Manuscript," MS pp. 249–55, MTP.

222:2 SLC to CC, March 14, 1909, "Ashcroft-Lyon Manuscript," MS p. 257, MTP.

222:17 *MTHL*, pp. 842–43.

222:27 "Ashcroft-Lyon Manuscript," MS pp. 100–06, 141–43, MTP.

223:2 *Ibid.*, p. 62, MTP.

223:8 IVL to Henderson, April 10, 1909, in my possession.

223:14 IVL to SLC, April 12, 1909, "Ashcroft-Lyon Manuscript," MS p. 122, MTP.

223:16 "Ashcroft-Lyon Manuscript," MS p. 120, MTP.

223:24 IVL to SLC, April 15, 1909, "Ashcroft-Lyon Manuscript," MS p. 136½, MTP.

224:7 "Note Bares Twain Attempt at Suicide," Los Angeles *Times*, April 15, 1951, I, 40.

224:14 CC to Mrs. Franklin Whitmore, August 5, 1910, MTM.

224:17 Rodman Gilder notes of an interview with Dan Beard, March 1940, MTP.

224:25 HHR to SLC, April 23, 1909, "Ashcroft-Lyon Manuscript," MS p. 165, MTP.

224:30 *HHR*, p. 662.

225:7 RWA to SLC, April 29, 1909, "Ashcroft-Lyon Manuscript," MS pp. 1a–1b, MTP.

225:20 Jean to SLC, March 5, 1909, MTP.

225:29 Fragment paged "98," Ashcroft-Lyon folder 2, MTP.

226:1 SLC to Jean, April 19, 1909, TS in MTP.

226:8 SLC to CC, March 11, 1909, "Ashcroft-Lyon Manuscript," MS pp. 254–55, MTP.

227:14 RWA to Henderson, May 27, 1909, in my possession.

227:19 *HHR,* p. 648.
227:26 "Ashcroft-Lyon Manuscript," MS p. 213, MTP.
228:4 RWA to SLC, June 3, 1909, "Ashcroft-Lyon Manuscript," MTP.
228:26 "Note" accompanying manuscript of *Is Shakespeare Dead?,* Folger
 Shakespeare Library, PH in MTP.
229:3 CC to Mrs. Franklin Whitmore, August 5, 1910, MTM.
229:30 *MTHL,* pp. 844–45.
229:36 DV #265, MTP.
230:24 "Ashcroft-Lyon Manuscript," MS p. 11, MTP.
230:35 *Ibid.,* MS pp. 394–95, MTP.
231:2 *Ibid.,* MS p. 418, MTP.
231:6 *Ibid.,* MS p. 28, MTP.
231:17 *Ibid.,* MS p. 34, MTP.
231:22 *Ibid.,* MS pp. 34–45, MTP.
232:21 SLC to Elizabeth Wallace, June 7, 1909, HEH, PH in MTP.
233:7 CC to SLC, July 9, 1909, MTP.
234:2 "Ashcroft Accuses Miss Clara Clemens," New York *Times,* August 4,
 1909, clipping in MTP.
235:9 "Ashcroft-Lyon Manuscript," MS pp. 355–56, MTP.
235:20 RWA to Stanchfield, July 30, 1909, Ashcroft-Lyon Folder 2, MTP.
235:27 All are preserved in Ashcroft-Lyon Folder 1, MTP.
236:32 RWA to Stanchfield, July 30, 1909, Ashcroft-Lyon Folder 2, MTP.
237:5 "Statement Submitted in behalf of Mrs. Ashcroft . . ." Ashcroft-Lyon
 Folder 2, MTP.
237:9 "Statement of Disbursements . . ." Ashcroft-Lyon Folder 2, MTP.
237:23 "Ashcroft-Lyon Manuscript," MS pp. 399, 421–22, MTP.
238:3 See *MTB,* pp. 1496–99.
238:12 *Ibid.,* p. 1519.
238:14 See IVL to Major Leigh, April 10, 1909, and Duneka to SLC, July 2,
 1909, MTP.
239:4 Item 281, Charles Hamilton Catalog 15, 1966.
239:33 "Ashcroft-Lyon Manuscript," MTP.
240:4 SLC to Stone, September 14, 1909, MTP.
240:13 June 25, 1910, MTM.
241:16 Rodman Gilder notes of an interview with Dan Beard, March 17, 1940,
 MTP.
241:28 "Report of Miss X," DeVoto Papers, Stanford University, PH in MTP.
242:4 Paine #278, MS p. 4, Washington University, PH in MTP.
242:11 *Mr. Clemens and Mark Twain,* p. 386.
242:19 Paine to Elizabeth Wallace, March 9, 1912, MTP.
242:25 *Ibid.,* March 22, 1912, MTP.
242:30 SLC to CC, July 18, 1909, TS in MTP.
242:32 George Harvey to SLC, May 5, 1909, referred to in "Ashcroft-Lyon
 Manuscript," MS p. 17, MTP.
242:34 University of Texas Library, PH in Ashcroft-Lyon Folder 2, MTP.
243:19 *MTB,* pp. 1521–22.
243:28 September 30, 1909, in my possession.
244:7 SLC to Mrs. Ogden, October 13, 1909, TS in MTP.
244:14 Johnston to SLC, October 6, 1909, MTP.
244:19 SLC to Mrs. Beatrice Benjamin, November 7, 1909, MTP.
244:31 SC to CC, July 18, 1909, TS in MTP.

245:2 Stormfield Guest Book, September 29, 1909, MTP.
245:35 November 7, 1909, in my possession.
246:10 DV #164, MTP.
246:17 December 21, 1909, in my possession.
246:21 *MTB,* pp. 1506–14, 1516–18, 1533–35.
246:23 An example of Paine's solicitousness is in a letter to Sir Arthur Conan
 Doyle, who attempted to rekindle SLC's interest in the Congo: "Mr.
 Clemens, who is not very robust these days, has asked me to reply to
 you concerning the Congo matter. He is deeply interested in the sub-
 ject; so deeply, in fact, that any intimate consideration of it excites
 and distresses him to a degree which we think dangerous. He there-
 fore does not permit himself to read any matter pertaining to the
 cruelties practiced there, or to write anything further on the subject"
 (Paine to Doyle, October 29, 1909, published in *Sir Arthur Conan
 Doyle: Centenary 1859–1959,* p. 73) .
247:4 *MTL,* pp. 833–34.
249:4 Jean to Marguerite Schmidt, November 20, 1909, in my possession.
249:8 *Ibid.*
249:26 October 19, 1909, in my possession.
249:30 S. K. Frantz to SLC, n.d., with marginal note for reply, MTP.
250:9 SLC to Frances Nunnally, December 14, 1909, TS in MTP.
250:14 SLC to Jean, December 6, 1909, TS in MTP.
250:33 *MTHL,* p. 851.
251:8 E. E. Loomis to SLC, June 11, 1909, MTP.
251:11 Booth & Alexander to SLC, June 1, 1909, MTP.
251:13 See Charles A. Watts to Lark, August 16, 1910, MTP.
251:17 Lark to Paine, December 11, 1909, MTP; Lark to SLC, January 4, 1910,
 MTP.
251:24 January 26, 1910, HEH, PH in MTP.
251:32 "Ashcroft-Lyon Manuscript," MS p. 166, MTP.
251:34 Loomis to Paine, November 6, 1909, MTP.
252:3 Lark to Loomis, November 9, 1909, MTP.
252:5 RWA to Lark, November 2, 1909, MTP.
252:14 Lark to Paine, December 11, 1909, MTP.
252:23 Jean to Marguerite Schmidt, December 21, 1909, in my possession.
253:3 New York *American,* December 25, 1909, Clippings File, MTP.
253:10 Gabrilowitsch cable to SLC, December 25, 1909, MTP.
253:26 *MTL,* p. 835.
253:36 Stormfield Guest Book, MTP.
254:8 *AMT,* p. 371.
254:13 "The Death of Jean," MS pp. 1–2, MTP.
254:14 *Ibid.,* MS pp. 18–19.
254:17 *Ibid.,* MS p. 31.
254:28 *AMT,* p. 376.
254:31 *Ibid.,* p. 378.
254:36 *Ibid.,* p. 380.
255:11 *My Husband,* p. 116.
255:27 December 28, 1909, MTM.
255:30 Mrs. Whitmore to SLC, January 3, 1910, MTP.
256:6 *Happy Island,* p. 136.
256:13 *Ibid.,* p. 137.

256:26 *The Twainian,* May 1943, 2:5.
256:28 SLC to CC, March 12, 1910, TS in MTP.
256:30 *MTL,* p. 843.
257:11 February 20, 1910, in the possession of Mrs. Robert Antenne, PH in MTP.
257:16 March 12, 1910, Hannibal Mark Twain Museum, PH in MTP; March 24, 1910, TS in MTP.
257:18 *MTL,* p. 844.
257:21 Lincoln National Bank to SLC, November 23, 1909, and April 16, 1910, MTP.
257:25 SLC to CC, March 6, 1910, CWB.
257:32 SLC to Paine, February 14, 1910, Wisconsin, PH in MTP.
258:17 Paine to SLC, February 6, 1910, PH in MTP.
258:19 *MTB,* pp. 1566–67.
258:26 *Ibid.,* p. 1552.
258:33 Notebook 39, TS pp. 2–4, MTP.
259:1 January 7, 1910, MTP.
259:2 Notebook 39, TS pp. 1–3, MTP.
259:8 *Ibid.,* TS pp. 6–8, MTP.
259:34 *The Twainian,* January–February 1948, 7:1–2.
260:5 *Enchantment,* p. 213.
260:7 SLC to CC, March 12, 1910, TS in MTP.
260:11 *MTL,* p. 842.
260:15 *MTB,* p. 1563.
260:24 Notebook 39, TS p. 6; *MTB,* p. 1558.
261:4 "Helen Allen Manuscript," DV #423, MTP.
261:10 Julian Street to Albert Bigelow Paine, January 2, 1912, HEH, PH in MTP.
261:27 *MTB,* p. 1571.
261:30 New York *Times,* April 22, 1910, p. 2.
261:33 Collier telegram to SLC, April 11, 1910, MTP; SLC to CC, March 24, 1910, TS in MTP.

EPILOGUE: THE LAST VOYAGE

265:3 *MTB,* p. 1575.
265:12 Paine to Mr. and Mrs. Allen, April 25, 1910, printed in *The Twainian,* January–February 1948, 7:3.
265:15 New York *Times,* April 22, 1910, p. 2.
265:17 In *MTB,* p. 1577, in facsimile; original in MTP.
265:22 CWB, PH in MTP.
266:17 *The Twainian,* January–February 1948, 7:2–3.
266:20 *MTB,* p. 1577; *MFMT,* p. 291.
266:25 March 12, 1910, HEH, PH in MTP.
267:11 *The Twainian,* January–February 1948, 7:3.
267:27 Joe Goodman to Paine, April 22, 1910, printed in *The Twainian,* January–February 1948, 7:3.
268:3 March 30, 1912, MTP.
268:11 In the possession of Bigelow Cushman, PH in MTP.
268:22 Paine to "Dear Bill" (William H. Briggs?), August 1, 1926, PH in MTP.

270:22 *MTN*, p. 319.
271:7 *MTHL*, p. 575.
272:34 *MTB*, p. 1579.
273:20 Kenneth Andrews, *Nook Farm: Mark Twain's Hartford Circle*, p. 237.
274:6 *MTB*, p. 1585.

INDEX

This index makes no attempt to record every appearance of the Clemens family and household in the pages of *Mark Twain: God's Fool;* only broad categories and general topics are included for the principals. A reader may trace Clemens' business affairs, publishing and literary projects, and social engagements by referring to his associates, co-investors, publishers, friends, and acquaintances.

73 74 75 76 77 10 9 8 7 6 5 4 3 2 1